THE BEST OF
BIRDS & BLOOMS
2005

THE BEST OF BIRDS & BLOOMS 2005

Editor: Heather Lamb
Art Director: Nathan Chow
Proofreader: Susan Uphill
Associate Editor: Deb Mulvey
Graphic Art Associates: Ellen Lloyd, Catherine Fletcher
Associate Artists: Connie Alenius, Maribeth Greinke
Photo Coordinator: Trudi Bellin
Assistant Photo Coordinator: Mary Ann Koebernik
Editorial Assistant: Marie Brannon
Executive Editor, *Birds & Blooms*: Jeff Nowak

Senior Vice President, Editor in Chief: Catherine Cassidy
President: Barbara Newton
Chairman and Founder: Roy Reiman

BIRDS & BLOOMS *BOOKS*
© 2005 Reiman Media Group, Inc.
5400 S. 60th St. Greendale WI 53129
International Standard Book Number: 0-89821-425-4
International Standard Serial Number: 1553-8400
Printed in U.S.A.

To order additional copies of this book, visit *www.countrystorecatalog.com* or call 1-800-344-6913. Learn more about *Birds & Blooms* at *www.birdsandblooms.com*.

Front cover photos: Top, from left: Paul Rezendes; RP Photo; Richard Day/Daybreak Imagery; bottom photo: Irene Jeruss
Back cover photos: From left, Ray Herrick/www.Racinphoto.com; Maslowski Photo; Mark Turner

WELCOME

The Best of Birds & Blooms 2005 is exactly that—the best stories, tips, projects and reader ideas from the past year of North America's most read magazine that celebrates beauty in the backyard.

Your favorite features and useful hints are here at your fingertips, organized into chapters and referenced in a complete index so you can easily find what you're looking for. No more paging through stacks of magazines!

Not only that, but we've included *14 bonus features* not found in the magazine. You'll learn how to plant carefree flowers…build the perfect birdhouse…stop squirrels…create a butterfly garden…attract birds with the right plants…and much, much more!

Everything you've come to expect from *Birds & Blooms* is right here—birds, flowers, butterflies, expert advice, reader ideas, backyard projects, beautiful photos and, most of all, fun. And now it's in one big, colorful and easy-to-use book. Enjoy!

Heather

Heather Lamb
Editor, *Birds & Blooms*

Magazine covers, from left: Richard Day/Daybreak Imagery; Jiang Jin/SuperStock; Irene Jeruss; Richard Day/Daybreak Imagery; Robert A. Lueck; Maslowski Photo

CONTENTS

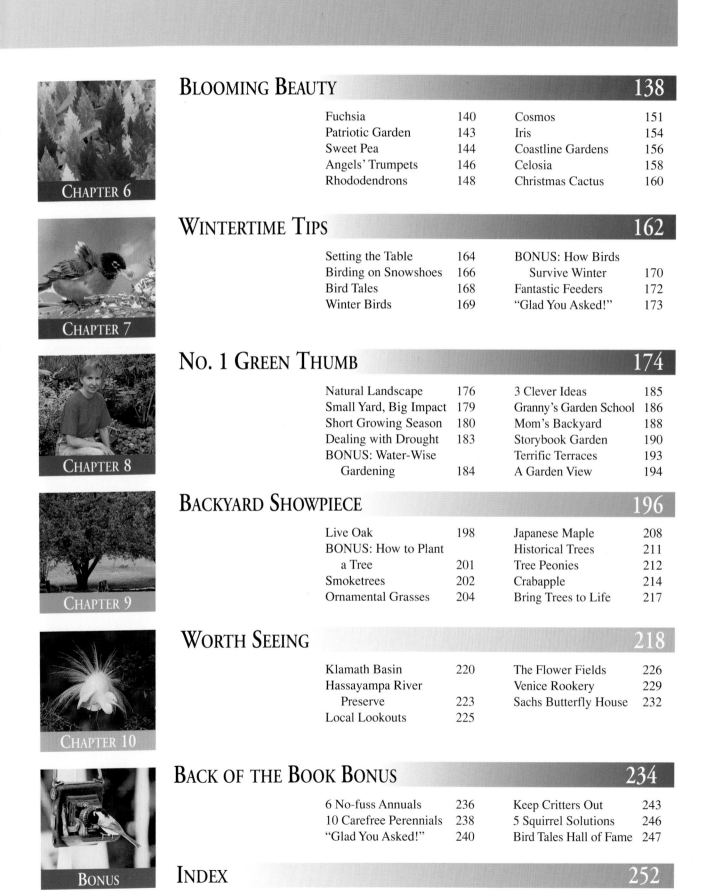

TOP BILLING

ORIOLES

They'll brighten your yard in spring.

By Jeff Nowak, Executive Editor

A flash of orange was all reader Helen Bratt from Ashton, Idaho needed to see.

"I knew right then that I had to grab my binoculars and field guide and get to the kitchen window quick," Helen says. "All my hard work of trying to attract the most colorful birds to my yard paid off when I spotted a brilliant orange and black Bullock's oriole in the lower branches of a lilac bush."

That kind of excited reaction is not unusual for first sightings of orioles. I remember when I lured these dazzling spring visitors to our backyard. The Baltimore oriole's uplifting whistle and eye-popping color (that's one at left) convinced me to do all I could to keep the bright visitors coming back to our yard every spring.

Jim Roetzel/Dembinsky Photo Assoc.

NOW YOU SEE THEM... now you don't. Orioles weave an intricate pouch nest (left) that conceals the birds and their young almost entirely. However, they'll eagerly come into the open to eat offerings of oranges, sugar water or grape jelly (below).

> ### READER TIP
>
> Attract orioles with orange halves, grape jelly or sugar water. In a pinch, chopped pears or apples and grapefruit will work, too. —*Helen Bratt Ashton, Idaho*

It doesn't matter where you live in the continental United States and parts of southern Canada, you should be able to attract a brilliant oriole to your backyard. You just need to know what they crave...and have some tree cover for their protection.

"I discovered orioles have an insatiable appetite for oranges, whether they're sliced up and set out in a pan, or halved and poked onto nails in a fence post or hanging log," Helen says. "The orioles are now regulars in our backyard."

No oranges? No worries...Helen also had success attracting orioles with grape jelly served in a small tuna can or a half grapefruit rind. She also uses chopped pears, apples and even the sugar water in hummingbird feeders.

Watch Orioles All Season

True, orioles have a sweet tooth. But it seems their craving for citrus wanes a bit—just about the time they start feeding their youngsters insects and caterpillars at the nest. But take this hint from contributing editor George Harrison, who has found the ticket to keeping Baltimore orioles coming to his backyard feeders in Hubertus, Wisconsin all summer long.

"Sugar-water feeders made for orioles seem to hold their interest throughout the season, up to the time they mi-

Bill Marchel; opposite page: Bill Marchel

grate south in early autumn," he says. "I use the same mix I put in the hummingbird feeder (1 part sugar to 4 parts water, boil, cool and serve). They never seem to tire of it."

Even though they're one of the most brilliant songbirds that visit backyards, all North American orioles belong to the blackbird family. (My youngest son even calls the Baltimore species the "Halloween bird", for obvious reasons.) Unlike other members in their family, however, they spend most of their time high up in the treetops rather than on the ground, where they'd be simple to spot.

When orioles return to their northern breeding territories, they look for tree cover and stay well hidden in their search of food, primarily spiny caterpillars, insects and fruits. The drab pale yellow females also build their incredible woven nests high above the ground.

"When the orioles arrive in spring at our place, they go tree to tree singing the whole time," says Debbie Richmond of Warren, Rhode Island, who has seen both Baltimore and orchard orioles in her neighborhood. "I don't think spring would be the same without hearing the beautiful song of the orioles when they arrive."

Reader Connie Storlie of Dennison, Minnesota has found an entertaining way to lure orioles out of the treetops so she can get a better view of the brilliant birds.

"I put out pieces of string or yarn and dog hair for them to use in their nest building," she says. "In the fall after the leaves drop, it's fun to go for a walk in the woods and see their carefully woven pouch-like nests dangling high in the trees."

Most nests of orioles (like the one on page 9) are true works of art and ingeniously engineered. The female skillfully weaves it from fibers of grasses, grapevines and milkweed, a process that may take up to 40 hours. Once complete, the nests are so intricate, they even close up like a drawstring purse when occupied by the parent or youngsters. Following the birds' sound is often the only way to locate the well-hidden nests. It's easier when the young become vocal and more demanding for food.

> ### READER TIP
>
> Want to spot an oriole's nest? In spring, set out short colorful pieces of yarn. Orioles may weave it into their nests, allowing you to see the pouches come fall.
>
> —*Connie Storlie*
> *Dennison, Minnesota*

Fab Five

There are nine different orioles that can be seen throughout the continental United States during the breeding months, but the most common are the Baltimore, Bullock's, orchard, hooded and Scott's. (All are featured in the profiles at right). Four other orioles—the altimera, Audubon's, spot-breasted and streak-backed—are rare sightings or have very small territories along the southernmost borders of the U.S.

The Baltimore and Bullock's orioles cover the largest area. Together, they span from coast to coast and are the most commonly seen in backyards. In the 1950s, scientists grouped these birds as one species, the northern oriole, because they often interbreed where their territories overlap in the Great Plains. But in 1995, the Baltimore and Bullock's orioles got their original namesakes back.

See the profiles to find out which oriole may visit your backyard. If you cover the basics—trees, fruit and sugar water—there's a good chance a blazing oriole will find its way to your backyard in spring.

Baltimore Oriole

The most popular of all orioles, the Baltimore oriole resides in an area from the Great Plains to the Atlantic Ocean. Its solid black hood and fire-orange plumage distinguishes it from others. It's the only oriole with a major league baseball team named after it and is the official bird of Maryland.

Scientific Name: *Icterus galbuba*.
Length: 8-3/4 inches.
Wingspan: 11-1/2 inches.
Distinctive Markings: Male has full black hood and fire-orange plumage. Female is drab yellow with dusky brown wings.
Distinctive Behavior: In a courtship display, a male bows, spreads its tail and lifts its wings to show its vivid colors.
Habitat: Deciduous woodlands, parks and backyard gardens.
Song: Short series of clear whistles in varied pattern.

Bullock's Oriole

The most common western oriole, the range of the Bullock's extends from the Great Plains to the Pacific Ocean. It looks distinctively different from the Baltimore oriole because it has a black cap, orange cheeks and large white wing patches.

Scientific Name: *Icterus bullockii*.
Length: 9 inches.
Wingspan: 12 inches.
Distinctive Markings: Male has a black crown, orange cheeks and large white wing patches. Female is mostly yellow with a gray back.
Distinctive Behavior: Pairs spend a lot of time together and will attack predators.
Habitat: Open areas with shade trees and backyard gardens.
Song: Short series of nasal-like whistles.

Orchard Oriole

The smallest of the oriole family, the orchard oriole resides east of the Great Plains, but is less common than the Baltimore oriole. The male has distinctive deep chestnut feathers. They'll spend lots of time in orchards, gleaning caterpillars and worms, protecting the fruits on the tree from damage.

Scientific Name: *Icterus spurius*.
Length: 7-1/4 inches.
Wingspan: 9-1/2 inches.
Distinctive Markings: Male has chestnut feathers and a black hood. Female is dusky yellow-green and gray.
Distinctive Behavior: One of the few orioles that nest in colonies. In Louisiana, 114 nests were once found on 7 acres.
Habitat: Orchards, open wooded areas and farmlands.
Song: High lively warble.

Hooded Oriole

This bright bird is common in desert suburbs of the Southwest, especially where there are fan palm trees, a favorite nesting area. Their black face and bib, and bright-orange head easily identify them. Males in the West are paler and more golden than the bright-orange ones residing in Texas.

Scientific Name: *Icterus cucullatus*.
Length: 8 inches.
Wingspan: 10-1/2 inches.
Distinctive Markings: Male has black face and bib. Female is drab gray and yellow.
Distinctive Behavior: Hangs upside down at times like a chickadee, as it probes blossoms for nectar.
Habitat: Woodlands and backyard gardens.
Song: Rapid, choppy, slurred whistles.

Scott's Oriole

Another oriole of the Southwest, the Scott's oriole can easily be spotted because its plumage is yellow and black instead of the trademark orange of its cousins. It has a black upper back and sings fast whistled phrases that resemble the western meadowlark.

Scientific Name: *Icterus parisorum*.
Length: 9 inches.
Wingspan: 12-1/2 inches.
Distinctive Markings: Male has black hood, breast and bright-yellow feathers. Females very drab gray with hint of yellow on belly.
Distinctive Behavior: Sings constantly during the daylight hours.
Habitat: Arid and semi-arid palm habitats.
Song: Low, clear, gurgling whistles like the western meadowlark.

■ Winter ■ Summer ■ Migration ■ Year-Round

How Birds Fly

Marie Read

It seems so simple for birds to take flight.

By Pat Kerr, Fraserville, Ontario

Ducking his head while wildly waving barbecue tongs in the air, my husband, Danny, tried to avoid a young purple finch as it fluttered and wavered above him before landing on our deck railing.

This was the first of many birds that we watched learn to fly that summer. Ironically, it was the same summer I started taking my own airplane flying lessons. All of it got me thinking about how it's so seemingly simple for birds to take to the air.

Tools of the Trade

For centuries, humans have envied our feathered friends' ability to fly. Greek legend warns man of his limitations by sharing the story of Icarus—the boy whose homemade wax wings melted when he dared venture too near the sun.

In reality, for a human to fly without mechanical help, it would require a breastbone 6 feet wide to support the equivalent muscle mass that birds require to fly.

For a bird, however, everything about its design supports flight—the wings offer lift and steering, and the tail helps slow a bird's speed during a landing. Even a bird's skeleton is designed to minimize drag as it's made up of mostly hollow bones that are filled with air.

If we compare a bird's wing to those on an airplane, the primary feathers (those at the end of the wing) would represent an airplane's propellers. When a bird flaps its wings, the primary feathers—which are the longest part of the bird's wing—push its body upward and forward.

The secondary feathers (closer to the body) are like the actual wings of an airplane. Whether gliding or flapping, the bird rigidly holds this part of the wing out from its body. This supports the bird's weight in the air and provides a steady lifting force as it constantly adjusts this part of the wing during flight.

As the bird flaps its wings downward, it holds its primary feathers (sometimes called "fingers") close to-

12

Richard Day/Daybreak Imagery

gether. This forces air down. When the bird brings its wings up, it opens the fingers and rotates them slightly to create the least air resistance. This repeatedly forces the air down, which provides lift for the bird. And as the air swirls out behind it, it pushes the bird forward.

As in aviation, wing shape determines flight style. Geese and ducks, for instance, have long broad wings. This, combined with a large muscle mass, allows for long-distance flights. They are the equivalent of nature's passenger jet, stable and powerful.

On the other hand, shorebirds—like terns and sandpipers (in top photo)—are more like gliders. They can ride ocean breezes for hours with their long narrow wings.

Though my delightful backyard songbirds aren't necessarily built for graceful gliding, their stout and short wings are made for mobility.

Backyard birds have many enemies, so the ability to maneuver and duck into the cover of a tree or shrub is lifesaving. Their finessed flight style could be compared to that of a trick plane or perhaps a crop duster.

A Perfect Landing

Flying was only half of the lessons the fledglings in our yard learned that summer. By far, the most complicated skill to master was landing. A trio of young rock pigeons provided my husband and me with an ongoing show of hilarious mistakes and mishaps when they unsuccessfully tried to stick their first few backyard landings.

The first pigeon to touch down stumbled forward. The second landed on its tail and just sat there for a moment, as if to consider how truly hard the ground was. The third overshot the "runway", tumbled forward and landed on its bill.

A little shaken, but certainly not discouraged, the doves tried again and again until, in a few short hours, their landings were perfect.

To their credit, my flight instructor reminded me that landing is the hardest part of flying. Landing safely requires judging one's speed while also determining the speed and direction of the wind. And then there are the proper wing adjustments that need to be made.

But I have to admit, it was gratifying to see that even our feathered friends have to practice a little.

Bill Marchel

Maslowski Photo

AIR "BORN". By nature's design, a bird's body is built for flight. Red-winged and yellow-headed blackbirds' stout wings provide ultimate mobility (far left), while sandpipers' long slender wings take advantage of ocean breezes (top). A great gray owl scanning a snow-covered field for prey (above center) and a male eastern bluebird coming in for a landing (above) flex their primary feathers.

WHOOPING IT UP FOR 'LUCKY'

By Bill Weber, Leesburg, Florida

As backyard birding experiences go, Gene and Tina Tindell's is hard to top. A few years back, a pair of wild whooping cranes nested in the 20-acre marsh behind their home. Even better, one of their offspring became the first chick from the United States to fledge in the wild in more than 60 years.

When the large white birds first arrived at Christmastime, the Tindells (above) weren't sure what they were. Then Gene spotted radio transmitters attached to their legs, and figured it wouldn't be long before they found out. He was right.

A state biologist visited the couple, explaining that the birds were part of an experiment to establish a non-migratory flock of whooping cranes in central Florida. The pair was part of a group raised in Maryland and released in Florida at 6 to 8 months of age.

Settling on the marsh was somewhat unusual, since it lies within the Leesburg city limits and is surrounded by people. Biologists think the cranes chose it for its open water—a local rarity after a 4-year drought—and plenty of natural food sources.

Gene and Tina think the explanation is much simpler.

"Gene puts out feed for his mallards, and these large birds passing by noticed and dropped in to help themselves," Tina says. "I called them 'Bonnie' and 'Clyde' because they came in and stole food whenever Gene put it out.

"Next thing we knew, they were building a nest. We got to watch it all—the courtship dancing, the nest building and the chicks hatching."

The Tindells were delighted when two chicks hatched in March—and devastated when a bald eagle plucked the youngest from the nest.

Great Escape for "Lucky"

"When the eagle stole that chick, it broke our hearts," Tina recalls. "We called the surviving baby 'Lucky' because he managed to escape the eagle and other predators."

When Lucky was 3 weeks old, the eagle returned—but this time the parents were ready. The mother crouched over her chick, wings spread, while Lucky's dad chased the eagle away. Three boys approached the edge of the marsh on bicycles later that day. Lucky's mother took no chances and shooed them away, too.

As Lucky grew and thrived, the Tindells reported their observations to scientists. They were fascinated by Lucky's diverse diet, which included grubs, worms, frogs, roots, snakes and snails.

One day, they watched the parents feed Lucky 37 different items in just 5 minutes!

Neighborhood Watch

While the Tindells watched and took notes, their neighbors helped protect the nestling by keeping kids, dogs, photographers and birders at bay.

When Lucky took flight for the first time that June, the Tindells likened it to watching a baby take its first steps. The scientists who'd been monitoring it called it a milestone. With only 400 whooping cranes left worldwide, Lucky buoys hope for the species' survival.

"We've learned a lot," says biologist Steve Nesbitt of the Florida Fish and Wildlife Conservation Commission. "There's every reason to expect that one day many more people will see whoopers raising young over most of Florida."

Marie Read

BELTED KINGFISHER

Unusual bird gets the catch of the day.

By Shirley Wilcox, North Manchester, Indiana

My friend fishes in the water near our home, and he's good at it. He's patient, and he rarely misses. But his technique has an unusual twist. When he spots his prey, he makes a loud rattling noise and dives into the water headfirst.

As you may have guessed, my friend is of the feathered variety—a male belted kingfisher. His favorite perch is a telephone wire near the water. When I go by, I don't think he even notices me. He's so intent on watching the water that he doesn't move.

When the kingfisher spies a fish, he zooms down at a sharp angle and lets out a call that has been compared to the sound of a large fishing reel. Sometimes he spears the fish, but usually he clamps it in his heavy bill. Then he flies up

to a safe perch, whacks his lunch against a tree limb, tosses it in the air, catches it and down it goes, headfirst.

Many Ways to Catch a Fish

Belted kingfishers prefer a perch that's exposed, like a telephone wire or a dead tree branch. They'll also hunt for fish by flying below the treetops to follow the course of a stream.

Sometimes they'll even hover 20 to 40 feet above the water before plunging below the surface, disappearing for several seconds before emerging.

In addition to fish, the belted kingfisher eats crawfish, frogs, tadpoles and insects. They're such swift fliers, they can even pick insects out of the air.

The belted kingfisher's scientific name, *Ceryle alcyon*, comes from Halcyone, a figure in Greek mythology. Halcyone was the daughter of the god of wind and became a kingfisher herself.

The name fits because belted kingfishers fly like the wind. Researchers have clocked their flight at 36 mph and as fast as 45 mph with a boost from a tailwind.

With its squat body, oversized head and tiny feet, the belted kingfisher does not look like a speed demon. Its blue-gray head seems too large—

READER TIP

To spot a belted kingfisher nest, look for a hole in the side of a bank near water. The nest itself is at the end of a tunnel that's 3 to 15 feet away from the entrance.

it's about one-third the size of its body—with an unruly crest of feathers.

Both males and females have white necks and blue-gray backs with matching collars. But the female's coat is showier, a rarity among North American birds. Females have a reddish band across the belly that extends down the flanks.

Hidden Home

Although a belted kingfisher can be easy to spot, finding its nest is another story. This bird values a private family life. It may nest in a hollow tree stump or trunk in a pinch, but it prefers a more protected burrow.

Nests are usually indicated only by a hole in the bank near a creek, pond or lake. The nest itself is at the end of a tunnel that's 3 to 15 feet from the entrance.

A pair of belted kingfishers can take up to 3 weeks to dig this burrow, excavating the soil with their bills and pushing it away with their feet.

For maximum protection and privacy, the birds place their nest at the end of the tunnel. It measures about 6 by 10 inches in diameter and is lit-

Rolf Nussbaumer

ONE BAND OR TWO. It's easy to distinguish the male belted kingfisher (above) from the female (like the one on page 15). Females have a reddish belly band in addition to the blue one. Both are talented anglers, sometimes diving underwater before appearing with their catch (below).

Marie Read

BACKYARD BIRDING BIO

Winter
Summer
Year-Round

Common Name: Belted kingfisher.
Scientific Name: *Ceryle alcyon.*
Length: 11 to 14-1/2 inches.
Wingspan: 20 inches.
Distinctive Markings: Bushy crest, dagger-shaped bill, white neck band and blue-gray collar. Females have a reddish belly band that extends to the flanks.
Distinctive Behavior: Watches for fish from exposed perches or hovers over water before diving for prey.
Habitat: Near water, including seacoasts and inland waterways, ponds and lakes.
Song: Harsh, loud "rickety-crick-crick-crick" call when diving for fish or moving between perches.
Nesting: Pairs build nests of fish bones and scales at the end of a tunnel in a bank. Females lay five to eight white eggs, which both parents incubate. They raise one to two broods per year.
Diet: Fish, tadpoles, shellfish, lizards, frogs, toads, snakes, turtles, insects, young birds, mice and berries.

tle more than a bed of fish bones and scales—items belted kingfishers are unable to digest.

The parents take turns sitting on five to eight glossy white eggs. When the eggs hatch, the sharing continues as both parents stick around to raise the young.

The nestlings remain in the burrow for several weeks. Once they develop feathers, you might spot them peeping from the mouth of their dark home.

Not-so-Common Cousins

The belted kingfisher inhabits areas near water throughout most of North America, and it's the only kingfisher that lives north of Texas and Arizona.

If you spot one, you probably won't see another in the same area except for its mate. Kingfishers are generally solitary and don't allow others to nest or fish in their territory.

Other members of the kingfisher family live in Africa, China, South America, Central America and the South Pacific, but most of these birds feed on insects instead of fish. Its Australian cousin, the kookaburra, is known for its raucous laugh.

The feathered friend in my yard doesn't laugh, he only rattles. But his rough song is music to my ears.

TUNNEL VISION. Kingfishers nest in burrows with nondescript entrances (like the one above), where the young (below) remain for several weeks. It can take up to 3 weeks for the adults to excavate the tunnels to these nests.

PINE GROSBEAK

John Gerlach

Take a second look at the "other" red bird.

Although the northern cardinal gets all the glory for being a bright spot in winter's snow, don't try to tell admirers of the pine grosbeak that their favorite bird is second-best. With rose-red feathers and a social nature, this striking species is quick to win over new fans.

Pine grosbeaks spend much of the year in the coniferous woods of Canada and the Rocky Mountains, seeking the tree seeds that make up the majority of their diets. When they wander into backyards, these northern birds are surprisingly friendly.

Carolyn Smyth of Cowley, Alberta experienced the pine grosbeak's gregarious disposition firsthand during a holiday visit to her parents' home in British Columbia.

"The beautifully colored pine grosbeaks—more than a dozen at a time—came every day to eat sunflower seeds at

"These northern birds are surprisingly friendly…"

the bird feeder," Carolyn writes (that's her with two male pine grosbeaks at top right). "Just for fun, we decided to try hand-feeding them. To our amazement, these birds were quite tame and would sit on our hands, eating as many as 30 sunflower seeds before flying off."

It's common for this slow-moving bird to remain still for long periods of time—a behavior often misconstrued as boredom. In Newfoundland, this behavior has earned it the regional nickname of "mope".

Follow the Food

Pine grosbeaks don't migrate, but in winter they'll move around looking for food, especially when there's a shortage of seeds or fruit in their summer territories. Sometimes they gather in enormous flocks of 100 birds or more as they wander the countryside.

During this seasonal movement, called irruption, pine grosbeaks enter areas of the northern Midwest and North-

east. The bird has even been spotted as far south as Texas, New Mexico and the Carolinas.

In backyards, smaller groups of pine grosbeaks eat at tray feeders or in gardens with abundant berry-producing trees and shrubs like mountain ash, crabapple, bittersweet and barberry. Michigan photographer John Gerlach, who provided the sparkling pine grosbeak portraits on these pages, says the birds visit his feeders in the state's Upper Peninsula from December to February.

"They like the sunflower seeds and typically come to the feeder in groups of at least 10 to 20," he says. "Because they're so tame, pine grosbeaks are one of the easier species to photograph."

Into the Woods

If you live in a wooded area with plentiful evergreens, maples and birches, you may spot pine grosbeaks searching for food among the branches.

The bird's scientific name, *Pinicola enucleator*, hints at this preferred habitat as well as its method of eating seeds. The first word is Latin for "inhabiting pine", and enucleator means "one who shells", which describes the bird's custom of husking pinecones.

Pine grosbeaks are similar in size and shape to the American robin. It's the biggest of the grosbeaks, larger than the black-headed, rose-breasted and evening grosbeaks.

The male's feathers are red with distinctive white wing

A REAL STANDOUT. The male pine grosbeak (far left) is a striking sight against a backdrop of snow, while the female (above) also exhibits a subtle beauty. These northern birds are a social species, even accepting handouts (at top).

bars, gray markings on its back and belly and a slightly forked tail. They also have a short dark eye line that some observers think gives the birds a squinting expression.

Females and juveniles possess the wing bars as well, but are grayish overall. Females (below left) have dusty yellow on their heads, while juveniles sport pale red crowns.

In addition to its colorful feathers, the male displays another lively characteristic—it's one of the few birds that sings beyond the breeding season. Many other species continue to communicate with non-musical calls, but male pine grosbeaks croon from high perches in the middle of winter. Their sweet warbling song sounds similar to the purple finch's melody.

Pine grosbeaks nest in late spring, constructing a loose cup of twigs and roots. After the female lays between three and five eggs, she'll incubate them for 2 weeks. During this time, the male feeds its mate while she stays on the nest. After the eggs hatch, both adults feed the young, which fledge in about 3 weeks.

Since the birds raise only one brood each season, they gather into winter flocks soon after the juveniles become independent, and may begin roaming for food again.

So as the weather cools, keep an eye out for a flash of ruby feathers at your feeders. You may be surprised, but certainly not disappointed, to discover it's the "other" red bird of winter, the pine grosbeak.

BACKYARD BIRDING BIO

Common Name: Pine grosbeak.

Scientific Name: *Pinicola enucleator.*

Length: 9 inches.

Wingspan: 14 inches.

Distinctive Markings: Males are red with gray markings. Both males and females have white wing bars and dark eye lines.

Distinctive Behavior: Tame and slow moving; will even accept seed offerings from your hand.

Habitat: Open areas and edges of coniferous forests, near water and in wooded backyards.

Song: A short clear musical warble, often compared to a purple finch.

Nesting: Bulky, loose nest. Female lays three to five blue-green eggs speckled with browns and grays.

Diet: Tree seeds, berries and insects.

Backyard Favorite: Sunflower seeds.

Winter
Summer
Year-Round

BICENTENNIAL BIRDS

Lewis's woodpecker and Clark's nutcracker share the spotlight with the famous explorers they're named after.

By Richard Patrick, Albany, New York

Clark's Nutcracker

Lewis's Woodpecker

In case you hadn't heard, 2004 was the 200th anniversary of one of the most fantastic adventures our country has ever pursued, Lewis and Clark's amazing "Corps of Discovery".

The mission—to discover a water route to the Pacific Ocean and explore the uncharted West.

During their journey from 1804 to 1806, Captains Meriwether Lewis and William Clark found more than that. The Corps discovered and documented more than 300 species of flora and fauna, including two birds that should become minor celebrities because of their famous namesakes.

A display case in the High Desert Museum in Bend, Oregon brought these interesting birds—the Lewis's woodpecker and the Clark's nutcracker—to mind. After studying the specimens in the modest showcase, I wanted to find out more about how these famous explorers first crossed paths with these birds.

In Lewis' Words

I learned Lewis first spotted the colorful woodpecker on July 20, 1805 near what is today Helena, Montana. That night he penned (reprinted here in Lewis' original words from his journals):

"I saw a black woodpecker (or crow) today about the size of the lark woodpecker as black as a crow. I indevoured to get a shoot at it but could not. It is a distinct species of woodpecker; it has a long tail and flys a good deel like the jay bird."

A year later, Lewis shot and preserved the hide of a black woodpecker. From its skin, he wrote a 500-word description of the bird, but didn't name it after himself. (It's the only zoological specimen that still exists from the entire Lewis and Clark expedition, and is a prized possession of Harvard's Museum of Comparative Zoology.)

Ornithologist Alexander Wilson eventually named the bird after Lewis in his 1811 book *American Ornithology*, published after Lewis' death. He also named three other birds from Lewis' expedition notes and collection—the western tanager, Clark's nutcracker and the black-billed magpie.

I recall seeing colorful Lewis's woodpeckers myself as we had lunch in Cottonwood Canyon in southeastern Colorado. There were several dining in nearby cottonwood trees. We had an outstanding view of their metallic greenish-black backs and pink bellies.

I must admit feeling a bit like Captain Lewis when I added that unusual bird to my personal "life list".

And Clark's Two Cents

Then there's the other occupant of the display case—the gregarious Clark's nutcracker, discovered by Captain Clark near Salmon City, Idaho. Clark recorded this in his journal on August 22, 1805 (in his original words):

"I saw to day [a] Bird of the woodpecker kind which fed on Pine burs its Bill and tale white the wings black every other part of a light brown, and about the Size of a robin."

You have to wonder if the explorers also discovered that nutcrackers are so tame, they'll readily take food from a human hand.

I recall my own experiences with the Clark's nutcracker at Bryce Canyon and Yellowstone National Parks 10 or so years ago. The birds were willing to "do lunch" with just about anyone.

No, the Clark's nutcracker and Lewis's woodpecker aren't your typical backyard birds. But even if you can't see them from your picture window, take time to open a field guide and study them. Then you'll appreciate that these birds, and at least two dozen other species in the book, were essentialy unknown until Lewis and Clark's remarkable adventure.

More Lewis and Clark Avian Discoveries

Black-billed magpie	Common poorwill
Brewer's blackbird	Greater-sage grouse
Glaucous-winged gull	Western grebe
Mountain quail	Western tanager
Pacific loon	Greater white-fronted goose
Pinyon jay	

Illustrations: Independence National Historic Park; paintings by Charles Willson Peale

"I saw a black woodpecker (or crow) today about the size of the lark woodpecker as black as a crow. I indevoured to get a shoot at it but could not. It is a distinct species of woodpecker; it has a long tail and flys a good deel like the jay bird."

—Meriwether Lewis

"I saw to day [a] Bird of the woodpecker kind which fed on Pine burs its Bill and tale white the wings black every other part of a light brown, and about the Size of a robin."

—William Clark

PURPLE MARTINS

"Their gurgling chatter fills the air..."

Roll out the red carpet for these backyard colonists.

So you think you have what it takes to "hang out" with purple martins? Lots of flying bugs for them to feast on...one of those cool apartment-style birdhouses... and a big tall pole for mounting.

Put it up and they will come. Right?

Not so fast—we're talking purple martins, one of the pickiest of all backyard birds. Put up a martin house or apartment that's not to their liking or in the wrong location, and you can expect to attract nothing but house sparrows and European starlings—public enemies No. 1 and 2 for the native martin.

Any way you slice it, purple martins are finicky. They want their houses placed just so. Follow the rules (see "How to Make Purple Martins Happy" on page 25), and they may stop for a closer look as they migrate north in spring. If martins find it to their liking, expect them to return year after year.

Good Neighbors

These stealthy birds are a real treat to have just out the back door. They're the largest bird in the swallow family, yet are more nimble on the wing than a fighter pilot. They catch many insects on the fly, and on rare occasions may land on the ground to pluck a bug.

The males are shimmering blue-black all over (see the one at left), while females and younger males have light grayish breasts. Their gurgling chatter fills the air from dawn until dusk. It's a sound that many purple martin landlords long for while the birds spend winters in Brazil and other South American areas east of the Andes. The birds will have soft sweet conversations with each other while perched on telephone lines, and will continue to chatter even as they fly.

"My grandfather had two martin houses on his farm, and my mom had two as well," writes Lynn Nash of Wichita, Kansas. "Come spring, she would have us watch for the scouts to arrive.

"I've been trying to become the third generation in my family to attract purple martins, with no luck," Lynn says, "but that hasn't stopped me from trying."

Purple martins have attracted the curiosity of bird lovers like Lynn for centuries because of their social nature. They nest in colonies of six to eight pairs, which can grow beyond 200 pairs when well established.

Native Americans were the first to attract these birds, hanging gourd houses near their villages. They thought the fearless birds would give chase to crows, keeping them from raiding their corn. Plus, the purple martins' huge appetites for flying insects kept flies and other pesky bugs under control.

Many of today's would-be landlords try to lure purple martins to their yards to help reduce the mosquito population. Much to their disappointment, martins feed primarily during the day and roost when mosquitoes are most active at night, making bats a better choice for mosquito control. But purple martins will devour a noticeable number of flies, beetles, moths, wasps, dragonflies and grasshoppers, which is why they're a friend to gardeners like Margaret Mason of Paris, Missouri.

"We've hosted purple martin colonies for years," she says. "When they leave for their winter grounds, we sud-

> **READER TIP**
>
> Make sure you have a martin house that's easy to lower so you can check for and clean out unwanted sparrow nests.
>
> —*Margaret Mason
> Paris, Missouri*

PURPLE PASSION. Purple martins are a hot commodity for backyard birders. They use mostly man-made housing, and nest in colonies that start with six to eight pairs, but may grow to a few hundred. Clockwise from left: A male shows off its rich iridescent color...a martin pair porch sits...a female feeds its young.

THE MARTINS ARE HOME. Purple martins can be a picky species. This martin house (above left) has everything purple martins want—an apartment-style nest box, with natural gourd houses for expansion of the colony and a roomy perch atop their glorious mansion. Above right, crushed eggshells, which provide calcium, attract these birds to backyards.

denly notice a lot more insects buzzing about our backyard."

Purple martins once primarily nested in cavities, like abandoned woodpecker holes in trees or cacti, but they soon became accustomed to man-made birdhouses. By the 1900s, very few martins were selecting natural cavities except in the West, where they still prefer more natural sites.

Purple martins arrive in North America from their winter grounds as early as January (see range map on page 25 for approximate arrival dates). The older males, called scouts, are the first to complete the journey.

Most of the time they'll return to the same house year after year, but are sometimes attracted to new sites. If there are colonies in your area, the odds of attracting birds to a new house greatly increase.

When putting up a new purple martin house, mount your nest box 10 to 15 feet off the ground and at least 40 feet from surrounding trees. Many people will place martin houses near water because there's plenty of open space and insects. (See diagrams at far right.)

Waiting for Residents

If you don't see immediate action at your martin apartment, don't get discouraged. Martin migration is a long drawn-out affair. Some later arrivals, primarily last year's young, won't even begin nesting until the end of June.

The female selects a male and its nesting cavity, and together each couple builds a nest. The females gather mud and sticks that they form into a platform lined with straw, feathers and paper. Males add green leaves, which some scientists think may help keep parasites under control.

The female incubates the eggs for just over 2 weeks until they hatch. Both parents work feverishly collecting insects and feeding the young until they leave the nest about a month

after hatching. In the South, purple martins may raise a second brood.

Despite all the attention they get from human friends, purple martins face some real challenges to their survival, primarily from nest-site competitors and predators.

Landlord's Responsibility

Responsible martin landlords protect their houses from house sparrows and starlings, two non-native birds that will drive martins from their nests, or worse yet, kill them.

The most effective way to keep starlings out is with a crescent-shaped entrance hole (pictured below). They work

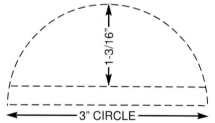

because starlings are too large to fit into the narrow entrance.

The height of the hole (1-3/16 inches) is critical. A hair too big, and starlings will get in. Too small, and the martins will be locked out.

House sparrows are a little more troublesome. But persistence is the key, says Margaret, who regularly patrols her boxes for these pests.

"Make sure you have a martin house that's easy to lower so you can check for and clean out unwanted sparrow nests," she says. "Martins make a very neat nest and a sparrow's is messy. After removing a sparrow's nests a few times, it usually goes away and you can reserve the apartment just for purple martins." ✒

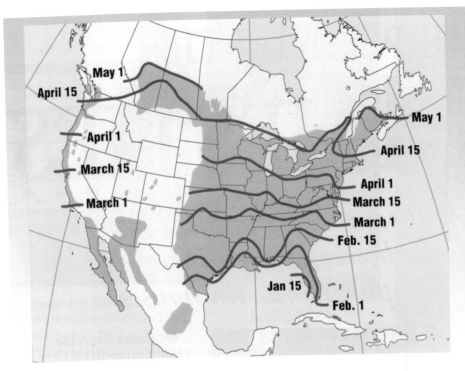

BACKYARD BIRDING BIO

Common Name: Purple martin.
Scientific Name: *Progne subis*.
Length: 7 to 8 inches.
Wingspan: 16 to 17 inches.
Distinctive Markings: Males are irides-cent blue-black all over, while females and juveniles have light gray breasts.
Distinctive Behavior: Nest in large colon-ies, usually in apartment houses or gourds.
Habitat: Open areas such as farmlands, parks and residential areas near water.
Song: Low, rich and liquid gurgling.
Nesting: Eastern birds primarily choose man-made housing. Western birds often nest in natural tree and cactus cavities. Females and males build platform nests in cavity; females lay four to seven white eggs.
Diet: Flying insects.
Backyard Favorite: Will eat crushed eggshells for calcium.

HOW TO MAKE PURPLE MARTINS HAPPY

1. Choose the right location. One of the major reasons people fail to at-tract purple martins is that they place the apartment or gourds too close to trees or buildings. Martins require a large open area. The diagrams at right show proper placement.

2. Use houses that make sense. Purple martin houses are large and need to be mounted 10 to 15 feet high. Make sure you're not trying to manage a 300-pound birdhouse from a stepladder. There are lots of specially designed telescoping or jointed poles to help lower the birdhouses.

3. Paint it white. Painting martin houses and gourds white will keep the compartments cooler in summer.

4. Track arrivals and departures. Martins usually return to their houses within a week or two of the time they did the previous year. Have your house ready, but keep the entrances closed (try plugging them with small paper cups) until you see some martins return. This will keep house sparrows out.

5. Protect your martin house from predators. Be sure to use baffles that keep raccoons, snakes and squirrels from accessing the birdhouse. Deeper 7-inch by 12-inch compartments also help protect the birds from hawks and owls, while grease on the pole stops fire ants.

6. Educate yourself. There's much to learn about purple martins, so be-fore you invest lots of money, time and hard work into your project, check out the information available on-line from the Purple Martin Conservation Association at *www.purplemartin.org*. If you don't have a computer, write PMCA, Edinboro University of Pennsylvania, Edinboro PA 16444, or call 1-814/734-4420.

Also, talk to other landlords in your area—they have a wealth of helpful information based on experience.

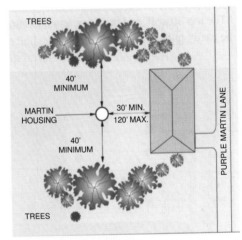

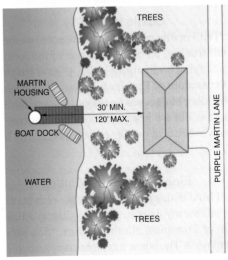

CAROLINA WREN

Don't let its small size fool you.

While the house wren often gets the glory because of its coast-to-coast territory and cute "Jenny wren" nickname, its Carolina cousin has striking good looks and the lung power to make sure it's not overlooked as a backyard favorite in the Southeast.

Of the nine North American wrens, the Carolina wren is the friendliest around people, often nesting in backyards. They're also one of the only wrens that visit bird feeders.

"Carolina wrens really seem to enjoy living in close proximity to humans," observes field editor Marlene Condon from Crozet, Virginia. Marlene's seen them in birdbaths and patrolling her garden for insects.

"To attract them, I put up an open shelf for them in a protected area," Marlene adds. "They nest on it during spring and summer and will sleep on it during cold fall and winter nights."

Carolina wrens have a knack for finding nooks and crannies to build their nests. It doesn't take long for them to pack mailboxes, rafters, gaps in woodpiles and stone walls with a massive collection of grasses, leaves and plant stems.

"Somehow, they always discover the clothing I hang on the clothesline," writes Jean Mitchell from Plant City, Florida. "One time after getting the clothes, I discovered a hysterical Carolina wren trapped in the pocket of a shirt! Since then, I always check the pockets and sleeves of our clothes before bringing them into the house."

Expanding Its Territory

At one time, Carolina wrens were strictly southern birds, inhabiting wooded and brushy areas in the Southeast. South Carolina even named the pint-sized bundle of energy its state bird.

But Carolina wrens will drift northward, especially during mild winters. Their territory has expanded to include New England and the upper Midwest, but

RIGHT AT HOME. The Carolina wren was a favorite even in colonial times. This bottle (above) is a design used to attract nesting wrens in colonial Williamsburg. They often nest in strange places—mailboxes, flower baskets and pockets on clothes that are hanging to dry.

Southwest and Pacific Coast.

Their bill is thin and pointed, ideal for catching insects. They're particularly fond of spider eggs found under eaves and in the cracks of decks. They'll also enter garages, carports and garden sheds to search crevices for food.

Unlike most wrens, Carolinas visit backyard feeders that offer suet, bird cakes or nutmeats, such as hulled sunflower seeds. Because they don't migrate, they're more likely to visit feeders in winter when the insect population drops.

Carolina wrens often roost in backyards, too. You'll see them in pairs above doorsills, in hanging baskets, birdhouses and even making use of abandoned robin nests.

"When they bed down in our rafters, the female is often cuddled up under the wing of the male," Jean says. "At least I assume it's the female, but it could be the opposite because both birds look alike."

Carolina wrens typically have the same mate from year to year. They're often seen together in backyards and maintain a year-round territory that typically covers a few acres.

These pairs will nest from early spring until late summer, raising as many as three broods in one season. Their bulky nests are often built in cavities. When they're in the open, the birds cover the top and make a side entrance.

The female incubates the speckled pink eggs and together both parents feed the nestlings. By 14 days, the young leave the nest—believe it or not, they're on their own!

That means more amusing bird-watching for readers living in the Carolina wrens' territory. After all, it takes a lot of personality to establish an identity among the crowded wren family. But the Carolina wren has certainly proved it's up to the task.

many birds don't survive when winters are harsh.

Carolina wrens are easy to spot, especially when they perch on an outstretched branch and belt out their distinctive repertoire. You just may hear them before you see them because Carolina wrens sing, robustly at that, all year long.

Their distinctive song, "tea-kettle, tea-kettle, tea-kettle", is attention grabbing, especially in winter when all is quiet.

"The males belt out a powerful song that belies their small size," Marlene says. "Since they sing all year, they're an absolute delight to have around. On very cold days, it's the perfect reminder that warm spring days are ahead."

Its alarm note is just as unique—a distinct buzzing noise that some have compared to the sound of a thumb being rubbed against the teeth of a comb.

Unique Good Looks

Carolina wrens are also the largest and most colorful eastern wren. They're stocky, measuring 5-1/2 inches from the tip of their bill to their cocked tail. And their plumage is a colorful rusty-brown with a distinctive white eye stripe (see it at far left) that's shared only by the Bewick's wren of the

> ## READER TIP
>
> To attract Carolina wrens, I put up an open shelf for them in a protected area. They nest on it during spring and summer and will sleep on it during cold fall and winter nights.
>
> —*Marlene Condon*
> *Crozet, Virginia*

BACKYARD BIRDING BIO

Common Names: Carolina wren, mocking wren and Louisiana wren.
Scientific Name: *Thryothorus ludovicianus.*
Length: 5-1/2 inches.
Wingspan: 7-1/2 inches.
Distinctive Markings: Stocky wren with white eye stripe and bright rusty-brown plumage.
Distinctive Behavior: Sings year-round and protects its territory all year.
Habitat: Commonly found in brush and heavy undergrowth in forests, parks, wooded suburban areas and gardens.

Song: Loud varied song. Often heard as "tea-kettle, tea-kettle, tea-kettle".
Nesting: Builds bulky nest of grass, bark, weed stalks, feathers and other materials in tree cavities, wood piles, sheds, flower baskets, pockets of clothes, mailboxes, etc. Female incubates five to six pale-pink eggs spotted with brown. Both parents feed the nestlings.
Diet: Primarily spiders and insects; eats some berries and seeds.
Backyard Favorites: One of the few wrens that visit bird feeders. Serve peanuts, suet, peanut butter and nutmeats.

■ Year-Round

Shed

Pool

Patio

House

PLAN A GREAT GARDEN

SECRET GARDEN FULL OF SURPRISES

This landscape has "curb appeal", and a private backyard with its own allure.

By Mary Massironi, Beaver Falls, Pennsylvania

The gardening bug bit my husband, Richard, and me when we moved to our new home. And it's a good thing it did.

The house was beautiful, but it had no green appeal whatsoever—not even one blade of grass on half an acre. Just mounds of dirt.

Our first objective was to establish a lawn. Once that happened, our focus turned to shrubs and trees.

To define and enclose the backyard, we planted 45 blue spruce around the perimeter. It took a few years, but now we have a beautiful green wall around the backyard. For the front yard, we chose shrubby pyracanthas and a 7-foot

hedge of upright Hicks yew (see photo, bottom right).

We chose a wide variety of trees that draw attention, such as linden, birch and maple. We also added lots of flowering trees, including magnolia, mountain ash, dogwood and cherry, which give the yard a luxurious feel when they bloom.

The trees and border plantings created the foundation for the backyard. Over time, we added garden beds and other enhancements. Every summer we tackled one more project on our long "to-do" list. Now we have flower gardens around every corner!

Let's Take a Tour

As you approach our front door, thick beds of impatiens greet you along the sidewalk, and annuals spill from window boxes and planters. Hanging baskets of more bright impatiens add color to a wooden fence that separates the front yard from the back.

Open the gate next to the porch to enter the secluded hideaway we call our "secret garden" (top). Lush annuals and perennials flank a stone path alongside a glass-enclosed porch. The yew hedge towers over the flowers, making this a very private and peaceful spot.

At the end of this path, you'll find a rustic wooden bench under a magnolia tree, one of our favorite spots to relax.

This area includes many things made by Richard, including an arbor he constructed from copper pipe (at left), several birdhouses and a whimsical chair he crafted from tree branches. A sidewalk through the gardens leads to our patio and swimming pool.

The backyard provides a haven for butterflies and hummingbirds all summer long. They love the combination of nectar-rich flowers I plant in my hanging baskets. We're convinced our porch is the greatest place in the world to watch nature.

Challenges Tackled

Our landscape has come a long way since we first saw those discouraging mounds of dirt, but it took a lot of work—and a few creative solutions.

Our biggest landscape challenge was dealing with the slopes in our front and back yards. The grades were too steep

BACKYARD HIDEAWAY. Impatiens and neatly trimmed yews (below) lead to the Massironis' front door. It's a prelude to the beauty out back, where baskets of impatiens brighten a fence (above) and pathways (at top and left) lead through bountiful flower beds.

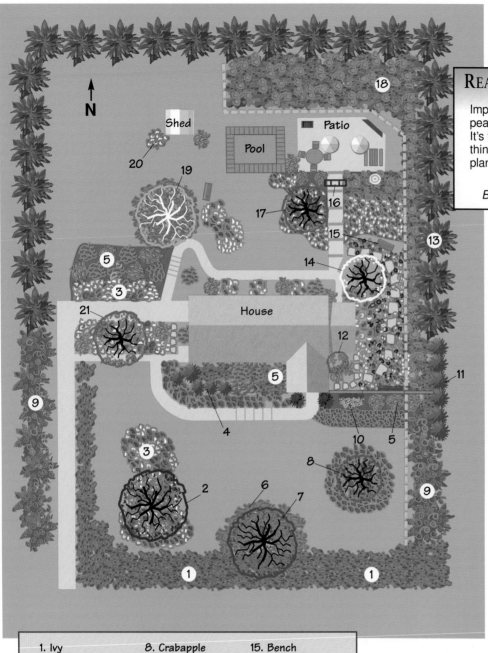

1. Ivy	8. Crabapple	15. Bench
2. Red maple	9. Pyracantha	16. Rose arbor
3. Annual/	10. Climbing rose	17. Linden
perennial beds	11. Hicks yew	18. Daylily
4. Yew	12. Dogwood	19. White birch
5. Rhododendron	13. Colorado blue	20. Hydrangea
6. Pachysandra	spruce	21. European
7. Sugar maple	14. Magnolia	mountain ash

while phlox, coneflower, lupine, bee balm, astilbe, hollyhocks, coreopsis, clematis and foxglove keep the riot of color going.

I also add annuals for long-lasting color. My standbys include impatiens, petunias, celosia, verbena, cosmos, vinca, daisies, geraniums, snapdragons and lantana. I plant many of them in containers or place them in hanging baskets.

Breath of Fresh Air

Scent is very important to us, so we added climbing roses and aromatic annuals like heliotrope. Even the magnolia and linden contribute to the heavenly aroma that permeates our yard.

Here are some of our best tips for gardeners who want to tackle their barren or difficult landscape:

● Whatever you're planting, whether it's flowers, trees or shrubs, enrich the soil first. Improving your planting bed with peat moss, humus or manure is the single most important thing you can do to help your plants' healthy growth.

● Know how large the plants you select will eventually grow. They may look small when you buy them, but they won't stay that way, so leave extra room.

● Proper spacing at planting time will keep your beds looking tidy, and save you the effort of moving or thinning plants later.

Our gardens do require a fair amount of maintenance, but for Richard and me, it's a labor of love. Passers-by often stop to compliment us on the way our place looks. We're always delighted to hear that other people enjoy our yard as much as we do!

to cut with a mower, so we found a way to keep them green and neat: We covered them with ivy.

On one bank in the backyard, we interspersed various colors of daylily with the ivy. Another bank is planted with more daylilies, plus rhododendrons and azaleas.

Curving flower beds placed around our trees provide color and form in the front yard. We included perennials with different flowering times to ensure continuous blooms throughout the season. Columbine and iris usher in spring,

DUST TO DIVINE

This couple struck gold by creating their own desert oasis.

By Beverly Podraza
Bisbee, Arizona

Once a copper mining boomtown, south-eastern Arizona's Bisbee is generally bust when it comes to lush garden landscapes. Built into the rugged mountainside of the ore-rich Mule Mountains, this charming city rests at an altitude of 5,300 feet and is part of the Chihuahuan Desert.

So when my husband, John, and I bought a house here in 1994, we felt fortunate that we at least had a green front lawn of Bermuda grass and a beautiful sycamore tree to offer a bit of shade.

On the other hand, the 30- by 70-foot side yard was an absolute disaster. A tacky canvas cabana, a pear tree on its last legs and a few patches of prickly weeds were all that covered this barren space that, much to our embarrassment, faced the street.

A Patio with Pow

Set on replacing the cabana, John built a screened-in "Arizona" room that features a see-through acrylic roof. A permanent place to house our hot tub, it's ideal for stargazing on those chilly Bisbee nights.

On the patio, just outside the Arizona room, we planted a Prince of Wales juniper and flanked it with color by adding two orange and yellow Dream roses. From there, it's a stone's throw to "Scarborough Fair"—a potted selection

of my favorite cooking herbs, which, of course, include parsley, sage, rosemary and thyme.

Then came the real problem. Our entire side yard was chock-full of caliche, better known as "poor man's concrete". A white calcium carbonate material, caliche takes years to form and occurs as solid layers or lumpy chunks in the soil in this area. Picks, hydraulic nozzles and dynamite are the typical methods for removal. But rather than try to determine what "might" grow in our soil, we decided to cover the majority of this area with decorative brick and rock.

So, to finish the patio, we used hexagon patio bricks and, little by little, were successful in covering the 30- by 12-foot L-shaped area.

Forging a Flower Bed

I then designed a plan for the rest of the yard that included an 8-foot-wide flower bed and a fountain.

Inspired by a quaint red farm pump we found at an antique store, we cut railroad ties into various lengths to edge the raised bed (that's it on page 39). John buried a soaker hose for easy watering and equipped the area with electricity. Once the fountain was in, we were ready to plant.

We started by planting patches of Sedum spurium, a drought- and frost-resistant ground cover (we prefer the Tricolor variety). This low-growing perennial keeps the soil in place during heavy summer rains. Plus, it fills in the gaps that our flowers—such as dahlias, verbena, petunias, salvia, snapdragons, pansies, moss roses and dianthus—leave during the colder winter months.

> ## READER TIP
>
> Rather than try to determine what 'might' grow in our caliche soil, we decided to cover the majority of that area with decorative brick and rock.
>
> —Beverly Podraza
> Bisbee, Arizona

A prized golden barrel cactus, a decorative bucket filled with strawberry plants and a giant dried agave flower stalk that displays our birdhouse collection (at left) were the perfect finishing touches to this colorful bed.

Setting the Scene

To add more interest to our yard, we created two theme gardens.

A whimsical farm scene (above) sits just under a thriving pecan tree at the far end of the yard. Upright railroad ties frame the free-form bed that includes an old wagon wheel, an antique tiller and a half barrel that spills over with shade-tolerant plants, such as pansies, English ivy and New Guinea impatiens.

Just behind this bed begins what we call "Desert Gulch". What

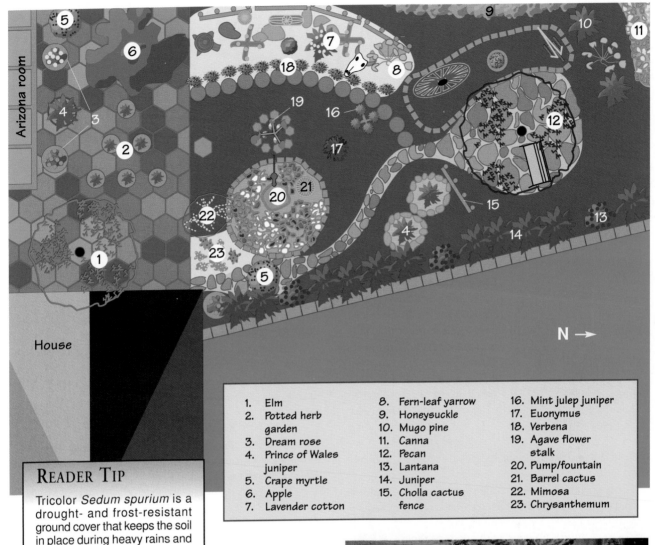

Arizona room

House

N →

READER TIP

Tricolor *Sedum spurium* is a drought- and frost-resistant ground cover that keeps the soil in place during heavy rains and fills in gaps between flowers.

1. Elm	8. Fern-leaf yarrow	16. Mint julep juniper
2. Potted herb garden	9. Honeysuckle	17. Euonymus
3. Dream rose	10. Mugo pine	18. Verbena
4. Prince of Wales juniper	11. Canna	19. Agave flower stalk
5. Crape myrtle	12. Pecan	20. Pump/fountain
6. Apple	13. Lantana	21. Barrel cactus
7. Lavender cotton	14. Juniper	22. Mimosa
	15. Cholla cactus fence	23. Chrysanthemum

started out as a 26- by 4-foot strip of bare ground, now includes an old tree stump, a deserted cowboy campfire and a sun-bleached steer skull (at right).

Strewn amid the cholla, rainbow and barrel cacti, the scene features other native plants like fern-leaf yarrow, lavender cotton and aloe vera.

Not only will these local desert inhabitants thrive in our caliche soil, but the colorful varieties require no shade and very little water.

The Big Cover-Up

To finish off the yard, John ordered a pallet of native lichen-covered flagstone, several bags of lava rock and a few yards of white quartz. He added the white quartz to Desert Gulch and spread the lava rock over the rest of the side yard.

Then he laid down the winding flagstone walkway that ends at a shady courtyard with an inviting park bench. We think it's the perfect place to take in the beauty our yard now offers.

In our eyes, we've created a true desert oasis.

THE DESERT IS IN THE DETAILS. A steer's skull accents drought-tolerant plantings in "Desert Gulch" (above). Other unique additions make their mark, like farm equipment (at top far left) and a dried agave stalk that displays birdhouses (far left).

'GLAD YOU ASKED!'

What's YOUR question for contributing editor Melinda Myers, our gardening expert?

Growing Lady's Slippers

I would love to have more of these pink lady's slippers (left) in my yard. Over the past 5 years, they've slowly multiplied from two plants to five. Is there a way to propagate them myself to help speed up the process?
— *Alan Shelor*
Salem, Virginia

Melinda: It won't be speedy, but you can start these plants from seed.

First, collect seeds in summer after the seedpod has reached full size and dried. Remove the seeds from the pod and sprinkle them on your planting site. Mark the location so you can avoid damaging the young seedlings—it takes several years for the plants to reach flowering size.

A friend of mine covers seeded areas with wire mesh for the first few years as extra protection for the seedlings (from squirrels *and* overzealous gardeners). Once the plants become established, remove the mesh in winter while the plants are dormant.

Save My Irises!

Last year, I lost most of my irises. The leaves turned brown and the rhizomes were soft and mushy. What caused this and how can I keep it from happening again?
— *Whynona Fenske, Wausau, Wisconsin*

Melinda: The iris borer is your culprit. To control it, it's best to first understand its life cycle.

This day-flying moth lays its eggs in the dried iris leaves each fall. The eggs don't hatch until spring, when the new leaves are 4 to 6 inches tall. The borer then enters the leaf and eats its way to the rhizome, where it feeds in early summer. The borer forms a pupa in the soil, and in fall emerges as a moth to start the process all over again.

So the best place to start is by cleaning up the old iris leaves in fall. This is the simplest defence against this pest, and with any luck, the lack of leaves should send the moths looking for a better place to lay their eggs.

Also, whenever you dig and divide your irises, remove and destroy any borers you find. Then cut out and discard damaged portions of the rhizome and replant the healthy portions for future blooms.

If these methods don't work, many gardeners have had success using predacious nematodes to control the borers. These microscopic parasites are sprayed onto the plant in spring, and they locate and feed on the borer.

Prevent Rabbit Raiders

Rabbits are a constant problem in my daughter's yard. What's the best way to keep them from munching on her flowers or vegetable garden?
— *Vivian Keyes*
Minot, North Dakota

Melinda: Fencing may not be pretty, but it's the most effective way to keep plants in and rabbits out.

The fence must be tight to the ground, have mesh small enough (like hardware cloth) to keep out baby rabbits, and be at least 4 feet high.

Applying repellents before the animals start feeding in spring and again throughout the season also can provide some relief. For your safety, use repellents that are approved for use on fruits and vegetables.

Some gardeners also report success using noisemakers, whirligigs and other moving or noisy devices to keep rabbits at bay.

Ultimately, persistence and a variety of deterrents are the keys to convincing rabbits to dine elsewhere.

Fresh Lilac Bouquets

Is there a way to keep cut lilac blooms fresh? After I bring mine in the house and put them in a vase, they begin to droop in a day or two.
— *Rebecca Johnson*
Millville, Pennsylvania

Melinda: It is frustrating to watch a fresh bouquet of lilacs quickly wilt. But you can increase the vase life of lilacs and other flowers by following these simple steps.

Collect flowers in early morning just as the dew is starting to dry, or in the evening. Carry a small bucket of lukewarm water and place the cut stems immediately in it to help keep the flowers fresh. It's best to harvest lilacs and other cluster-type flowers before all the flower buds have opened.

Once inside the house, remove the lower leaves that would be submerged in water and recut the stems on a slant before putting them in the vase. You also can split the woody stems of lilacs and other shrubs. This will help increase their water intake.

Then make sure the vase is always filled with clean water, add a preservative for extra insurance and enjoy!

Dahlias for the South

I'm looking for a dahlia variety that will grow well in the South. I've tried planting them in numerous locations, but the plants and tubers can never make it through summer. Can you help? —Paul Daniels, Waco, Texas

Melinda: You may want to try these two unique varieties that are hardy in Zones 7 to 10. One is the Mexican Cutleaf dahlia (*Dahlia dissecta* var. *sublignosa*), which grows about 30 inches tall with spikes of single lavender-pink flowers atop fine textured foliage.

For a big statement in the garden, try the Giant Tree dahlia (*Dahlia imperialis*). It grows about 9 feet tall and looks like a tropical tree in the landscape. The single pink flowers open late in the season.

Both plants are available through the Plant Delights Nursery catalog. Call 1-919/772-4794 or visit *www.plant delights.com*.

Mystery Plant

My mother always called this plant "monkey faces". She had one of her own years ago, and this one (at left) is about 15 years old. If I protect it in winter, it returns in spring bigger than before and then blooms all summer. Can you tell me its real name?
—Sue Goodwin
Pine Mountain, Georgia

Melinda: This beauty goes by several common names, including cupid's bower and hot water plant. Botanically speaking it's known as *Achimenes*, a native of Mexican and Central American forests.

Gardeners in northern regions subject to hard frost should bring this plant indoors for winter. Then you can grow it like a houseplant or store the dormant rhizome in a cool dark location.

Once outdoors, provide it with full sun and moist well-draining soils. Southern gardeners should select a location with a little afternoon shade.

In the Pink

My sister-in-law spotted this pink-blooming strawberry plant (left) in her garden. What caused the flowers to change from the typical white color?
—Dianna Justice
Lebanon, Oregon

Melinda: It's not always possible to pinpoint *why* a plant developed a new characteristic. However, these types of unexpected changes keep the plant world interesting, sometimes resulting in the introduction of new varieties.

The spontaneous changes in leaf shape, flower color or other features are called sports. This may be what happened to your sister-in-law's plant. In fact, there's an ornamental strawberry with pink flowers that's known as Pink Panda. This pretty strawberry is grown for its flowers but rarely bears fruit.

Mother's Planting Method

My mother used a unique planting method I hope you can help me duplicate. She cut long strips of newspaper, then carefully stuck seeds on the paper and planted these strips in the garden. Her flowers came up looking perfect. But here's my question: How do I attach the seeds to the paper strips? —June Crowley, Horton, Missouri

Melinda: The commercial garden industry took this homemade idea to the marketplace with seed tapes, which were popular in the early 1980s. They made planting smaller seeds easier, ensured proper spacing and eliminated the need for thinning young plants.

To duplicate your mother's method, you can create a "glue" of cornstarch or flour. Here are two recipes I know:

Mix 1 cup flour with 1/4 cup water until the mixture is the consistency of pancake batter. Dab the "glue" on strips of newspaper or paper towel at the proper spacing for your chosen seed.

Place the seeds on the glue and allow to dry. Once you plant it, the flour mixture dissolves, the paper decomposes and the seeds sprout at the proper spacing.

You also can use a cornstarch mixture. Add 1 tablespoon cornstarch to 1 cup cold water, then heat over medium heat, stirring constantly to prevent lumps. Remove from heat as it boils and forms a gel. Cool to room temperature before use.

Rooting Roses

Can you tell me how to root a rosebush cutting? I've tried, but always end up with a dried-up stick rather than flourishing roses. —Lucille McNeal, Elora, Tennessee

Melinda: Timing is everything. You should take the cuttings as the first set of blooms is starting to fade. Make a

4- to 6-inch cutting and remove the flower and lower leaves. Then dip the cut end in a rooting hormone, which is available at most garden centers. This encourages the stem to grow roots while inhibiting rot.

Place the cutting in moist sand, vermiculite or a well-drained potting mix. Loosely cover it with a plastic bag and place it in a warm location away from direct light.

The cutting should root in several weeks, then you can transplant it into a container of potting soil. Move it to a sunny location and water as needed. Once new growth appears on the stem, use a diluted solution of flowering plant fertilizer.

Then pat yourself on the back—you've successfully rooted your first rose!

Spring Surprise

Every year, this plant (left) springs up in my yard. It resembles a hyacinth, but has no scent. What is it?
—*Margie Casey*
Norwich, New York

Melinda: This blooming beauty is commonly known as a wood or Spanish hyacinth. You may find it listed under several botanical names including *Hyacinthoides hispanica*, *Endymion* or *Scilla*.

No matter what you call it, this beauty makes a nice addition to the perennial garden. This hyacinth look-alike is shade tolerant and can grow in a wide range of soils. Hardy in Zones 4 to 9, plant it in fall with other spring flowering bulbs.

Toppling Flowers

My recent crop of zinnias and gladiolas were quite spindly. The zinnias grew 5 feet tall and the glads reached 6 feet. The stems were so weak they could barely support the blooms, even with the help of stakes. What happened?
—*Jo Smith, Summerville, South Carolina*

Melinda: Lack of light or excess nitrogen can cause the growth you describe, so take a look at the conditions in this garden area.

Have your trees matured and started shading these plants? Perhaps a new fence, shed or other addition is blocking some much-needed sunlight.

Next, take a soil test to find out what, if any, fertilizer is needed. Avoid high-nitrogen fertilizer that can promote excess growth.

And finally, monitor the soil's moisture. Excess rain or watering can lead to the spindly growth you've noticed as well as certain disease problems.

Coneflower Seeds

I often admire the purple coneflowers (like the ones at right) growing in my neighbor's yard. Can you plant them using seeds from the cone tops?
—*Patty Duffield*
Strange Creek,
West Virginia

Susan M. Perren

Melinda: Yes, and anyone growing purple coneflowers probably would be happy to share the offspring of these prolific seeders.

Collect seeds in fall, and sow outside or store in the refrigerator over winter. Stored seed can be started indoors or planted directly outdoors in spring.

You won't see flowers until the second season. Also, the offspring of hybrids may look different than the parents.

Help for Hollies

How can I tell the difference between male and female holly shrubs? I've recently learned I need to plant both in order to get berries.
—*Ernest MacKay*
Economy, Nova Scotia

Melinda: A close look at the flowers will reveal the differences between them. The male flower has a straight stem and a flower containing pin-like structures called stamen. These contain the pollen to pollinate the female flowers.

The female flower has a swollen base in the center—similar in shape to a vase—which contains the eggs. Once pollinated, these will develop into the red holly berries.

If it seems like too much trouble to determine what type of holly you have, simply add another pair of holly plants to your yard. Some nurseries sell both male and female plants in one container to avoid confusion.

Start with an Acorn

A friend of mine offered to give me some of her acorns so I can grow new trees. How do I plant them?
—*Ann Fearns, Lecanto, Florida*

Melinda: Thanks for taking on the task of planting oaks that future generations will enjoy.

Harvest and plant acorns as soon as they ripen. You will get the best results by picking acorns from the tree when the nut turns brown. Or collect firm and insect-free nuts as soon as they hit the ground.

Plant the acorns 2 inches deep in rows in a garden area that you've amended with organic matter. Cover the bed with wire mesh to prevent rodents from digging up the acorns. Once young saplings appear, they can be transplanted in early spring to a permanent location.

ANYTHING BUT PLAINS

These gardeners didn't let the harsh Kansas weather dry up their backyard plans.

By Theresa Beilman, Wichita, Kansas

Mother Nature sure doesn't make it easy to garden in the Great Plains of Kansas.

We live in a climate that can be 20° below in winter and 110° in summer...with watering restrictions. Then there's our infamous wind!

But over the past 30 years, my husband, Vern, and I have learned how to work with the weather to create a backyard that makes us proud.

Much of our garden is made up of hand-me-down plants from neighbors and friends. Not only did this help us save

money while putting our six children through college, it also meant the plants already were "Kansas-tested". If they'd survived for other gardeners in our area, we figured they should work for us, too.

If there's one thing I've learned over the years, it's not to mess with success—if it grows, leave it!

Take the Heat

Given our harsh gardening conditions, plants recommended for full sun do well here in partial shade. Hardy lilies

READER TIP

Given our harsh conditions, plants recommended for full sun do well here in partial shade. —*Theresa Beilman Wichita, Kansas*

grow beautifully, as do purple coneflowers, phlox, bee balm, cannas and old-fashioned annuals like zinnias, marigolds, morning glories and moss roses. I fill shady areas with columbine, hostas and foxgloves.

Irises are a trusty standby in Kansas, offering striking blooms in early summer and nice foliage for the rest of the growing season.

A couple plants have surprised us. I managed to grow azaleas by tucking them among the shelter of daylilies on the north side of the house. And a Japanese maple also has thrived, while other gardeners I know have watched theirs struggle.

Because I start planting the gardens as early as February, I protect the young starts at night with sheet plastic draped over stakes and anchored with rocks.

Vern also built a cold frame (above right, left photo), and he's a master at nurturing seedlings, so many plants get a head start in the protection of our miniature greenhouse.

Let the Wind Blow

One thing we've found is that sturdy wooden or stone fences are an absolute necessity. These offer some protection from the wind, especially for tall perennials.

Still, there are many times we can't protect our flowers. One year we lost most of our columbine after a storm covered the entire garden with 3 inches of solid ice. And my pride and joy is a Nelly Moser clematis, but we know that one severe winter or summer could wipe this beauty out.

In addition to the harsh weather, we also face extremely dry summers. So we water judiciously and select plants and lawn grasses—like zoysia—that can tolerate a little drought.

We use a lot of homemade mulch, leaves and lawn clippings to enrich the flower beds. The soil here is hard-packed clay, so it really benefits from this added organic mater-

HAND-ME-DOWNS. The Beilmans made the most of what they had—whether it was donated plants or a former tree-house ladder (above) that now displays geraniums. At top, from left: a fountain accents a shady spot; a cold frame protects early seedlings; the back patio provides a relaxing retreat.

ial. We have a large compost area that we've disguised by planting morning glories on lattice in front of it.

A Place to Relax

I've tried to create several private spots in our garden, which is sometimes difficult because of its small size. One gravel path leads to an out-of-the-way bench, fountain and planter boxes beneath a redbud tree. It's a favorite place for us to sit with our grandchildren and cool off (that's it on page 45).

Even when our six grandchildren aren't visiting, there are reminders of them—and our children—everywhere in the garden. A ladder propped against the maple tree (far left) once served our boys' tree house. Now I use it to display potted geraniums. I anchored the containers to the rungs with nails through the drain holes.

We also made sure to leave room for the grandchildren's swing set, and the clothesline I once used is still there, screened with clematis-covered lattice.

Although gardening in this part of Kansas isn't a breeze, we've discovered plenty of ways to breathe life into our little plot.

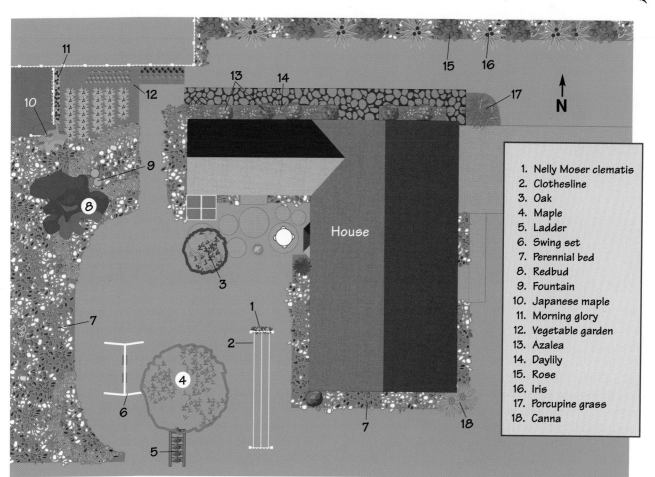

1. Nelly Moser clematis
2. Clothesline
3. Oak
4. Maple
5. Ladder
6. Swing set
7. Perennial bed
8. Redbud
9. Fountain
10. Japanese maple
11. Morning glory
12. Vegetable garden
13. Azalea
14. Daylily
15. Rose
16. Iris
17. Porcupine grass
18. Canna

WHAT TO KNOW BEFORE YOU SOW

Photos: Alan and Linda Detrick

These timely tips will help your seeds get growing.

By Andrew Hind, Gilford, Ontario

Starting your garden plants from seeds packs a big pay-off. Mainly, it's cheaper than buying established plants. But besides the savings, starting your own seeds also gives gardeners a deep sense of satisfaction and, if you live in a harsh climate like I do, it can give you up to a 10-week head start on the growing season.

But before you rush out to buy a new supply of peat pots,

there are several things to consider before you push that first seed into a container filled with potting mix. Follow these tips, and you'll likely have lots of blooming success.

● **Select the right seed.** How do you choose from the hundreds, if not thousands, of seed varieties available? Do your research first. Consider how long it takes for seeds to sprout, germination percentage (how many seeds will sprout), number of days until harvest, disease resistance, soil and sun requirements, plant size and, for vegetables,

expected yields. Choose seeds that match your needs, and the conditions of your planting bed.

● **Pick a winner.** Look for award-winning seed varieties. (This information is usually highlighted on the packet.) These are seeds that have performed well in horticultural trials, making them the safest bet. New disease- and drought-resistant varieties of old favorites are good choices, too.

● **Read the directions.** Seed packages contain a wealth of vital information, such as starting dates and growing conditions, but many gardeners don't even bother to look on the back.

● **Give 'em a bath.** An overnight water bath helps seeds germinate faster. Hard-shelled seeds, such as morning glories and sweet peas, benefit from this process. But some gardeners soak all their seeds to speed up germination. You can plant the next day.

● **Don't overbuy.** Seeds can remain viable as long as they're kept in a cool dry place, but they do degrade over time. For the best results, only buy the seeds you expect to use during the coming season.

● **Let there be light.** Seedlings need lots of light to grow. A south-facing window works well, but the consistency of grow lights is even better. These special lights provide intense illumination to speed up the germination process.

● **Keep your cool.** Most seeds need warm temperatures to sprout—a consistent 69° to 75° Fahrenheit (21° to 24° Centigrade). Higher temperatures can damage the seeds, and cooler ones may prevent germination. Once seedlings emerge, reduce the temperature between 55° and 60°F (13° to 15°C) overnight and 65° to 70°F (18° to 21°C) during the day to prevent leggy growth.

Keep these tips in mind, and your seeds will blossom into a healthy, bountiful garden…and that's the most rewarding payoff of all.

HOW TO SAVE YOUR OWN SEED

It's a great way to get more plants—for free!

By Melinda Myers, Contributing Editor

Collecting, storing and starting seeds can add a new dimension to your gardening. Many seed-savers pass them down through generations, like any other family heirloom. Some gardeners want to preserve old varieties, while others simply try their hand at saving seed for next year's crop. Whatever your reason, start with the end result in mind.

Select seeds from healthy plants that have the color, size or fragrance you want. A good basis of desired characteristics will increase your chances for desirable offspring.

Keep in mind that only self-pollinated plants will "come true" from seed with offspring that look like the parent. But even then, a few surprises can be fun, and may result in something better than expected—or at least a topic for conversation.

My favorite cross-pollinating plants are squash. When I worked for the Extension service, every fall my office was filled with squashes of unusual shapes and colors. Gardeners would bring them in to be identified and ask if they were safe to eat. I remember unique combinations like a white acorn squash, a green zucchini with yellow spots and many other interesting mixes.

I explained to the puzzled gardeners that the seed they saved from last year's crop had been pollinated by another variety. The offspring kept a few characteristics from each parent, producing a unique squash. I assured them that

> ### READER TIP
>
> When collecting seeds, write down the details about what you've gathered. Record important information, such as seed source, date collected, cleaning procedure, storage treatment and germination success. These records will help you repeat successes and avoid duplicating any failures.

Collection Tips

EXTEND your seed collection time and increase your success with these simple techniques:

- Place a paper or cloth bag over the seed head as it nears maturity. This will reduce the number of seeds lost to birds, squirrels and gravity, as they may drop to the ground before you have time to harvest them.

- Cut the stems, bundling them together, and cover seed heads with a paper bag. Use a rubber band or string to secure the bag and trap the seeds inside.

- Pour the seeds out of the bag and continue with the cleaning and drying process.

RDA Inc./GID

these unusual vegetables were safe to eat, and then we had some fun making up names for them.

Collect seeds once the fruit matures or the seedpods dry on the plant. Timing is important, because collecting seeds before they ripen can result in poor germination or even none at all.

Seeds in fleshy fruits like berries, tomatoes and crabapples are best harvested when the seed is fully ripe or slightly overripe. Scoop out the seeds and eat or compost the rest of the fruit. Place the seeds, pulp and water in a bowl or jar of water. Set the mix aside to ferment for several days.

The pulp and bad seeds will float to the top. Scrape this away, pour off the water and save the larger seeds in the bottom. Rinse, then spread those seeds on newspaper to dry for several days. You can also try picking out the seeds with a fork. Rinse off the pulp, then dry.

Collect dry seeds from plants like coneflowers, and those in pods like yucca, after the pods or seeds dry. That's about a month after the flowers fade. Cut off the flower heads and move indoors to clean them. Loosen dried seeds from the stem. Break pods apart to release the seeds inside. Remove any debris or poorly developed seeds. The seeds may look dry, but give them a few more days to dry thoroughly before you pack them away for winter.

Place dried seeds in an envelope, label the contents and place them in a dry airtight jar in the refrigerator. This will keep the temperature consistent and the seeds dry. Wet seeds may begin to sprout in the fridge instead of your garden.

Source: *Birds & Blooms' Ultimate Gardening Guide*, by Melinda Myers. To order, visit "Marketplace" at *www.birdsandblooms.com*.

WHAT A VIEW! Family heirlooms, like a milk cart from her grandparents' ranch (left), overflow with flowers; a fence post birdhouse and an arched bridge (above) accent the back creek and provides a haven for birds like this tree swallow.

a flower-draped arbor, so we can enjoy the birds while we relax.

The birds also frequent the little stream that meanders through one corner of the property. A tree swallow nests near the creek every year in a fence post birdhouse (above right) just in front of our footbridge.

Last year, a couple of mallard ducks were our favorite guests. They'd bathe in the creek, then waddle to the bird feeders to eat the leftovers that had dropped to the ground.

So far, we've attracted more than 20 bird species to our yard, including chickadees, nuthatches, flickers, pileated woodpeckers, scrub and Steller's jays, towhees, waxwings, tanagers and grosbeaks. Hummingbirds are welcome, too. Some years, they surround the sugar-water feeders in droves.

Different Duties

Now that our yard has matured, we don't have to pull thistles anymore—but with 76 roses and 14 flower beds, we still have our hands full. To make watering easier, we installed a sprinkler system to ensure that our lawn and

> ### READER TIP
>
> We use a solution of water with a squirt of mild dish soap to blast aphids off the leaves.
>
> —Lyda Behnke
> Mount Shasta, California

many flower beds receive enough moisture.

Deadheading the flowers is our biggest daily task, but fighting aphids runs a close second. We use a solution of water with a squirt of mild dish soap to blast these little culprits off the leaves.

When the garden is in full flower, we enjoy our little paradise so much that it's hard for us to leave it. We don't want to miss anything—a special bloom we've been waiting for, some young birds leaving the nest, or harvesting our scrumptious fruits and vegetables at their absolute peak.

During summer, we sometimes relax on the deck into the wee hours of the morning so we can listen to the sounds of crickets and other night creatures—including the bear that occasionally finds its way into our yard to eat the fruit from our trees!

Through the years, we've changed things around and moved several trees and shrubs to new locations. But we find great joy in being able to care for this wonderful home and yard.

And come spring, I'll plant a few pansies in the front yard...just as my grandmother always did.

HEAVEN ON A HILLTOP

Fierce weather didn't deter this reader.

By Jane Maxwell Dysinger, Sugar Loaf, New York

From our vantage point, we can see north to the Catskill Mountains and west to the Delaware Valley. Living on top of a hill offers some great views, but the summer sun can be relentless, and the winter winds are downright brutal.

Yet, by planting sun-loving flowers and amending the unforgiving clay soil, I've managed to create whimsical gardens that are drought tolerant and vibrant, despite the elements.

Where It All Began

Using a pickax, I dug my first flower bed in 1992. After weeks of unearthing and removing wheelbarrows full of fist-size rocks, I decided to use them to define flower beds and pathways instead.

I also started a compost pile. I added kitchen scraps, such as coffee grounds, vegetable clippings and eggshells, as well as 5-gallon buckets of horse manure collected from the local racetrack. Even the fallen leaves from my mother's yard ended up on the pile. Eventually, I had enough compost to begin to enrich the soil.

Then came the fun part. I planted all types of sun-loving perennials, including daisies, lilies, lambs' ears, yarrow, lavender, lady's mantle, love-in-a-mist, spiderwort, hollyhocks, black-eyed Susans, bee balm, tansy, poppies, veronica and baby's breath. These plants have to be tough because once a flower is established in my garden, the only water it gets is what Mother Nature provides.

Yesterday's News

Because the yard used to be grassland, weeds and invasive grasses are always trying to take over the flower beds. I ex-

perimented with everything short of chemicals, until I discovered the benefits of mulching with moistened newspaper topped with wood chips. Not only does this method stunt weed growth and keep the soil moist, but it's good for the environment, too.

Each fall, I make

ETHEREAL ESCAPE
Jane Maxwell Dysinger (below) created a colorful retreat with sun-loving plants and whimsical garden art like the cherub (above left).

> ### READER TIP
>
> Improve the soil by mulching with moistened newspaper and wood chips. Not only does this method stunt weed growth and keep the soil moist, but it's good for the environment, too.
>
> —*Jane Maxwell Dysinger*
> *Sugar Loaf, New York*

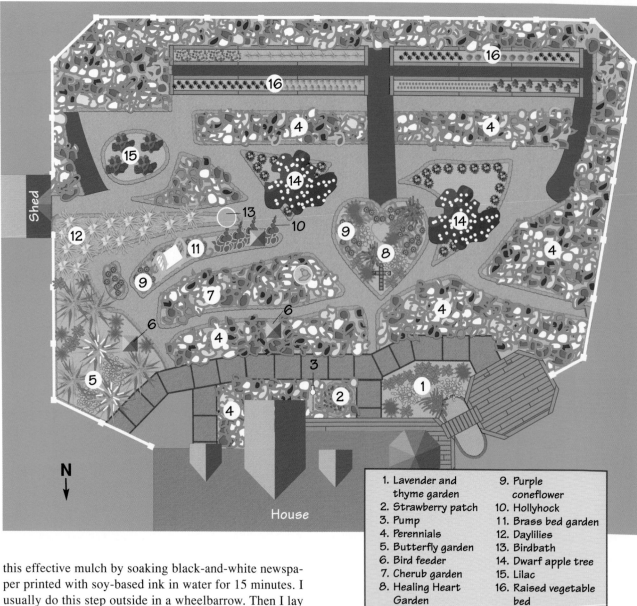

1. Lavender and thyme garden
2. Strawberry patch
3. Pump
4. Perennials
5. Butterfly garden
6. Bird feeder
7. Cherub garden
8. Healing Heart Garden
9. Purple coneflower
10. Hollyhock
11. Brass bed garden
12. Daylilies
13. Birdbath
14. Dwarf apple tree
15. Lilac
16. Raised vegetable bed

this effective mulch by soaking black-and-white newspaper printed with soy-based ink in water for 15 minutes. I usually do this step outside in a wheelbarrow. Then I lay the newspaper (about 15 to 20 sheets thick) in my flower beds, making sure there are no gaps for weeds to poke through.

Once it's down, I cover the paper with 2 to 3 inches of inexpensive organic mulch before topping it with a thin layer of more attractive wood chip mulch.

When I want to plant, all I have to do is cut through the newspaper (after it's been moistened) and dig my hole. I also mulch existing flower beds by spreading paper around established plants. I'm just careful not to place it too close to reseeding annuals, as I don't want to snuff out the seeds for next year's blooms.

While many people consider their gardens a backdrop to their house, I consider my house a backdrop to my gardens.

That includes the "butterfly garden". Each season, it attracts several species of these flying flowers. They just love my Summer Beauty butterfly bush, with its rosy-pink flower spikes. The monarchs flock to my milkweed. Because it's the larval host plant for these beauties, I just let it reseed

VIEW FROM THE TOP. Winding pathways link a series of flower beds in Jane Maxwell Dysinger's hilltop backyard (above), which includes features like a brass bed garden that eventually blooms with marigolds, and a heart-shaped memorial garden (below left).

through the garden each year, so there's always plenty.

Serene Themes

A stone cherub (on page 53) is the centerpiece for one of my most colorful beds. In early spring, iris and chives surround the statue given to me by a fellow gardener. In summer, white garden phlox, yellow coreopsis, white clematis, red hot poker, pink Asiatic lilies and rust-colored gaillardia are familiar inhabitants of this garden.

Then there's the "brass bed garden". Inspired by a bed that was headed for the junkyard, my friend Diana suggested we add it to the garden. It took only 15 minutes to assemble, and we planted yellow and orange marigolds into

READER TIP

For a sunny garden with less work, select tough sun-loving flowers. You'll cut down on watering requirements later.

the crate-filled mattress and used begonias for the "pillow".

I also created two heart-shaped gardens. One is a 24- by 36-foot herb garden that I named the "Healing Heart Garden". Filled with purple coneflower and a variety of thyme and lavender, it sits in the center of my backyard.

Memorial Garden

The other heart-shaped garden is in memory of my sister-in-law, Joan Valentine. Located in the front yard, it's the first garden you see (at left) as you come up the driveway. Two stone benches offer perfect views of both sunrise and sunset. Yellow daffodils, pink begonias, mother of thyme and Silver Mound artemisia are reflected in the silver gazing ball that sits in the garden's center.

Today, my flower beds are home to over 150 different plants, and if the past is any indication of what's to come, I look forward to watching my gardens grow even more in the years ahead.

GARDEN OF IDEAS

Readers share all the creative ways they make backyards special.

"Gourdeners" Stay Busy With Crafty Creations

LOOKING FOR something new for landscaping and crafting? Birdhouse gourds are a two-for-one package.

The white-flowered vines beautify the garden during the growing season, and after their fruits cure and dry over winter you can turn them into…well, just about anything.

Joan Pruiksma from Warrenton, Virginia says her friend Kay May uses gourds to make birdhouses, containers, instruments and more (see photo below).

"Kay decorates many with wood-burned designs," Joan says. "For others, she leaves the dried seeds inside to make musical instruments. Even the smallest ones are turned into canisters with cork or corncob stoppers."

Kay's largest gourd, which she calls "Big Mama", is decked out in a straw hat and a necklace made of dried gourd seeds, of course.

On the opposite coast, Jack and Lorene Trimble of East Wenatchee, Washington didn't know what to do with their bumper crop of gourds. After drying and cleaning them, Jack decided they made perfect canvases for their outdoor paintings (top).

"The first thing I tried was an elk. Then we moved on to flowers and birds," Jack says. "We also turned quite a few into painted snowmen. It's amazing what you can do with gourds if you take the time."

USING THEIR GOURDS. Readers have found lots of unique ways to transform a bumper crop of birdhouse gourds into one-of-a-kind creations.

Easy Winter Pond Care

I'VE BUILT a lot of water gardens over the years and am often asked if waterfalls and fountains need to be turned off in wintertime. My answer is always an emphatic, "No!"

As you can see from the photo above, leaving your waterfall and fountain on in winter can provide all kinds of beauty and open water for your bird sanctuary.

People also ask me what to do with their fish and plants in the wintertime. Some water gardeners take their fish indoors, but it really isn't necessary. If your pond is 36 inches or deeper, your fish will be fine throughout winter because they "hibernate" in the bottom as the weather gets cold. You don't even have to feed them (nor should you for their own good).

Perennials like water lilies, water iris and arrow plants should be moved to the deepest part of the pond for winter. As for annuals, some reseed in their bottom debris, while others need to be replaced.

—*Rob Harris*
Campbellsville, Kentucky

56

Living Christmas Trees Give for Years to Come

WANT TO ENJOY your live Christmas tree long after the holidays? Then consider purchasing a balled-and-burlapped tree that you can replant in your yard after the celebration.

To increase your chances for successfully planting a "live" Christmas tree in your yard, here are some tips from the International Society of Arboriculture:

● Dig a planting hole before the ground freezes. Store the removed soil someplace where it won't freeze, like a garage or shed. Fill the hole with straw and cover it with boards for everyone's safety.

● Choose a location in your backyard that's big enough for a mature tree. Some evergreens can reach 50 feet in height, with a 20-foot spread, so give them plenty of room.

● Select a tree with a moist soil ball, not a frozen one. Store the tree in your garage for a few days to minimize the stress of bringing it into the warm indoors.

● Keep the tree in your house no more than a week, so it doesn't dry out. Put the tree back in the garage for a few days, then plant it in your prepared hole, using the dirt you stored to fill the hole. Water thoroughly, and watch your Christmas tree take root and grow!

RP Photo

Little Sprouts Grow with Elementary Garden Club

MAGIC BULBS. Students at Strafford Elementary School help science lab teacher Debbie Burks (above) plant flowering spring bulbs. At left, the principal's husband, Garnall Cigdill, offers a hand.

HERE AT Strafford Elementary School, where I teach, three other teachers and I started a garden club for students in grades one through five. The only requirement for membership is simple—an interest in "playing in the dirt"!

At our first meeting, we gathered seeds, talked about the plants we had at home and discussed ideas for sprucing up our school's existing garden. We moved dirt and rocks, turned over the soil in the garden beds to see what was there and got rid of the weeds that were trying to take over.

The students' energy and enthusiasm has rubbed off on others, too. We wrote letters to seed companies, and they sent the children seed packets for next season. Our principal's husband recruited two friends to put in a new sidewalk near the garden. A local business even donated a truckload of topsoil.

Since then, we've received a grant from the Missouri Conservation Department and have added a water garden, 16 benches and lots of native wildflowers. —*Linda Maune Strafford, Missouri*

Creativity in Bloom

IT'S AMAZING what you can do with a little dirt and a dose of imagination. Just check out these clever container ideas sent in by our readers. Instead of heading for the garden center, they used homemade or recycled containers to make one-of-a-kind planting pots for their backyards.

Want to try it yourself? Take a peek in your garage or basement. You might be surprised at how easy it is to turn castoffs into blooming treasures.

S.S. MARIGOLD. "This flower box (above) is a miniature fishing dory," writes Wayne Smith of Shelburne County, Nova Scotia. "My brother-in-law, Fulton Goreham, built the boat for his wife, Mildred. He's a retired fisherman and enjoys building these miniatures. It certainly brightens up the yard."

SHORT STUFF. "Last year, I recycled old boots and a pair of blue jean shorts to make planters (above)," says Anne Sacher from Leonardo, New Jersey. "I made the most of the planting space in the shorts by adding flowers to the pockets, too. We had a lot of heavy rain here in spring, but the gazania in these planters weathered it well."

Colorful Pathway

WHEN WE MOVED into our house about 5 years ago, a pathway of broken concrete slabs led to our front door. But the plain pieces looked drab and ugly.

My wife works with stained glass as a hobby, so she solved the problem by transforming the concrete pieces into colorful mosaic stepping-stones. The stones at the walkway's outer edge feature flowers, and those on the inside depict birds (see photo at right).

The project took about 2 years to complete (there are 82 pieces!), but the results are well worth it.

—*Boyd Sensenich Jr., Beaufort, North Carolina*

TIDBITS

Make Your Own Pot Holes

WANT TO ADD drainage holes to that pretty clay container? *Birds & Blooms*' resident handyman, Cliff Muehlenberg, came up with this simple method.

Using *light* pressure, drill a 1/8-inch hole with a normal wood bit. You can also use a bit designed for drilling holes in glass.

Increase the size of the hole by using progressively larger bits. This gradual method helps keep the clay from cracking. If you want to enlarge the holes even more, file off the edges with a round rat-tail file—the coarser, the better. Stop periodically to wash off the file with water and wipe it dry.

Create Your Own Sparklers

LOOKING for a Fourth of July garden decoration with "flare"? Try transforming dried flower heads into sparklers. *Birds & Blooms* Field Editor Royce Pendergast of Orange, Texas sent us this photo (at right) of her unique idea.

"I cut the stems of my spent agapanthus flowers and spray-painted them red, white and blue," she writes. "Gathered into a holiday display, they looked just like exploding fireworks!"

Gardens Come to Life

MANY GARDENERS liven up their landscapes with simple flowers. These readers, however, went a step further and used colorful blossoms to create garden figures that are larger than life.

A horse figure in Manitowoc, Wisconsin (top) so impressed Josie Bochek of nearby Sturgeon Bay that she had to stop and take a few pictures.

"Whenever we travel through Manitowoc, we always drive past this garden to see what's new," Josie says. "On one trip, we were surprised to see this beautiful begonia-covered horse. The eyelashes were made from spider plants. What a labor of love!"

Marilynn and Frank Kathrein of McMinnville, Oregon have an eye-catching "flower lady" (left) that keeps watch over their front gate. They keep her interesting by frequently updating her "wardrobe" during the year.

"She changes with the seasons," Marilynn says. "In summer her skirt bursts with Wave petunias, and at Christmastime, we drape her with white lights and add a bouquet of red carnations."

The topiary, made of tree moss over a metal frame, even has a name—"Sabrina".

Some garden sculptures are happy accidents—like Gia Spoor's "flower train" (below) in Worthington, Indiana.

"It started when my husband and I put up a trellis for morning glories near my old honeysuckle vine," Gia explains. "I added golden star melampodium to add color on each side, and pink pampas grass at the end."

All aboard!

Sandbox a Shady Retreat For Budding Naturalists

OUR BOYS love birds, so we created a "sand house" where they can play and enjoy nature at the same time.

My husband removed the original tarp roof and attached lattices to the corner posts. We planted birdhouse gourds next to the house to provide shade for the boys as they play. And we love seeing the gourds resting on the roof in fall.

I added other plantings the boys would enjoy, such as sunflowers, zinnias, cottontail grass and red salvia for the hummingbirds. For a fall display, we planted ornamental corn.

Wind chimes with bird and butterfly designs hang throughout the sand house. There's also a birdhouse that hosted a wren family and small feeders crafted by our sons.

On the large chalkboard at the back of the house, the boys often draw creative pictures of the nature scenes they see.

We've enjoyed this project so much and have received many compliments on it. But the highest compliment is that our sons play there all summer long. —*Natalie Fontes Charlton, Massachusetts*

THEY ROSE TO THE CHALLENGE

New surroundings and a helpful neighbor spurred their gardening aspirations.

By Nita Aston, Lewiston, Idaho

PAVING THE WAY. Nita and Dave Aston (at left) welcome birds into their yard with a birdbath and feeders (above) among a mix of perennials and roses.

Our gardening adventure began 20 years ago, when our family moved from the sunny southern California climate to the beautiful, but wetter and cooler, state of Idaho.

It was late winter when we arrived. And even though we didn't expect a yard ablaze with colorful flowers, we hoped spring would uncover little crocus, yellow daffodils or pink tulips. Alas, it did not happen.

However, our backyard did yield one rather large plant that a knowledgeable neighbor identified as rhubarb. We certainly had a lot to learn about gardening.

Seeing our disappointment with the backyard's condition, our gardening neighbor began sharing her wisdom—and her plants—with us. At the time it seemed impossible

to make our yard look as lovely as hers, but we accepted the challenge.

Little Sprouts

During our first few years in Idaho, my husband, Dave, and I were too busy raising a family to spend a lot of time raising plants. But as the children grew up and moved out, we began to tackle yard projects with vigor.

First we planted trees and shrubs. The trees we liked most were flowering dogwoods and Japanese maples, which provided beauty without being too big.

Next we dug out grass to create room for curving flower beds. We made an island in the middle of the lawn and planted three rosebushes, Mary Rose, Summer Snow and Sunsprite. Over the years, roses became a common feature in our yard.

> **READER TIP**
>
> Create a pattern with inexpensive gray and red pavers for an attractive patio that doesn't break the bank.

I also wanted a place to entertain, so Dave designed and built a patio area (that's it at top). He used inexpensive gray and red pavers to create a pattern of 4-foot squares. He left four open squares for plants, which brings the garden right onto the patio. This is especially nice for fragrant flowers.

Our next project came about because we found some free bricks. We decided

MADE IN THE SHADE. The Astons' newest garden area borders a shady path (above center). The colorful plantings lead to a relaxing bench (right) that sits in the leafy embrace of a Japanese maple. At top, roses and a towering butterfly bush flank a paver patio.

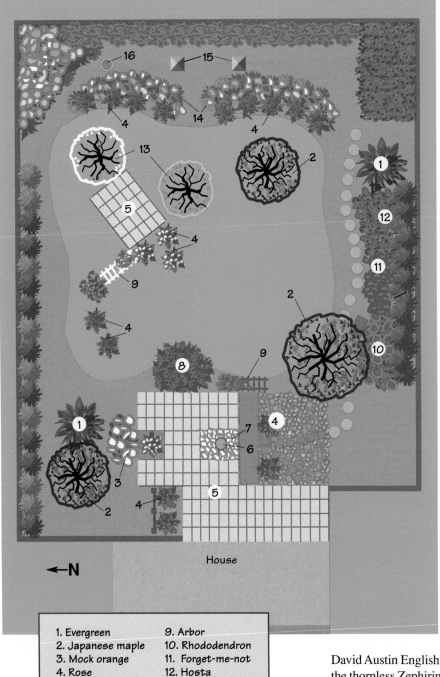

1. Evergreen
2. Japanese maple
3. Mock orange
4. Rose
5. Patio
6. Sundial
7. Alyssum
8. Butterfly bush
9. Arbor
10. Rhododendron
11. Forget-me-not
12. Hosta
13. Dogwood
14. Perennial garden
15. Bird feeder
16. Birdbath

on, we decided to choose mostly pastel colors like pink, lavender, light blue, white and soft yellow. This created a serene and peaceful atmosphere.

However, if we see deep-red or orange flowers we really want to try, we put them in our "wild garden" for a season or two. That lets us try them out before adopting the flowers into the rest of our garden.

We've also realized the importance of different shades of green to complement the other hues in the landscape. One of our favorites for this is lady's mantle (*Alchemilla mollis*), a perennial with large lobed leaves and tiny greenish-yellow flowers.

We're also more selective about our roses. In our early exuberance, we'd planted about 40 hybrid roses. They were beautiful and healthy during the first 2 years. But the third year, they developed every possible blight—black spot, mildew and rust, along with an infestation of aphids.

Now most of our roses are floribundas, shrub roses, rugosas and David Austin English roses. We also have climbing roses like the thornless Zephirine Drouhin, graceful William Baffin and Dream Weaver.

Alive with Activity

We don't have to spray the roses for disease anymore, so birds regularly visit the garden to feast on the aphids and other insects.

Birds also flock to our birdbaths and feeders. The hummingbirds have even found us, along with robins, doves, quail, sparrows, goldfinches and many other species that we have yet to identify.

Recently, a friend told us visiting our backyard was like being in a park. That really made us feel accomplished, especially considering where we started.

Now we enjoy being able to share our knowledge—and plants—with friends and neighbors.

to use them for another small patio to connect the white dogwood tree to our "rose island". Dave built an arbor beside it, where we planted silver lace vine, which is a lovely focal point when in bloom.

Last summer we started working on a shade garden as well, planting varieties like astible, Jacob's ladder, hostas and rhododendrons.

Learn as You Go

In the beginning of our gardening endeavors, we planted any color of rose or perennial that we liked. Later

6 EASY-TO-GROW BACKYARD ROSES

Carefree Beauty

Height: 5 to 6 feet.

Blooms: 4- to 4-1/2-inch rosy-pink semi-double flowers.

Bloom time: Mid-season and repeats.

This plant was one of the finest bred by the late Dr. Griffith Buck's program at Iowa State University. He wanted roses that could meet the challenge of Midwest gardens—blazing hot summers and frigid winters.

Carefree Beauty can blanket your garden with its beautiful fragrance.

New Dawn

Height: Climbs 12 to 20 feet.

Blooms: 3- to 3-1/2-inch blush-pink double flowers.

Bloom time: All season.

This climbing rose is easy to train on a trellis or fence because its canes are light and flexible—just watch out for its large thorns.

New Dawn, introduced in 1930, is packed with blooms that have an aroma like ripe peaches. It was the first plant in history to receive a patent.

Knock Out

Height: 3 feet.

Blooms: 3- to 3-1/2-inch ruby-red single flowers.

Bloom time: All season.

When it comes to no-muss, no-fuss roses, Knock Out tops them all.

Knock Out produces brilliant single blossoms all summer long that are "self-cleaning", which means there's no need for removing or "deadheading" faded flowers to encourage more blooms.

The Fairy

Height: 2 to 3 feet.

Blooms: 1-1/2- to 2-inch bright-pink double flowers.

Bloom time: Midsummer until frost.

The Fairy is a small compact shrub rose that forms a mound about 3 feet tall and wide. It's an excellent rose to grow in the perennial garden or in large containers such as a half whiskey barrel.

It produces flowers that look like tiny boutonnieres all summer, even if ignored.

Flower Carpet

Height: 12 to 30 inches.

Blooms: 1-1/2- to 2-inch single or double flowers, depending on variety.

Bloom time: All season.

The Flower Carpet series of roses bloom profusely and are among the easiest plants to maintain.

These ground cover roses can produce more than 1,000 blooms in a single season, covering an area 3-feet square. They're also beautiful in hanging baskets and pots.

William Baffin

Height: 8 to 12 feet.

Blooms: 3- to 4-inch deep-pink flowers with a splash of white.

Bloom time: Midsummer and repeats.

This Canadian rose comes from the popular Explorer Series, bred for extreme cold hardiness. The vigorous rose has a large spread and jaw-dropping clusters of flowers. It brings life to fences and trellises, and has proven to be suited for gardens throughout North America.

BACKYARD BIRD HAVEN

Main Photo: Michael Shedlock; Birds on sunflower, Hugh P. Smith Jr.

HOW TO ATTRACT BIRDS

*Put out the welcome mat
for your feathered friends.*

By Anne Pink, St. Paul, Minnesota

When you brought that expensive bird feeder home, were you expecting instant Christmas-card images—flashes of bright-red northern cardinals and frosty blue jays—just outside your picture window? Are you still waiting for them to appear?

No doubt it's a great idea to liven up your backyard. But it takes more than a feeder to turn a ho-hum backyard into a bird haven. To achieve it, you're going to have to know the basics of "birdscaping".

Just what does that mean?

Birdscaping is providing everything feathered friends need to survive right in your backyard. Do a good job, and your chances of attracting lots of winged activity increase remarkably.

That means you're going to have to do more than just set out food and water. You'll also have to add plants that provide suitable places for nesting and cover from weather and predators.

Combine these ingredients, and you're on the way to establishing a complete ecosystem for feathered friends. (See "Calling All Birds" on page 69).

Where to Start

Even if you're starting from scratch, the good news is you don't have to plant an entire meadow or forest, nor does your flower bed or border have to have that wild unkempt look. You just have to select the plants most desirable to native songbirds. Here are some suggestions to get started:

● **Evergreens**, primarily conifers, are a key element for birdscaped backyards. They provide dense shelter and well-hidden nesting sites, as well as food from their seed-producing cones.

Incorporate conifers into your landscape by anchoring them to flower beds, then design around them. Most importantly, consider the size of your planting area. Many evergreens grow more than 60 feet tall and spread 20 or more feet wide, but there are evergreens suitable for every space and growing condition. Before you dig the hole, know exactly how large your plant will eventually get.

● **Deciduous shrubs and trees**, plants that lose their leaves in autumn, are the second most important element to a bird-friendly landscape. If you have limited space, consider small ornamental trees. Many produce berries for food, as well as flowers in spring and gorgeous colors in the fall. Some bird species will use the crotches, where branches meet, for nesting (above photo).

● **Ornamental grasses**, native or not, are a real treat for birds because they provide both seeds and shelter. They combine beautifully with evergreens and flowers, and come in all sizes, shapes and colors. Another benefit: The only annual maintenance needed is a trim back in spring.

(Be aware that while most grasses form clumps, some

THE RIGHT STUFF. You can attract more birds to your yard by selecting a variety of plants for food and cover. Sunflower (above) attracts feasting birds like American goldfinches and house finches. Black-eyed Susans and annual red fountain grass (at far left) also produce seeds for food. At top, a male yellow warbler tends a nest sheltered in protective cover.

seed prolifically and should be avoided or used carefully.)

• **Perennials** provide nectar and seed sources for backyard birds. Some, like purple coneflower and black-eyed Susans, supply both.

For gardeners who prefer a well-manicured look, it takes a little effort to refrain from cutting the plants back in fall. It's better to leave the seed heads stand so the birds can get to the food when they need it most—in winter.

For an effective perennial garden, plant flowers that bloom at staggered times so you have continuous blooms. Good combinations include wood geraniums and columbine for spring, bee balm and phlox for mid-season and asters and sedums for August and beyond. But don't stop there…the combinations are endless.

• **Annuals** bloom all summer long and some are top-notch nectar sources for hummingbirds and butterflies, so save some space for them. Even common inexpensive plants like zinnias, sunflowers and petunias are welcome additions to a bird-scaped garden.

• **Birdbaths** are essential to a bird garden, since avian species need water for drinking and bathing. Water that moves and splashes in fountains or ponds will draw more birds to your backyard because of the sound, but a simple shallow dish or birdbath (right) can be inexpensive and effective. Add a heater in wintertime.

• **Birdhouses and feeders** will attract even more birds into your backyard. House wrens and purple martins are about the only birds that will nest in a swinging birdhouse, so most should be post- or tree-mounted. Feeders should offer a variety of food, including seed, suet and sugar water.

How you arrange these bird-friendly elements is entirely up to you. If your yard is small, consider putting lower plants around the foundation, creating a "stadium effect" (pictured above). Or ask a neighbor to share a garden that straddles the property line. This will split the cost and labor.

For larger properties, create clusters that lead the birds to feeders near your house, so you can see the activity from your favorite windows.

As you can see, birdscaping isn't rocket science, but it does take a little research and planning to select trees, shrubs and flowers that serve the birds' needs. But your efforts will be rewarded…with those Christmas-card images you've been dreaming of.

> **READER TIP**
> Water that moves and splashes in fountains and ponds will draw more birds to your backyard because of the sound.

DIVE IN. A heated birdbath (above) is a great way to attract birds, like this American goldfinch. At top, plant groundcovers, shrubs and trees according to height to create a "stadium effect". This makes for unobstructed bird-watching from indoors.

CALLING ALL BIRDS

LIKE ANY SUCCESSFUL RECIPE, you'll need the right ingredients to attract more birds to your backyard. The basics are food, water, cover and places to raise young. Here's a list of what you can add to encourage more winged activity at your place:

● **Fruit-, nut- or seed-bearing trees and shrubs.**

A northern mockingbird perches on red cedar.

Cherry
Crabapple
Dogwood
Hawthorn
Highbush cranberry
Holly
Mountain ash
Mulberry
Raspberry
Red cedar (Juniper)
Serviceberry
Sumac

● **Shrubs and conifers that provide shelter, protection and nesting areas.**

Fir	Mesquite
Hemlock	Rhododendron
Juniper	Pine
Manzanita	Spruce

● **Perennials and annuals that provide seeds and nectar sources.**

Asters	Purple coneflower
Bee balm	Red-hot poker
Coreopsis	Salvia
Cosmos	Sedum
Goldenrod	Sunflower
Joe Pye weed	Zinnia
Marigold	

● **Vines for cover and nest sites.**

American bittersweet	Honeysuckle
Clematis	Trumpet vine
Grape	

● **Birdbaths for bathing and drinking.**

● **Feeders providing seed, suet and sugar water.**

Ground feeders	Post-mounted feeders
Hanging feeders	Tabletop or tray feeders

● **Birdhouses for cavity-nesting birds.**

● **Brush piles for shelter, nesting and protection.**

5 PLANTS BIRDS LOVE

Birds can't resist this garden.

Illustration: Larry Mikec

Want to add some winged activity to your backyard? Use this easy-to-follow planting diagram for five bird-friendly plants that offer the nectar, seeds and berries feathered friends love.

To use all these plants, you'll need an area in full sun that's about 10 feet by 10 feet, leaving at least 5 feet from nearby buildings for the tree to grow. Or, just add a few of the plants to your already existing flower beds!

Allegheny Serviceberry (1)
Botanical name: *Amelanchier laevis.*
Size: Up to 25 feet tall and wide.
Hardiness: Zones 5 to 9.
Bird-friendly benefits: Large berries appear in early summer and are irresistible to many birds, such as American robins, cedar waxwings, northern cardinals and blue jays. Some people call these trees juneberries.

Liatris (2)
Botanical name: *Liatris spicata.*
Size: 3 feet tall and 18 inches wide.
Hardiness: Zones 4 to 9.
Bird-friendly benefits: Also called gayfeather or blazing star, this flower attracts hummingbirds to its spikes of lavender, rose or white flowers. American goldfinches, tufted titmice and other seed eaters savor its seed heads.

Serbian Bellflower (3)
Botanical name: *Campanula poscharskyana.*
Size: 6 inches tall and 24 inches wide.
Hardiness: Zones 3 to 9.
Bird-friendly benefits: Deep-purple bell-shaped flowers on trailing stems make this a colorful ground cover that's a favorite of hummingbirds.

Midnight Wine Weigela (4)
Botanical name: *Weigela* 'Midnight Wine'.
Size: 24 inches tall and wide.
Hardiness: Zones 4 to 9.
Bird-friendly benefits: This dwarf cultivar of weigela has purple leaves and pink flowers that attract hummingbirds.

Black-Eyed Susan (5)
Botanical name: *Rudbeckia fulgida.*
Size: 36 inches tall and 18 inches wide.
Hardiness: Zones 4 to 9.
Bird-friendly benefits: Numerous seed-eating birds enjoy the seed heads at the center of this flower's bright-yellow petals. Some birds you might see are house finches, chickadees and American goldfinches.

FANTASTIC FEEDERS

These three pages are full of ideas to serve birdseed with style.

Birdie Buffet

"I MAKE yard art, and this combination bird feeder and birdhouse (right) is one from my latest creations," writes Bill Toler of Thornton, Texas. "It brightens the area around our home and attracts plenty of bird activity."

All Aboard

"I DESIGNED this oriole feeder (above) to look like a railroad tunnel, complete with tracks and a red handcar that holds grape jelly," writes Maynard Paul of Bloomington, Minnesota. "The ends of the tunnel are painted to look like stone, and the white guardrails make suitable perches."

A Feeder That Rocks

"THIS FEEDER (below) combines my love of rocks, wood and birds," says Kirk Starin of Fowlerville, Michigan. "It's 8 feet tall and holds about 10 days worth of food. I wrapped a Slinky around the pole to keep squirrels from climbing up and stealing the birdseed."

Family Tradition

"MY HUSBAND, B.K. (above), has built many birdhouses and feeders, but this one has special meaning," says Judy Hiatt of Kearney, Missouri. "It represents the grain mill and elevator my father owned for more than 40 years. B.K. worked for Daddy as a teenager, and then managed the mill for 3 years before it was sold. It brings back great memories."

In Their Sunday Best

"MY SON, James, built this bird feeder (above) for me and installed it in my backyard where I can see it from the kitchen windows," says Cecil King from St. Amant, Louisiana. "The steeple lifts off for easy filling, and the protected vestibule helps keep the food dry. Clear windows allow me to see when it's time to replenish the seed.

"Cardinals are frequent visitors to the feeder, so we joke that it must be a Catholic church."

Bright Idea

"A PIPE sticking out of the ground from our well was an eyesore, so I built this 6-foot-tall lighthouse around it with a bird feeder on top (at left)," says Joe Zampella of South Berwick, Maine. "The plastic center that holds the food is painted yellow to look like a beacon."

It's Uncanny!

"A LOCAL MAN, Tony Baumann, makes these wonderful feeders (right) from cans that we save at the school where I work as a cook," says Bridget Klebel of Green Isle, Minnesota. "I help feed the kids, and he helps feed the birds. Even when my feathered friends aren't there, my little tin man makes me smile."

Throwing Birds a Curve

"MY WIFE AND I help out at a county park, where one of our duties is to maintain a Frisbee golf course (it's like regular golf, but uses Frisbees to hit targets)," writes Cecil Smethers of Grants Pass, Oregon. "As you might guess, we find a lot of unclaimed Frisbees, but I didn't want to throw them away. That's why I came up with the idea to make them into bird feeders (below).

"Each feeder uses two Frisbees and an old plastic jar to hold the seed. Birds of all sizes love the feeders, and everyone thinks it's a terrific idea. They even supply us with extra Frisbees!"

Thomas Trains The Squirrels

"MY DAUGHTER Becky is a huge fan of Thomas the Tank Engine, so my father, Patrick Martin, made this squirrel feeder (left) for her," writes Susan Sebring of Bartonsville, Pennsylvania. "He based his design on a squirrel train feeder he saw in a past issue of *Birds & Blooms*. As you can see, he did a fantastic job. We've seen as many as four squirrels riding Thomas at once. It's very entertaining."

On the Cheep

"ALTHOUGH it's made from inexpensive materials, this goldfinch feeder (right) really works," says Mary Millard of Morpeth, Ontario. "I started with an old tennis ball can and drilled holes in it to accommodate wooden dowels for perches. I added several smaller holes to dispense thistle seed and then hung it up using an extra coat hanger.

"This simple feeder would be a great project for kids to build."

Heavenly Host

"I FOUND the plans for this replica of Paris' Notre Dame Cathedral (above) in a book called *Architectural Birdhouses* by Thomas Stender," writes Norman Watson of Phoenix, Arizona. "I revised the design to make a feeder, replacing the center entrance with a window. I've since converted other plans in the book to make feeders modeled after an Aztec pyramid, the Chrysler Building and the Parthenon."

New Life for Old Stump

"MY HUSBAND, Ralph (left), built this feeder and placed it on the stump of a huge pine tree we had to cut down," writes Linda Martell of Burton, Ohio. "It's 4 feet wide and holds a lot of seed, so daily refills aren't necessary. We placed it right outside our bay window and next to our porch, so we have many opportunities to view the various birds that visit."

Sea Food

"A HISTORIC seacoast home inspired my father, Fred, to build this double-duty bird feeder and house (above)," says Betty Williams of Groton, Connecticut. "He sketched the original house, located in Noank, Connecticut, then set about building this replica.

"To fill it, he removes the 'widow's watch' at the top and pours feed down a chute. It holds about 25 pounds of sunflower seed! During the 10 years it has stood in his yard, the feeder has attracted a lot of attention—from birds and people."

Giving Squirrels the Slip

"I WAS TIRED of squirrels eating all the food from my feeders, so I came up with this squirrel-proof design," writes Richard Blatt of Columbus, Ohio. "I built this feeder (above) and mounted it on a 1/4-inch piece of Plexiglas, then edged it with wood.

"Now the squirrels can climb up the pole, but they can't get into the food. The Plexiglas is too slick for squirrels to grasp, and the wide platform prevents them from reaching around to climb onto the feeder."

Ready to Ride

"THIS FEEDER (left) was a cooperative effort," writes Mrs. Ed Carpenter of Capac, Michigan. "Our son built the flatbed for the corncobs, and some family friends added the detailed tractor, which is a replica of the one my husband drives. We placed the feeder in our backyard, where both squirrels and birds hop aboard to dine."

BUILDING CONFIDENCE WITH EVERY BIRDHOUSE

For these young men, an artistic enterprise taps their hidden talents.

It started with a simple idea. Mark Pelletier, who is a day program teacher at a foster home for young men with behavioral disabilities, often took his students on woodland hikes. They loved observing wildlife, so Mark thought they might enjoy crafting some simple birdhouses.

Armed with materials left over from his son's Cub Scout project and a few basic tools, Mark introduced his students to birdhouse building.

At the time, his only goal was to help them improve their motor skills. But the project quickly expanded into something much more exciting.

Over the past 7 years, the students have created more than 2,300 stunning one-of-a-kind birdhouses. They sell the houses throughout Maine and on the Internet, and interest is so great that the builders have trouble keeping up with demand. They craft all the houses from recycled and found objects, making each one a unique work of art.

The project provides the "Birdhouse Guys", as Mark calls them, a small income. More importantly, it gives them a sense of accomplishment and pride.

"I once saw a T-shirt with a saying that read, 'Art saves lives'," Mark says. "I'm not sure who said that, but there's some truth to it."

Opening Up

The students are residents of Brown's Foster Home in Gardiner, Maine, a long-term residential facility for teenage boys and young men. Most are autistic and nonverbal.

"Communicating is a very scary thing for them," Mark explains. "The birdhouses give us a focal point we can work on together, without a lot of pressure. It's had an incredible impact on all of our lives. It's given them a way to communicate with us—the guys who are facilitating this job—and for us to communicate back to them."

Construction materials run the gamut from spare barn siding and trim board to antiques and tree fungus. Each roof is

74

THE "BIRDHOUSE GUYS" construct over 300 nest boxes each year (like the ones above). The builders (far left) are, first row, from left: Ben Brendahl and Aaron Bridgham; second row: John Williamson, Kevin Francis, Keith Keller, Tim Barton and Graham Weston; third row: facilitators Curt Brown and Mark Pelletier.

shingled with pinecone scales, which are the operation's trademark. For perches, the builders use a remarkable array of found objects—clothes hooks, skeleton keys, silverware, parts from a saddle stirrup, furniture handles and more.

Mark's favorite customer comment came from a woman who purchased a house with a golf club perch. "Is this guaranteed to get a birdie?" she asked.

Attention to Detail

The birdhouses are so striking that many buyers purchase them for indoor display, but they're designed for outdoor use, with careful attention to sizing, entrance hole placement and

"They're so proud of what they're doing…"

ease of cleaning. The shingles are attached with waterproof adhesive, and the roofs are dipped in spar varnish for a durable finish.

The birdhouses have been displayed at the Portland Museum of Art, the state capitol, Bowdoin College and the Maine Festival, an annual celebration of the arts. Some are a little rough around the edges, with occasional bent nails or dents, but Mark says that only adds to their character.

"We're always a little surprised by the finished product," he says.

Mark supervises the students with three other staff members. The builders work at their own pace, turning out 300 to 400 birdhouses a year.

"They enjoy what they're doing so much that it's sometimes hard for the rest of us to keep up with them," Mark says. Each house is numbered, dated and stamped with the operation's logo, Recycled Reflections.

Community support for the project has been tremendous, Mark says.

"This has sort of become an identifying symbol of our place," he says. "Our friends and neighbors drop off bags of pinecones. Everybody wants to get involved. People have just been so great at supporting us."

Enthusiastic Reception

"The school brings by kids for tours, and they help us put together a birdhouse. Our guys just beam. They're so proud of what they're doing."

Mark is an enthusiastic booster of his students' efforts, and is delighted to have played a small role in their growing success. As for the birdhouses, Mark is as awed by them as anyone else.

"They're not just birdhouses," he insists. "They're works of art."

Editor's Note: *Recycled Reflections birdhouses are available on-line at www.recycledbirdhouse.com or call 1-207/582-1103.*

NEW LIFE. These builders use recycled objects to create one-of-a-kind birdhouses. Above, from left, Aaron and Tim select wood; Graham and Mark attach a perch; Keith, Tim and Kevin set up a birdhouse at the home.

come back to this tree every year, pecking out more holes for homes. Recently, I noticed a family of squirrels had taken up residence, too. Both species continue to live there in harmony.

Nature sometimes amazes me. That hurricane devastated my property and caused millions of dollars in damage. But at the same time, it provided a place for two species of wildlife to come together and live peacefully.

—David Florence, Sumter, South Carolina

Cagey Idea

A FRIEND gave us a birdcage, knowing my wife, Lee, and I enjoy birds. What she didn't know, however, is that we prefer outdoor birds that roam free.

Not wanting to waste this thoughtful gift, my wife converted it into a bird feeder (below). After fashioning some

large openings so all types of birds could use it, she covered the cage's sharp edges with split pieces of hose.

We fill the bottom of the cage with wild birdseed and hang it under our patio, so we can watch all the winged action from our living room window. *—Jerry Piro Sun Valley, California*

Stop Window Collisions

SEVERAL YEARS AGO, we discovered a way to stop the birds from crashing into our picture window. We found a large piece of red cloth mesh and securely attached it to the outside of the windowpane.

It's practically invisible from inside. And we don't notice it when we're in the yard either. Since the first day we put it up, we haven't had a single bird fly into our window.

—M.J. O'Brien, Milwaukee, Wisconsin

A Growing Birdbath

THIS BIRDBATH (left) is both attractive and practical. The plants create a serene atmosphere while providing a little protective cover for the birds as well.

I created it using two plastic flowerpot bases. I filled the outer one with soil and placed goldmoss sedum in it. Then I put the other base inside it and added water. The birds love it, and I like photographing them in this natural-looking setting.

—Jan Steitz, Antioch, Illinois

Cleans with a Twist

I USE THE metal twist-ties from bread packages to clean the tiny ports in my hummingbird feeder. They work better than any scrub brush I've tried. *—Virginia Bice Metz, West Virginia*

These Feeders Are Free

I USED to throw away the plastic trays from frozen entrees like lasagna until I thought of using them for a project the birds would love.

I make the trays into hanging birdbaths! I place them in the trees close to their feeders. Now the birds can eat and bathe in a place that's secure from predators. It's an inexpensive and fun project. *—Ruby Paul Four Oaks, North Carolina*

Critter Control

SQUIRRELS were driving me nuts until I found a peaceful

way that we could all live together. The birds get their own feeders, and so do the squirrels. Now each one seems to stick to eating in their own territory.

I also provided a separate feeder for one "special" squirrel—an albino that has visited for the past 6 years (at left).

It's actually a dog feeder, but it works perfectly for squirrels. I fill it with corn, and our ghost-like companion eats from it every day.

—Kathy Kroeger, Savage, Minnesota

Tips for Safe Flying

WHILE we might enjoy large picture windows and glass doors, they can pose a real hazard for birds.

Not only do many birds fly into them because the glass surfaces reflect the outdoors so perfectly, but male cardinals, robins and other birds actually attack their reflections—which they regard as rivals—during mating season. They'll often do this repeatedly.

Carrol Henderson of the Minnesota Department of Natural Resources recommends placing a silhouette of a diving falcon in the upper corner of the glass to scare off birds. You can also hang colored strings or ribbons 4 inches apart in front of the glass to break up the mirrorlike image. Another quick temporary solution is to rub soap on the outside of the window.

Because some window injuries occur when songbirds fly away from a feeder or birdbath in fright, consider moving these features at least 20 feet away from the closest windowpane. Or bring them very close to the house so birds won't have enough momentum to hurt themselves.

—Tom Kovach, Park Rapids, Minnesota

Create Your Own Bird Habitat

EVEN AS NOVICE birders, we knew our yard wasn't going to attract a lot of feathered friends. With no trees nearby and only a few shrubs, just adding a feeder would not cut it.

So we solved this problem by creating miniature "bird environments" near our feeding stations.

At the corner of our summer porch (above), we planted a blue spruce, a clematis vine and low-growing shrubs. Then we added a birdbath as well as sugar-water, tube and tray feeders. The tray feeder is mounted on PVC pipe to keep squirrels from climbing to the seed.

We added another haven a little farther from the house by placing a second tray feeder near a blue spruce. Then we added a wishing well that holds a birdbath and two feeding trays. In just a couple of days, this area was bustling with winged activity.

We're very happy with these small havens, and apparently the birds are, too. We've attracted and photographed more than 22 different species in our first year.

—*Ed and Patricia Leland, Van Wert, Ohio*

Keep Birdseed Dry

AS AN avid woodcrafter, I enjoy tackling challenges and making new projects. So when I was faced with a bird-feeder dilemma, I got out my tools and went to work.

Every time it rained or snowed, the seeds in our two feeders got wet and clumped together, generally making a big

mess. Cleaning up that stuff wasn't fun!

I finally got tired of the situation and created roof extensions from some wood I had handy, then nailed them in place on the feeders (see photo at left). Now, the feed stays dry—and we enjoy the birds rain or shine!—*Earl Schember Gagetown, Michigan*

Thanksgiving Leftovers

MY HUSBAND and I have been feeding birds year-round for a long time and get great pleasure out of watching the different species.

Last Thanksgiving, we decided to give our outdoor friends a little treat. I had leftover bread set aside to make stuffing and didn't use it all. Instead of tossing the bread, I crum-

bled the slices and scattered them outside for the birds to enjoy. A bold blue jay was one of the many takers.

It was a great way to make sure our leftovers didn't go to waste. —*Barbara Morrison, Shirley, Massachusetts*

Bluebird Bonanza

EACH YEAR, bluebirds make nests in the two bluebird houses on our property and enjoy the mealworms we put out on a tray on our deck railing—a mere 8 feet from our big picture window.

They stick around for a long time. We took this picture (below right) of a flock that stopped by in fall.

All we have to do to get the birds' attention is step outside the door and whistle. They know that means it's time for dinner!

It wasn't always like this, however. We had to do a little coaxing first. After we mounted the blue-bird houses, we put out a tray of meal-worms on a table in the yard for a couple of days.

Slowly, we moved the tray closer and closer to the house until it was on the deck. By that time, the birds felt comfortable enough to come near the house—and we've been enjoying the view ever since! —*Dolly Smith Meredith, New Hampshire*

No More Spills

KEEPING PIGEONS away from my bird feeder had been a constant struggle. They'd gather below the tube feeder because there was always seed on the ground.

Here's how I took care of the situation: First, I put a cork in the narrow end of a plastic funnel. Then I drilled two holes on opposite sides of the wide end and slid a dowel through the holes.

The last step was to connect the dowel to the tube feeder with S hooks. The funnel catches the seed—and I can easily remove the cork to clean the funnel when I need to.

Since I came up with this contraption, the pigeons have vanished. —*Mary Porbeck, St. Louis, Missouri*

Gone to Seed

WHEN THE BLOSSOMS of my outdoor hanging annuals died last year, I sprinkled birdseed over the soil and hung the plants in the dwarf apple trees where lots of birds live. They loved it!

They had a safe place to eat, where no predators could get to them, and when it rained, the water flowed through the soil and out the drainage holes, so the seed didn't stay wet.

Now I don't feel so bad about the annual demise of my summer annuals. —*Karin Ericson, Grand Isle, Vermont*

HOME TWEET HOME

Readers share their most creative birdhouse ideas.

Where It All Began

"I BUILT my first birdhouse while visiting a friend in Florida who likes woodworking," says Gunter Hille of Midland, Ontario. "Together we worked on this Swiss chalet (above), and I've since created many more birdhouses of my own."

Made of Memories

"MY HUSBAND, Robert (that's him above), loves to build birdhouses and feeders," says Patti Aldrich of Dover, Arkansas. "Since he lived in Germany for 21 years, he built this birdhouse to remind him of his wonderful years there. Whenever he wants to reminisce, all he has to do is look up."

You've Got Mail

"I BUILT this dainty domicile (right) from an old mailbox I was going to convert into a flower box," says Dickie Huff of Elliston, Virginia. "When I started the project, I realized that if I made the flower section smaller, there would be enough room to accommodate a birdhouse. When we have feathered tenants, I always make sure to put up the flag to show it's occupied."

Winds Haven't Changed

"THE WINDMILL I used as a model for this birdhouse (above) is still pumping water in Friesland, the province in the Netherlands where my wife and I grew up," explains Gordon Kuipers of North Haledon, New Jersey. "I used to ride my bicycle past it everyday when we were dating—over 50 years ago."

What a Character
"AS A CARICATURE ARTIST, I do lots of faces at various events throughout the year," writes Keith Parker of Charleston, West Virginia. "I couldn't resist putting my likeness on a gourd when a friend gave me one to paint. I gave it back to her as a gift."

Glorious Nut
"MY BROTHER Clayton Rollins of Cobden, Ontario turned several of these acorn birdhouses on a lathe," writes Susan Swan from Clinton, British Columbia. "I was thrilled when he gave me one. I couldn't wait to get home and decorate it with my favorite birds and flowers—hummingbirds and morning glories."

A Taste of the Far East
"MY MOTHER-IN-LAW, Jennie, loves Asian decor, so I created this Asian-themed birdhouse for her," says Teresa Briggs of Grove City, Ohio. "Now the birds in her yard can also enjoy a bit of her favorite Far Eastern style!"

South-of-the-Border Abode
"THERE'S ENOUGH ROOM in this hacienda (above) for two bird families," writes Gerry Vincent of Bailey, Colorado. "There's an entrance hole in each front window—I painted them black so they'd blend in. The house unscrews from the base for cleaning. I originally built it for an auction, but couldn't part with it. Now I have this and more than a dozen other birdhouses in my backyard."

On the Cob
"FOR YEARS, my husband has been making me wren houses, and they're always original designs," says Mrs. Harold Holden from Grayslake, Illinois. "But even I was surprised when he presented me with this ear of corn (left)! I only used two colors to paint it; the finish my husband applied brought out all the different tones in the unpainted wood. The wrens in our yard are going to love it."

Dollhouse Digs

"ONE CHRISTMAS morning when I was 4 years old, my parents surprised my sisters and me with a hand-crafted dollhouse," shares Kristen Whitcomb Pochipinski of Colorado Springs, Colorado. "Through the years, we've moved it around until it found itself in the hands of my two young boys (in the photo above, Ty and Tanner, plus new arrival, Travis).

It didn't take long for it to become a target for their hockey practice, so I knew I had to find a way to preserve this special gift. With that in mind, I split it into three parts, restored its original colors and had a family friend reshingle the roof. The next Christmas, the recycled dollhouse became birdhouse gifts!"

Aged to Perfection

"I PAINT BIRDHOUSES and each one has a one-of-a-kind design," says Judy Tamagno of Muncy, Pennsylvania. "I spend about 2 weeks on every house because of all the details I like to add—I just can't stop."

Four for the Family

"BUILDING birdhouses is my newest hobby," says Tom Westrich of Racine, Wisconsin. "I have four children with families and homes of their own, and I decided it was time to build a special birdhouse for each of them, including a phone, clock, train and Southwestern hacienda."

Not a Broken Home

"AFTER INSTALLING a tile floor, I wanted to make good use of the scraps," shares Jerry Little of Georgiana, Alabama. "I came up with this idea for a tiled birdhouse. The chimney is made of pebbles from our flower bed, and the top is thin cedar strips."

Carving a Niche

"IT MAY NOT look like it, but this expressive birdhouse is made entirely out of wood (except for the pan hat)," write Mr. and Mrs. Paul Allen of Bushkill, Pennsylvania. "Our son, Russell, who lives in New Jersey, carefully carved the face from a tree trunk and then painted it. We think it's pretty unique."

Quirky Cork Cabin

"With all of the wine corks I've collected throughout the years, it was easy to create this unique birdhouse," writes Bruce Bohnsack of Fargo, North Dakota. "This quaint cabin required 130 recycled corks!"

A Celebration of Seuss

"THIS six-apartment birdhouse (above) was built to honor the centennial of the birth of Dr. Seuss, as part of a fund-raiser for Junior Achievement," writes Roger Meyer of Chattanooga, Tennessee. "It's based on the house of a character in *The Lorax*. The cleaning door on each of its six nesting spots is marked with a Seuss-like poem about the bird for which the compartment was built."

Log Lodging

"MY HUSBAND created the pattern for this log house (right) from a picture on a Christmas card," says Anna Rice of St. James, Missouri. "We originally meant to use it to build a holiday gingerbread house, but my husband thought it would make a rustic birdhouse, too. The finished product has six nesting compartments and plenty of charm."

'GLAD YOU ASKED!'

What's YOUR question for contributing editor George Harrison, our birding expert?

Migration Mystery

How do migrating birds, like purple martins, find their way back to the same birdhouses year after year?
—*Frank Bartel, Flagler Beach, Florida*

George: Purple martins, and most migratory birds, are genetically programmed to know where to migrate in fall, and where to return in spring.

Hummingbirds are the most amazing examples of this. Adult hummers leave their breeding grounds before their youngsters of the season are ready to make the long flight. That leaves the 2-month-old juveniles alone. Because of their genetic programming, they know when to leave, where to fly, when to stop and how to return the following spring. Amazingly, it works.

Shared Parenting

Before we could take down our Christmas wreath one spring, two bird pairs built nests in it. House finches claimed the center hole and American robins took the top. It made for some wonderful bird-watching.

Then one day we spotted something remarkable—an adult robin feeding the finch babies (see the photo above). Can you explain this unusual behavior?

—*Margaret and Allen Denney, Huntington, Indiana*

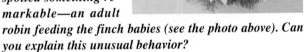

George: This behavior is not as unusual as you might believe. The urge to feed young is so strong in parent birds that they will even feed the young of other birds.

The American robin nest was located so close to the house finch nest, that when the parent robin saw the open and begging mouths of the finch babies, it instinctively fed them.

This kind of behavior will sometimes even occur after young birds have left the nest.

Birdseed Ball Recipe

I'd like to make birdseed balls to hang on the trees in our yard. Do you have a good recipe?
—*Alma Poate Los Angeles, California*

George: Here's a recipe I cooked up at home.

To make one seed ball, add two 1/4-ounce envelopes of unflavored gelatin to 1/3 cup of water in a saucepan. Stir over low heat until the gelatin is dissolved and the mixture is clear.

Stir in 1-1/4 cups of birdseed—whatever the birds in your backyard enjoy. Make sure it all gets coated with the gelatin.

Then with damp hands, pack the mixture into a small round-bottomed plastic container and chill until solid. Remove from the container, and hang it from a tree with wire or string.

Protection from Hawks

Ever since we spotted a hawk in the neighborhood, the bird activity around our feeders has declined. How can I protect songbirds from this hawk so they'll return to our backyard?
—*Frank Cox, Midwest City, Oklahoma*

George: There are two hawks that are common in backyards across America—the larger Cooper's hawk and the sharp-shinned hawk. They look almost identical, except for slight a difference in size, and the Cooper's has a slightly rounded tail. Both prey on feeder birds.

Since state and federal laws protect all hawks, there is no legal way to get rid of them. However, one solution is to provide sufficient natural cover near your feeders. You can create quick cover without waiting for plants to grow by using a discarded Christmas tree or a small brush pile.

This will give the songbirds a place to escape danger, and your birds should return to eat at your feeders even if a hawk is present.

Gazing Ball Dilemma

I've heard gazing balls can confuse birds. Is this true?
—*Bonnie Parton, Denham Spring, Louisiana*

George: The problem with gazing balls is that birds see their reflections in them. During breeding season, this appears to be another bird that has invaded its territory.

As a result, the real bird will fight the reflection in an attempt to chase it away.

Identity of Owl

While I was vacationing in Harpswell, Maine, I spotted this owl (at right). Can you tell me what it is?
—Kelly Kramer
Gaylordsville, Connecticut

George: This is a fledgling great horned owl. Though it sports some white down, it's already as large as its parents, yet still depends on them for food. Appearing to have recently left the nest, this nocturnal fellow was probably just cooling its heels until dark, when dinner would be served.

Takeover by Pigeons

How can I discourage pigeons from pillaging my bird feeders and making a mess of my property? I miss watching all the other birds that used to visit my yard.
—Gail McDonald, Millis, Massachusetts

George: Pigeons and other large birds can be a problem at bird feeders. One solution is to build or purchase feeders that are surrounded by wire mesh that's too small for large birds like pigeons to enter.

Mesh with 1-1/2-inch holes should do the trick, while allowing smaller birds, such as finches and chickadees, to hop through and enjoy a meal.

Strange Sighting

We spotted this bird (below) relaxing on our deck one fall. Can you identify our mystery guest?
—David and Joene Bohlmann, Dedham, Iowa

George: Your visitor is a common nighthawk, a member of the nightjar family that includes whippoorwills. We usually see nighthawks in late August, when they migrate south in large numbers during early evening.

This bird spends much of its time darting through the air in pursuit of insects, so perhaps the one you saw was resting after a busy evening in flight.

Where Do Goldfinches Go?

We've noticed that for a month in fall and spring the goldfinches vanish from our feeders. Does this have something to do with molting?
—Ron and Judy Lane
Independence, Kansas

George: Although American goldfinches grow a new set of feathers during molting periods in fall and spring, they continue to visit feeders during this time.

However, goldfinches do travel around within an area whenever they're not nesting, and often seem to have completely disappeared.

Even when these birds are abundant at feeders, they're actually moving a great deal—so much so that the goldfinches frequenting feeders in the morning are usually different birds from those visiting the same feeders in the afternoon.

Bird's Don't Use Birdbath

I received an aqua-colored concrete birdbath as a gift. It's located near a small tree, but I haven't seen one bird use it in 2 years. Any idea why?
—Gilberta Cism
Harpursville, New York

George: Your birdbath problem is most likely the aqua color. Birds might not recognize the bath as containing water because it looks so different from natural water sources.

I would suggest that you paint the basin a sand-like color.

Should Sugar Water Be Red?

I've heard you're not supposed to add red food coloring to the sugar-water mixture (above) for hummingbirds. Is this true?
—Florence Neilson, Duchesne, Utah

George: One of the older red food colorings was found to be toxic to birds, but with the new formulations, I don't believe that's still true.

However, it isn't necessary to dye sugar water for hummingbirds under most circumstances. The feeders usually have red or orange parts, which provide enough color to attract hummingbirds or orioles.

Clear sugar water (one part sugar to four parts water) will work just fine.

Woodpecker Won't Stop

For the past several years, woodpeckers have pecked large holes in the siding of our house. Owl decoys don't scare them away. Do you have any other ideas?
—Bill Campbell, Versailles, Missouri

George: To the woodpeckers, your house is just another way to make sound. They often drill on houses—or trees, utility poles, antennas, etc.—to declare their territory to other woodpeckers. The noise also helps them attract and keep mates. In other words, the tapping is the woodpecker's song.

There are many ways to prevent woodpeckers from drilling on houses. You can scare them with noise or hang shiny strips of Mylar, tinsel, aluminum or metal on your house. I've even heard of home owners squirting woodpeckers with water from their garden hose. Another strategy is to cover the area with netting or wire.

It takes persistence, but it should pay off when the woodpeckers move on to find more hospitable territory.

Best Shrubs for Birds
We'd like to plant a small tree or shrub in our yard to provide shelter and perhaps even food for birds. Do you have some suggestions? —Karen Lester
Wyandotte, Michigan

George: If you only have room for one tree or shrub, plant an evergreen. This will provide protective cover for the birds and remain a haven for them throughout the year. Any kind of pine, spruce or cedar will work.

Food-producing trees and shrubs lose their leaves in winter, so they don't offer year-round cover like evergreens do.

How to Attract Bluebirds
We have several bluebird houses in our yard, but tree swallows always get to them first. How can we attract bluebirds (like the ones below) instead? —Darle Whitfield
Little Orleans, Maryland

Hubert Brandenburg

George: The easy answer is to put up more bluebird nest boxes so there's enough housing for both tree swallows and bluebirds. But the more difficult problem is keeping swallows out of all the houses.

One way is to use a style of bluebird house that isn't typically acceptable to tree swallows. Those with an open top or an angled bottom, for example, may discourage swallows.

Save Some Grapes for Us!
Every year, my father's grapevines produce an abundance of fruit—but the birds quickly devour it. We've put netting over the vines, but that hasn't worked. Do you have any ideas?
—Mary Mattox
Ridgeway, South Carolina

George: You're correct to try netting. This is the best deterrent against birds eating any kind of fruit. But it's essential to use it correctly.

The netting has to cover the entire plant loosely, not wrapped so tightly that the birds can get to the fruit through the netting.

Grapevines should be covered with netting that can be se-cured with stakes in the ground to keep the birds from moving it to get at the grapes.

Sterilizing Eggshells
Should I sterilize eggshells before setting them out for birds or mixing them into bird cakes? —Erin Hanson
Berwick, Maine

George: It's not necessary to sterilize eggshells before offering them to birds for calcium. Birds have tough digestive systems.

The eggshells they eat in the wild aren't sterilized, nor is the grit, salt or other minerals that are typical parts of their diets. Actually, the shells from chicken eggs are generally cleaner than the shells birds eat in the wild.

One Feeder or Two
Do I have to keep a separate feeder for finches, or can I mix nyjer (thistle) with the wild bird food and black-oil sunflower at my other feeders?
—George Mills
North Bend, Oregon

Gordon Bergstresser

George: Go ahead and mix all the seed together.

In fact, finches will eat most of the seeds in a wild bird food mix, as well as the nyjer seeds. Nyjer is usually kept separate only because the seeds are so small.

Specialized finch feeders have tiny ports (like the one above) that keep these seeds from falling out.

Call of the Robins
Each morning, we hear American robins in our yard make a coarse rasping call. Do you know what they're doing?
—Ethel Brott, Englewood, Colorado

George: This rasping call is the American robin's alarm call. Robins are very nervous birds when they're nesting, and any little threat, like a dog, cat or person walking through the yard, will cause the robins to become alarmed.

Will Red Pepper Work?
I've heard crushed red pepper will keep critters out of birdseed. Will this work, and is it safe? —Betty Hostetler
North Augusta, South Carolina

George: Red cayenne pepper will keep mammals off your bird food, although if they're hungry enough, they will eventually eat it. However, the spice won't affect the birds, since they don't have well-developed senses of smell or taste.

As an alternative, serve your bird treats in a feeder surrounded by a wire cage, or use squirrel baffles.

If the baffles are large enough, placed high off the ground and the feeder is away from trees and buildings to prevent mammals from jumping onto it, they should work.

HOMES BY THE YARD

Florida couple creates big bright birdhouses.

By Roland Jordahl, Field Editor
Pelican Rapids, Minnesota

Sometimes wrong turns happen for a reason. That's how my wife, Patty, and I stumbled upon Dave and Judie Johnstone's wonderful "birdhouse yard" in Port Charlotte, Florida one winter.

After finding ourselves in an unfamiliar part of town, we drove past their home and couldn't help but gape. Colorful, uniquely styled birdhouses of every size and type fill their yard.

Dave and Judie moved to Port Charlotte about 7 years ago. Since then, they've remodeled their home and yard, but the most important addition was a garden workshop and shed. This is what led to their passion for creating birdhouses.

A Huge Hobby

During the day, Dave works in the construction business. But at night and on weekends, he's usually in his shop.

He began building birdhouses as a change of pace from his other woodworking projects, like making toys for their grandchildren. However, this hobby quickly grew into something more—and the size of the birdhouses grew, too.

Some of the houses weigh 100 pounds, and the biggest ones tip the scales at 300 pounds. Dave admits he sometimes gets carried away. To move one particularly large birdhouse out of the shop, he had to remove the door!

Once in the yard, the houses attract the attention of various winged visitors. All birds are welcome, but Dave gets a little nervous when the woodpeckers show too much interest.

Dave uses various structures as inspiration, from castles and historic lighthouses to rustic churches and barns. Then he crafts each house from cabinet-grade 3/4-inch plywood so they last.

While Dave is the master builder, Judie is the artist. She adds the finishing touches—giving the houses their dramatic paint jobs. She applies three coats of exterior paint so the colors will remain bold and strong for years.

Judie draws on her sewing and quilting experience to come up with delightful color schemes. She uses lots of bright pastels and other vivid hues that complement the Florida landscape.

HOUSING PROJECT. Dave and Judie Johnstone have created a jaw-dropping birdhouse neighborhood in their Port Charlotte, Florida backyard (above photos). Dave does the building and Judie is the artist. They think big...some houses weigh over 300 pounds!

Collection Is Growing

Dave isn't responsible for all the birdhouse construction, however. Judie creates purple martin houses from the gourds she grows. Once the gourds have matured, she allows them to dry, cleans out the insides, cuts entrance holes for the birds and adds drainage holes in the bottom. Then the gourds are ready for Judie's special creative touches.

Both Dave and Judie have wonderful imaginations, and it shows in their finished projects. No two birdhouses are exactly alike, and they're always thinking of new ones. Dave guesses there are at least 30 to 35 houses in the yard right now...but you can bet he's busy dreaming up the next big thing. ✒

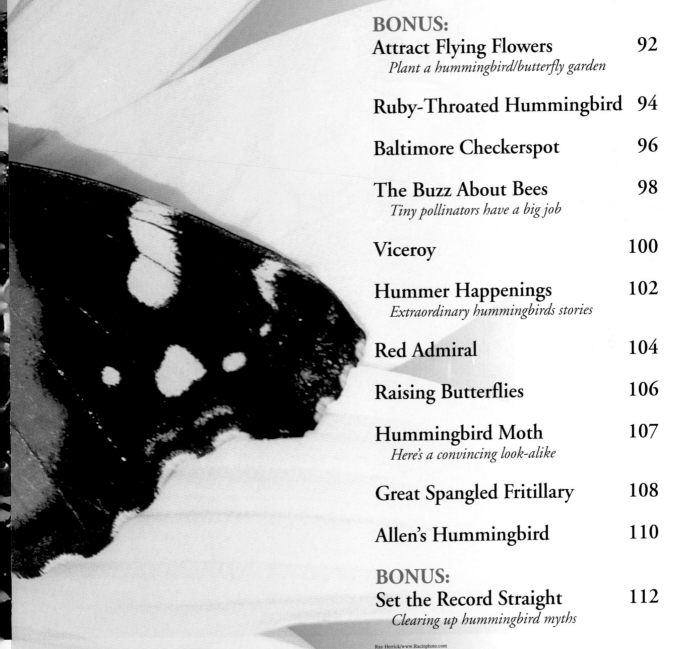

WINGED WONDERS

Ray Herrick/www.Racinphoto.com

89

HOW TO ATTRACT
FLYING FLOWERS

SuperStock

By Melinda Myers, Contributing Editor

We all like pretty butterflies, and to see more, we need to attract the caterpillars they come from. So it's important to include food sources for both.

Colorful flowers such as phlox, coneflowers, marigolds and zinnias make attractive additions to the garden and great food sources for the adult butterflies. For added protein, place some rotten fruit in a small container.

For the larvae (caterpillars), add some butterfly weed, parsley, licorice vine and dill. Use a variety of plants, so that while the caterpillars are eating one plant, the neighboring plants will mask the damage until they're finished eating.

Include several plants of each so you have plenty of food for unexpected guests. My friend Arlene Kaufman, Master Gardener and butterfly garden expert, was overwhelmed by a large number of swallowtail butterflies one season. Once the swallowtails devoured her parsley, she bought several bunches of it to supplement their diet. This usually isn't necessary, but those butterflies seemed to know Arlene would take care of them all.

Butterflies prefer a sunny location out of the wind. Include a few stepping-stones or warming stones, too. The butterflies need to spread their wings and warm their bodies before taking flight. It's also fun to watch.

Trees and shrubs should be planned into your butterfly garden, because they can provide shelter, nectar for butterflies, food for the larvae and egg-laying and pupating sites.

And don't forget the water! You've probably come across butterfly drinking parties called "puddling". You can build your own puddle with a bucket, sand and water. Bury the bucket in the ground. Fill with sand, then fill with water. Some gardeners put a few stones in the middle.

Once your butterfly garden is established, don't be too quick to tidy up the place. Eggs and cocoons are often hidden on branches and stems. A thorough garden cleanup may eliminate the butterflies you're trying to attract.

For the Birds

Hummingbirds feed on the nectar of various flowers. They usually prefer brightly colored trumpet-shaped flowers such as fuchsias and trumpet vines. Some gardeners add a hummingbird feeder to guide the birds to the nectar-rich flowers in their gardens.

Shelby Carter

Many gardeners supplement their natural hummingbird feeder—their gardens—with a commercial one. Mix 1 part sugar into 4 parts boiling water. Do not use honey, as it spoils easily. Cool the solution and fill the feeder. Replace it after 2 days to prevent fungus from forming. Soak the feeder in a diluted bleach solution, rinse, dry and refill.

Once you start feeding and enjoying the hummingbirds, you'll find it hard to forget to fill their feeders.

TWO DO-IT-YOURSELF HUMMINGBIRD FEEDERS

WHEN A RACCOON destroyed one of our hummingbird feeders last year, we needed to act fast because dozens of hummers were swarming around our one remaining sugar-water feeder. I quickly made a new one from a plastic soda bottle in about 20 minutes.

Just cut three or four V-shaped notches in the rim of a 16-ounce plastic soda bottle (pictured far left). Mark the neck to show where the notches are. Screw on the cap, unscrew half a turn and mark the cap to line up with the notches. On these marks, drill holes from inside the cap with a 5/32-inch bit.

Find a larger jar lid—red if possible. If there is a plastic seal on the inside of the lid, remove it. Sand the inside of the lid and top of the soda cap with 60-grit sandpaper. Attach the soda cap to the center of the lid with hot glue or silicone.

Create a wire hanger. Be sure it swings out of the way

Plants for Hummingbirds and Butterflies

Hummingbird (H)		Butterfly (B)		Butterfly Larvae (BL)	

Trees

Birch (*Betula*)	B, BL	Butterfly weed (*Asclepias tuberosa*)	B, BL
Black cherry (*Prunus serotina*)	BL	Cardinal flower (*Lobelia cardinalis*)	H, B
Crabapple (*Malus*)	BL	Columbine (*Aquilegia*)	H, B
Elm (*Ulmus*)	BL	Coneflower (*Echinacea*)	H, B
Hawthorn (*Crataegus*)	BL	Delphinium (*Delphinium*)	H, B
Hickory (*Carya*)	BL	Lupine (*Lupinus*)	H, B
Willow (*Salix species*)	BL	Penstemon (*Penstemon*)	H, B
		Phlox (*Phlox*)	H, B
		Salvia (*Salvia*)	H, B

Shrubs

Azalea (*Rhododendron* species)	H, B	
Blue mist spirea (*Caryopteris*)	H, B	
Butterfly bush (*Buddleja* species)	H, B	
Juniper (*Juniperus*)	BL	
Lilac (*Syringa species*)	B	
Mock orange (*Philadelphus*)	B	
Spirea (*Spiraea*)	B	
Viburnum (*Viburnum*)	B	
Weigela (*Weigela*)	H, B	

Annuals

Cosmos (*Cosmos*)	B
Dill (*Anethum*)	BL
Fuchsia (*Fuchsia* species)	H, B
Licorice vine (*Helichrysum petiolare*)	BL
Lobelia (*Lobelia species*)	H, B
Marigold (*Tagetes* species)	B
Parsley (*Petroselinum*)	BL
Pot marigold (*Calendula officinalis*)	B, BL
Salvia (*Salvia*)	H, B
Snapdragon (*Antirrhinum*)	B, BL
Stock (*Matthiola*)	B
Sunflower (*Helianthus annuus*)	H, B
Verbena (*Verbena bonariensis*)	H, B
Zinnia (*Zinnia* species)	B

Vines

Honeysuckle vines (*Lonicera*)	H, B
Trumpet vine (*Campsis radicans*)	H, B

Perennials

Aster (*Aster*)	H, B
Bee balm (*Monarda*)	H, B

Source: *Birds & Blooms' Ultimate Gardening Guide*, by Melinda Myers. To order, visit "Marketplace" at *www.birdsandblooms.com*.

---

so you can stand the bottle up when filling. (I used 22-gauge electric fence wire.)

Fill the feeder with sugar water, put the cap back on, then unscrew half a turn or until the liquid dribbles into the lid.

It might take hummingbirds a couple days to figure out how to use this type of feeder, but ours got the hang of it quickly. They even sit on the rim and drink.

—*Cindy Sexton*
Monroe City, Missouri

WE DON'T SEE many hummingbirds here in western Nebraska. So when one territorial hummingbird chased two others from our feeder, I made nectar feeders (right) from bouillon jars so each bird could have its own.

To assemble, I cleaned the small jar before drilling a 1/16-inch hole in the center of the red plastic lid. Then I added four or five more holes around the perimeter, about 1/4 inch from the edge.

To hang it, I threaded a short length of string through the top hole, filled the jar with sugar water and screwed on the

cap. I keep the jars full, so the hummers can reach the solution easily.

For a nice perch, I wrapped a piece of firm but flexible wire just below the lid and bent it out a half an inch.

The hummers like these feeders, and I do, too. They're cheap, reliable and the best part is I can clean them in the dishwasher!　—*Linda Bussell*
Imperial, Nebraska

RUBY-THROATED HUMMINGBIRD

One look at a male ruby-throated hummingbird, and you'll know how it got its name. A distinctive scarlet patch, called a gorget, on the male's throat is its most prominent marking. Females don't have the signature patch, but sport the same metallic green backs as the males.

This winged wonder is tiny, even by hummingbird standards. The bird measures 3-3/4 inches from the tip of its bill to the end of its tail and weighs a scant 1/10th of an ounce.

Despite their small size, ruby-throateds are tireless fliers. Each year, these birds migrate up to 2,000 miles to and from

"It's the only hummingbird species regularly found in the East..."

southern Mexico and Central America. And many use a route that takes them over the Gulf of Mexico, traveling more than 600 miles nonstop!

These gorgeous birds are found anywhere east of the Mississippi River and north of Florida. In fact, it's the only hummingbird species regularly found in the East, so if you spot a hummingbird in this region, chances are it's a ruby-throated.

READER TIP

Make your own sugar water for hummingbirds by mixing 4 parts water with 1 part sugar. Boil, cool and serve. Store leftovers in the refrigerator for up to a week. Change feeder nectar every 3 to 5 days.

Nesting season for ruby-throated hummingbirds is between late March and early June. The males are fearless protectors of their home territory, but they're especially vigilant during this time. They'll defend an area that averages 1/4 acre in size, chasing away any intruders—including those at nearby sugar-water feeders.

After building tiny cup-shaped nests 10 to 20 feet off the ground, the female lays two tiny eggs that are the size of navy beans. The eggs hatch within 2 weeks and the young are on their own at about 3 weeks of age. Any longer and they might not fit in the nest!

HUMDINGER: Do you know how fast ruby-throated hummingbirds can move their wings?

Answer: Up to 200 times per second.

Ray Herrick/www.Racinphoto.com

BALTIMORE CHECKERSPOT

W hen you see a Baltimore checkerspot, chances are its wings will be unfolded, displaying this butterfly's distinctive black and orange markings.

Most butterflies tend to perch with wings closed because the muted colors on the underside of their wings provide camouflage. But the Baltimore can be bold—it has another means of protection. This species feeds on plants that make it distasteful to predators.

The Baltimore checkerspot takes its name from both the checker-like pattern on its wings and its striking hues. Black and orange were the colors on the family coat of arms of George Calvert, the first Lord Baltimore, who helped establish the Maryland colony. The similarly striking Baltimore oriole (see pages 8-11) also takes its name from Calvert.

A Northeastern and Midwestern species, the Baltimore

Tom Allen

checkerspot frequents backyards from Nova Scotia and Maine west to Minnesota and south to northern Arkansas and Georgia. They typically measure 1-5/8 to 2-1/2 inches, with the northern butterflies being on the small side.

A favorite host plant for Baltimore caterpillars is turtlehead, which thrives in wetlands and bogs and offers the protection of its plant toxins. But the caterpillars feed on other plants, too. Popular choices are honeysuckle, white ash, false foxglove, penstemon and English plantain.

The young larvae feed in large groups, weaving a tent-like web around themselves for protection. They then hibernate over winter before maturing into 1-inch-long black caterpillars with orange stripes and black multibranched spines (see above).

After only 6 to 10 days in the chrysalis, the butterfly emerges, typically between May and July. You might even discover one in your garden. Just look for the butterfly showing off its spots.

BUTTERFLY BRAINTEASER: In addition to their bright colors, what's another reason the Baltimore checkerspot is so easy to see?

Answer: They fly quite slowly.

VICEROY

Quick! Name that butterfly. No, it's not a monarch — it's a viceroy, a convincing imposter whose look-alike guise protects it from predators.

Like monarchs, viceroys have black-veined orange wings with white spots at the borders. What sets the viceroy apart is an extra black line curving across the hind wings. This subtle distinction is overlooked by most birds, which steer clear of monarchs because their milkweed diet makes them unpalatable. Since viceroys look very similar, they're spared from becoming lunch as well.

Tom Allen

Clever camouflage protects the viceroy throughout its life cycle. The eggs mimic leaf growths, the caterpillars have slightly fearsome-looking "horns" (see photo at left) and the chrysalides resemble bird droppings. Over winter, hibernating viceroy caterpillars hide in plain sight by wrapping themselves in bits of leaves attached to branches.

Viceroys are slightly smaller than monarchs, with wingspans of 2-1/2 to 3 inches. In flight, they alternate between wildly flapping and gliding.

You'll find this butterfly throughout the United States and Canada, with the exception of the West Coast. In the southern U.S., viceroys have darker mahogany-colored wings, appearing more like the queen butterfly, another milkweed eater.

Willow leaves are the preferred food for the caterpillars, so they seek out open water or moist marshy areas. If willows aren't available, they'll eat the leaves of aspen, poplar, apple, cherry and plum trees in meadows and wooded areas.

As adult butterflies, viceroys feed on the nectar of thistle, aster, goldenrod and Joe Pye weed, as well as tree sap and overripe fruit.

In most regions, you're likely to spot viceroys and their caterpillars between April and September. In warmer areas, they're often in flight year-round.

READER TIP

Distinguish the viceroy from the monarch by looking for the black line curving across the viceroy's hind wings.

BUTTERFLY BRAINTEASER: Do you know which state named the viceroy as its official state butterfly?

Answer: Kentucky.

Chapter 4 • Winged Wonders

HUMMER HAPPENINGS

Readers' encounters with nature's shimmering jewels are truly amazing.

Surprise Development

DURING FALL MIGRATION, I took this photo (below) of a beautiful male Costa's hummingbird sitting on a friend's feeder. Imagine my surprise when I developed the film and found that a broad-billed hummer had begun sparring with the Costa's at the moment I snapped the picture.

During migration, it's quite common to see several species sharing the same feeder. Note the juvenile black-chinned hummingbird that's looking on.

I've taken hundreds of photographs of hummingbirds. It's amazing how many times the images I capture aren't exactly what I saw when I snapped the shutter. They move so fast!

—*Donald Sowieja*
Tucson, Arizona

Time for a Refill

A FEW YEARS AGO, I was exercising in my swimming pool when a hummingbird swooped over me and hovered about 10 inches above my head. Then it flew to the empty sugar-water feeder, poked it and came back to hover over me again. It did this about four times before I finally got the message.

I got out of the pool to fill the feeder. As soon as I hung it up, the bird started feeding.

A little while later when I was back at my exercises, I noticed the hummingbird flying up and down the length of the pool, as if it were performing a thank-you dance for me! —*Barbara Billert, Carrollton, Georgia*

Feeding a Crowd

OUR FRIENDS Milton and Ruth Klotzbach of Goleta, California took this picture (above) of hummingbirds at their feeder. I'd never seen so many feeding together before. The photograph was taken at dusk, when the hummers gather in swarms. —*Margaret Kinnaird, Santa Barbara, California*

Handheld Birdbath

AFTER A PERIOD of hot dry weather, I noticed my poinsettia was wilted. When I started watering it with the hose, a hummingbird flew over and landed on my arm to watch the spray. I was so stunned I couldn't move!

After perching on my arm for several seconds, the bird flew straight into the mist. For a full 15 minutes, my little friend hovered and zoomed through the spray.

Totally soaked, it took a break on a nearby tree limb. It shook off and then flew right back for a second shower. I never expected such a great thrill in my own backyard.

—*Cathy Congdon, Saint Marys, West Virginia*

Nursed to Health

AS A NURSE, I'm accustomed to helping others. But I didn't think one of my patients would ever be a tiny hummingbird!

One day, at the end of my shift, an employee told me there was a hummer under a shrub outside. It seemed to be in shock, breathing hard with its tongue hanging out. Fearing it was close to death, I brought the hummingbird into the hospital and carefully placed it in a denture cup.

I filled a syringe with dextrose and placed a small drop on its tongue. To my surprise, the little bird perked up and immediately started drinking!

I took the bird home in the cup and put it in a safe spot in my hummingbird garden. I checked on it every 15 minutes. It became more alert with each visit. After several hours of recuperating, it finally flew away.

I like to think that it's enjoying my garden with the many other hummingbirds that regularly visit.

—*Janet Hodziewich, Rochester, Massachusetts*

High-Rise Nest

I SNAPPED this photo (left) of a hummingbird with two little ones in a nest built in a ficus tree on our front porch.

The female constructed the nest 4 years ago and returns to it every year and adds on. I think she's turning it into a high-rise!

The ficus is in a flowerpot right next to our front door. When the mom's on the nest, we enter our house through the garage or back door so we don't disturb her.

—*Kay Saindon, Long Beach, California*

Cool Advice

WHEN I FOUND a hummingbird nest on the ground and discovered two babies inside it, I called the local nature center for advice.

They suggested I poke holes in the bottom of a whipped topping container, nail the tub to the tree it had fallen from and put the nest inside. With luck, the mother would find the nest and babies and return to it.

I followed these instructions and began keeping vigil. After several hours, I finally heard the mother hum past. Sure enough, she found the nest and was reunited with her hungry babies. —*Gloria Kelly, Augusta, Michigan*

A Closer Look

MY 9-YEAR-OLD daughter was inspecting a fuchsia plant on our deck, gently holding one of the flowers, when a female ruby-throated hummingbird flew toward the nearby sugar-water feeder. To our surprise, the hummer passed the feeder and came to drink right out of the flower Michelle was holding!

When the bird finished, it decided to inspect Michelle, flying so close that its wings brushed her cheeks.

We named this hummingbird "Little Lady", and she regularly visited, often peeking into our picture window as we dined.

One day when I was wearing a bright-colored blouse, Little Lady flew to me for a closer look and almost landed in my lap. I could feel her wings brushing against my forearm as she hovered. It was a close encounter of the *bird* kind!

—*Candiss DelCastillo, Prescott, Wisconsin*

Finger Food

FOR A FEW EVENINGS last summer, the hummingbirds were on a feeding spree in our backyard. The males were chasing each other, and whenever one tried to perch, another would shoo it away.

With all this buzzing about, I decided to try to get one to land on my hand while it fed. After sitting for only 10 minutes, I was rewarded by the tickling of tiny feet on my finger (see photo above). After that, the hummers returned again and again.

The following evening, my parents and one of my sisters shared the same unforgettable experience.

—*Nathin Peters, MacDowall, Saskatchewan*

Come and Get It

WHILE REFILLING my feeder, I wondered if the birds would continue to eat while I held it. Lo and behold, they did!

It started with one brave little hummingbird, but I eventually counted nine flying around me, each waiting their turn. At one time, I had four on the feeder, with three of them using my fingers as landing pads!

After my husband noticed what was going on, he snapped some pictures and had a chance to hold the feeder, too.

—*Kristin Tague, Graham, Washington*

Sorry, Wrong Number

EARLY ONE MORNING, I was tending to garden chores when I noticed a hummingbird flitting around the morning glories. When I stopped to watch, I must have caught its eye, too. The bird flew within a foot of me, inspecting my bright-pink T-shirt, which had a big yellow flower on it

I told him, "Sorry, fella, but you don't want this flower," and off it went. I think it understood me! —*Sherry Moran*
Caledonia, Michigan

RED ADMIRAL

R ed admiral butterflies are true people-pleasers. Distinctive red-orange stripes on the forewings make them easy to spot, plus they'll perch on humans.

The red admiral gets its name from its wing bars, which resemble the rank stripes on a Navy uniform. It's one of the most common butterflies in North and Central America, with a range extending from central Canada into Guatemala.

In northern climates, red admirals appear in spring as they migrate by the millions to their breeding grounds. From Florida west to Texas, red admirals are visible year-round.

Sometimes called the alderman butterfly, you'll find this species near forests, streams and shorelines, moist fields, marshes, parks and meadows. Their wingspan is 1-3/4 to 2-1/4 inches.

Once red admirals stake out turf, they remain there for days or weeks at a time. Males may patrol their territory 30 times an hour to flush out intruders and watch for potential

"They migrate by the millions to their breeding grounds…"

mates. If humans wander through, the butterflies often land on their shoulders—behavior they'll repeat for days on end.

Red admirals feed when it's sunny, seeking out sap, fruit, clover, nectar and dung. They're more frisky at dusk or just before thunderstorms, chasing each other or painted lady butterflies, which belong to the same family.

Tom Allen

The females lay eggs on nettle, false nettle, pellitory or hops. The barrel-shaped eggs hatch into 1-1/4-inch black, reddish-brown or yellowish-green caterpillars with yellow stripes and branching spines (left).

To attract red admirals, plant hops under a trellis to provide a place for the eggs and caterpillars. Then add asters or butterfly bush to coax the adult butterflies to stick around.

BUTTERFLY BRAINTEASER: The red admiral can see a wider range of colors than many butterfly species. Do you know why?

Answer: Their eyes have four color receptors, which respond to red, green, blue and ultraviolet light.

ALLEN'S HUMMINGBIRD

For a bird that's less than 4 inches from the tip of its bill to the tip of its tail, the Allen's hummingbird certainly carries lots of attitude.

During the breeding season, males defend their territories as if they have the stature of a bald eagle. The male usually perches on a twig overlooking its territory, and will give chase to any winged intruder, including red-tailed hawks and American kestrels.

You'd expect a bird like this to be named after Napoleon rather than 19th-century naturalist Charles Andrew Allen, who spent his life collecting hummingbirds and many other natural history artifacts.

The Allen's hummingbird is nearly identical to the rufous hummingbird, with lots of orange in its plumage. But the Allen's has a green crown and a back that's more than half green. Most impressive is the brilliant scarlet to orange "gorget" (throat) above a bright-white vest.

Allen's hummingbirds breed in a very narrow range along the Pacific Coast, from southern California to southern Oregon. While humans have developed much of its natural territory, Allen's hummingbirds have amazingly adapted to these newly formed urban and suburban habitats. In fact, this bird has expanded its range because there's more landscaping with both exotic and naturalized nectar plants.

> ## READER TIP
>
> You might hear a male Allen's hummingbird before you see one. Listen for the metallic whine they make while in flight.

Adult males are often heard before they're seen. They make a metallic whine while in flight, created primarily by sharp points on its wings. The bird also makes various sounds during its courtship display. Some scientists believe these unique sounds are a substitute for songs.

During these courtship flights, the male flies in a J-shaped pattern. He rises 80 feet in the air, then dives toward a perched female before ascending again 25 feet up and hovering there.

These birds gather nectar from flowers, eat sap at sapsucker holes and catch insects in mid-air. Sometimes they'll even pluck insects and spiders from webs.

HUMDINGER: What month do male Allen's hummingbirds begin migrating to North America from Mexican winter grounds?

Answer: In January; they'll breed from February to July.

SET THE RECORD STRAIGHT

Hugh P. Smith Jr.

We get so many questions about hummingbirds, we wanted to share some answers with you.

How to Make Sugar Water

I've been told several ways to mix sugar water for hummingbirds. What is the best way?
—*Arlene Heinlein*
Caro, Michigan

Commercial mixes are available, but it only takes a few minutes in the kitchen to make your own. Here is the simple recipe:

Combine 4 parts water with 1 part sugar (for example, 4 cups water to 1 cup sugar). Then boil for a minute or two.

Connie Toops, author of the book *Hummingbirds: Jewels in Flight*, suggests this method to make it even easier:

"I measure sugar into a large glass container, boil water, add it to the sugar and stir rapidly until it dissolves. Often I make a large batch and refrigerate the excess syrup, which keeps well for at least a week."

Sweeter syrup mixes should not be offered, nor should mixtures made from honey or sugar substitutes. Honey spoils quickly and can be fatal to the birds, while sugar substitutes offer them no nutrition.

Hot or Not?

Why do I need to boil the sugar water that I serve to hummingbirds? —*Nancy Tinker, Hibbing, Minnesota*

Boiling the water helps the sugar dissolve quickly and prevents fermentation of the liquid.

Don't forget to completely cool freshly made nectar before offering it to hummers.

"Dye-ing" to Know

Is it unsafe to add red food coloring to hummingbird nectar? —*Clarice Brainard, Prescott, Arizona*

This has been a controversial issue with people who feed hummers since Red Dye No. 2 was declared unsafe for humans and recalled by the Food and Drug Administration in 1975.

Now, all red dyes on the market have been approved as safe for both humans and animals.

Since most hummingbird feeders you can buy at the store

ALL NATURAL. Kathryn Kolb of Dyersburg, Tennessee proves that red dye is not needed in nectar to attract hummingbirds. Most sugar-water feeders have red parts to catch their eye.

have red plastic flowers or parts on them, dye is not necessary to attract them.

However, planting red flowers and hanging a hummingbird feeder near them is a great way to invite the birds to your feeder. Once they're feeding regularly, begin moving the feeder closer to a window (a little at a time) for better viewing.

Keeping Feeders Clean

I have a hard time cleaning the mold out of my hummingbird feeders. Is there an easy way? —Nancy Cole
Houston, Texas

Reader Kathleen Wing of Bradford, Pennsylvania shares these suggestions:

"I use a cotton swab (pipe cleaners work, too) to remove fungus from the feeder ports," she explains. "And for stubborn stains, try using sand and water (then shaking) to scour the feeder."

Also, hanging hummingbird feeders in shady areas should help slow the growth of mold.

Fall Migration

Do hummingbird feeders have to be removed in the fall to encourage birds to migrate south? —Pat Schmauss
Sneads Ferry, North Carolina

No. Nothing will entice hummingbirds to stay longer than their instincts tell them. In fact, many hummingbirds begin migrating even when there are plenty of nectar flowers and insects still available in northern regions for food.

Adult hummingbirds will generally migrate weeks ahead of the younger ones, who follow later. Hummingbird feeders left up may actually help serve as refueling stations along

the way for birds journeying southward.

On the West Coast and in the Southwest, hummingbirds will stay year-round and feeders may be kept up all the time.

Clearing Up a Myth

Some people say hummingbirds migrate on the backs of geese. Is this true? —Alexandria Beaumier
Krakow, Wisconsin

When it comes to hummingbird legends, this one is perhaps best known.

Eleanor Collins of North Kingstown, Rhode Island reports documented evidence of this reprinted book titled *Hand-Taming Wild Birds at the Feeder* by naturalist, artist and taxidermist Alfred Martin.

In it writes, "One evening a friend called at my studio and laid a Canada goose on the table, then took a ruby-throated hummingbird from his tobacco pouch and placed it on the goose.

"'Al,' he said, 'I shot this goose down this morning and when I picked him up, this little fellow rolled out of his feathers. He was still alive but died in my hand.'"

Alfred was impressed. In fact, he reasoned, "I am just as sure that ruby-throated hummingbirds will ride a goose as I am that aviators ride planes."

Local legend or fact, this story has been well told throughout the years.

However, there is no scientific proof to confirm hummingbirds will actually hitchhike on the backs of geese.

Since scientists have determined the two birds migrate at different times, go to different winter grounds, live in different habitats and have been observed migrating on their own, this story raises questions.

On the other hand, Mother Nature does do some strange things. So, who knows?

SEEING RED. Hang a hummingbird feeder near red and nectar-producing flowers in your yard.

THIS BIRDHOUSE HAS CLASS

Inspired by a reader's photo, we developed a simple plan that you can customize.

By Cliff Muehlenberg
Editorial Assistant

Readers send lots of photos of backyard birdhouses, and as a weekend woodworker, I love to study them all. Once in a while one catches my eye, and I just have to build it for myself.

That was the case with this schoolhouse birdhouse sent by Patty and Bill Martin of Bonita Springs, Florida. The one-room birdhouse ranked high on my wife's cuteness meter, and I could tell it was easy to assemble, even for the first-time birdhouse builder. Best of all, I knew this basic design could be easily customized. I can see it now... the perfect birdhouse fishing shanty ...general store...church...or firehouse. You decide.

START BUILDING!

1. Enlarge the front/back wall pattern at right by 200% on a copy machine, then enlarge it about another 154% to a final height of 10-1/4 inches (copiers may differ, so final enlargement could vary).

Cut two pieces of board 11 inches long. Tack the two boards together using four 1-1/4-inch brads. Tape the pattern to the boards. Cut out the pattern with your saber saw.

2. Cut the pieces for side walls.

3. Create the windows with a chisel. Start by tapping an outline,

RP Photo

Here's What You'll Need...

- ❏ One 6-foot 5/8-inch x 6-inch cedar fence picket
- ❏ 1-1/2-inch finishing nails
- ❏ 1-1/4-inch brads
- ❏ One #6 1-1/4-inch galvanized wood screw
- ❏ Wooden match sticks
- ❏ Acrylic paints
- ❏ Decorative items (available at most craft and hobby stores)

Recommended Tools...

- ❏ Saber saw or hand saw
- ❏ Chisel
- ❏ Hammer
- ❏ Drill
- ❏ Hand plane
- ❏ Combination square
- ❏ Nail set
- ❏ Hot-melt glue gun

then chisel a smooth even surface about 1/16 inch deep. Paint chiseled-out surfaces black.

4. Nail the sides to the front and back. Set the nails just below the surface.

5. Cut the four roof pieces to size. Cut one edge of the lower roof pieces at a 45° angle.

6. Cut and plane to a thickness 1/4 x 1/4 inch trim for the door frame. The window trim is made from wooden matchsticks. Paint the trim on all sides.

7. Cut wood 1/8 inch thick for the door and shutters (you'll also want to cut the chalkboard at this time if you're making the schoolhouse birdhouse). It can be planed to 1/8 inch or sawn to this thickness on a band saw. Exact thickness is not important.

Make one piece that is large enough for all the pieces to be cut from it. Cut the door and shutters to size and paint.

8. Glue on shutters, door and all trim pieces. Nail on front porch and add a small step below the door made from a scrap piece of door trim.

9. Cut the birdhouse floor to fit. Drill four 1/4-inch holes near the corners for drainage.

Recess the floor 1/4 inch. Predrill a hole on the back wall of the house for a 1-1/4-inch screw, which holds the floor in place. Add additional support to the floorboard by drilling pilot holes about 1-1/8 inches deep on each side for a finishing nail. The nail heads will stick out so you can remove them when cleaning.

10. Glue on roof pieces. (Note the vent space above the lower roof. This keeps the house cool in summer.) When glue is set, nail in place. Also glue awnings over windows.

11. Drill an entry hole approximately 6 inches above the floor. Use 1-1/8 inches for wrens and 1-1/4 inch for chickadees. Decorate as desired and let dry before hanging it in your backyard.

If a bird takes up residence, you've passed the test!

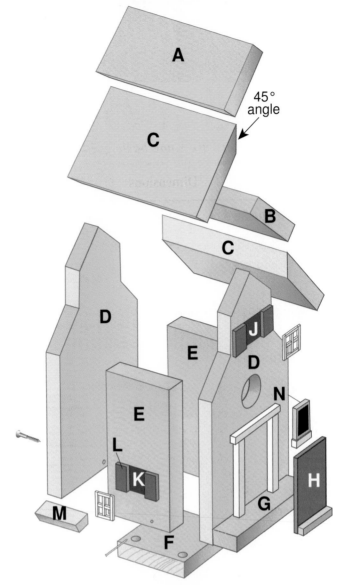

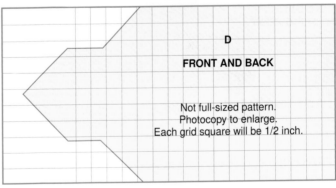

D

FRONT AND BACK

Not full-sized pattern.
Photocopy to enlarge.
Each grid square will be 1/2 inch.

CUTTING LIST

Part	Name	Qty.	Dimension
A	upper roof	1	3-5/8" x 6-3/4"
B	upper roof	1	2-3/4" x 6-3/4"
C	lower roof	2	3-1/8" x 6-3/4"
D	front/back	2	5-1/2" x 10-1/4"
E	side walls	2	4" x 6-3/8"
F	floor	1	cut to fit

OPTIONAL DETAILS:

Part	Name	Qty.	Dimension
G	porch	1	1-1/4" x 5-1/2"
H	door	1	1/8" x 1-3/4" x 4"
J	front window	1	chisel 1-1/4" square
K	side windows	2	chisel 1-1/4" x 1-1/2"
L	shutters	6	1/8" x 3/4" x window height
M	awnings	2	3/4" x 3-1/4" with a 15° bevel on one side
N	chalkboard	1	1/8" x 1-1/4" wide x 1-3/4" high

BUILD YOUR POTS A HOME

Here's What You'll Need...

❑ One 8-foot 2 x 4
❑ One 8-foot 1-inch x 8-inch No. 2 pine board
❑ One 16-inch x 48-inch piece of 3/8-inch or 1/2-inch plywood
❑ 2-inch galvanized deck screws
❑ 2-inch, 1-1/2-inch and 1-1/4-inch finishing nails
❑ Five 6-inch clay pots
❑ Waterproof construction adhesive

Recommended Tools...

❑ Table saw   ❑ Clamps
❑ Saber saw   ❑ Compass
❑ Power drill
❑ Combination square

1. Find five 6-inch clay pots. You may want to buy new ones from a single source to ensure the pots have the same diameter.

2. Cut the piece of 16-inch x 48-inch plywood to a width of 14-1/2 inches. Then cut the plywood with 45° angles on each end (see illustration below).

   Be careful with this board so the pointed corners do not chip when moving it in your work area.

3. With a compass, draw a circle 5-7/8 inches in diameter (2-15/16-inch radius) onto a piece of heavy cardboard or scrap wood. Cut out the circle and check your clay pots for fit. Adjust the diameter if necessary until the lip of the pot sits on the surface of the test piece. Then set your compass for the radius of that hole.

   Use the compass to lay out the remaining holes on the plywood as shown in the illustration below, then cut out each one with a saber saw.

4. Rip two lengths of 3-inch-wide board from the 8-foot 1-inch x 8-inch board. (Be sure to use a push stick when ripping boards. This will keep your hands a safe distance from the blade.) These become the trim boards around the plywood top.

5. Cut the trim boards to size. You will need to make 45° bevel cuts on each board. See diagram below for the approximate length of each trim board and to determine the direction the angles should be cut. Notice the side trim boards have parallel angles and the front and back boards have opposing angles. (See step-by-step method on following page.)

6. On a flat surface, lay the trim pieces around the plywood top to make sure they fit together snugly, but don't attach them to the top just yet. Simply mark the depth of the plywood onto each trim board with a pencil. (Do this rather than measure since not all 1/2-inch plywood is exactly 1/2 inch thick.) Later, you will mount support boards along these lines to hold the plywood top flush with the trim boards (see step 8).

7. From the remaining 1-inch x 8-inch board, rip a strip

* Trim board dimensions are approximately 1/2 inch longer than needed. Cut to fit using the method shown at the top of the next page.

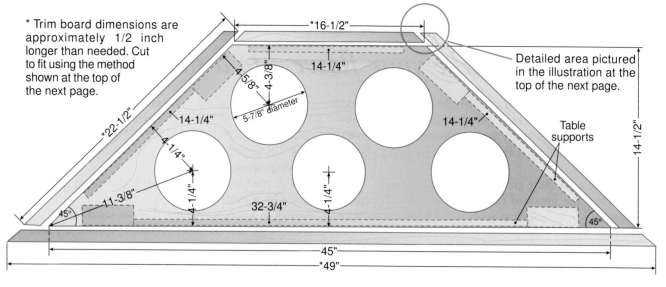

Detailed area pictured in the illustration at the top of the next page.

Table supports

*16-1/2"
14-1/4"
4-5/8" 4-3/8"
5-7/8" diameter
*22-1/2"
14-1/4"
14-1/4"
4-1/4"
4-1/4"
11-3/8"
32-3/4"
4-1/4"
45°
45°
14-1/2"
45"
*49"

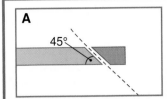
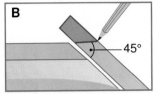
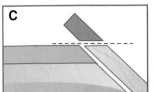
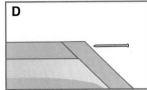

Step 5: To help determine where to cut 45° angles on the trim boards (shown above): **A.** Start by cutting a 45° angle on one piece. **B.** Place it in position, lay the next piece in place and mark where to cut it. **C.** Trim the board. Repeat these steps for the rest of the trim pieces. **D.** To attach the trim, clamp (as shown below), drill pilot holes (make sure they go partially into the next piece) and nail at the corners and into the plywood top with 2-inch finishing nails.

3/4-inch square (use a push stick) and cut the following table supports:
- One piece 32-3/4 inches long
- Three pieces 14-1/4 inches long (for the other sides)

8. Center the longest and shortest supports on the front and back trim boards and attach them below the pencil line made in step 6. Glue and nail with 1-1/4-inch finishing nails.

   Mount the side supports as indicated in the illustration on page 120 so they do not interfere with the legs.

9. Attach the side trim boards to the plywood top with 2-inch finishing nails. Predrill the holes almost the full length of the nail into the plywood.

   Fastening angled pieces can be tricky, but clamping them to your workbench or table will make it much easier (see illustration at right).

10. To make the legs, cut four 17-1/2-inch pieces (they can be longer if desired) from a 8-foot 2 x 4. Add an optional 45° bevel cut to face inward at the bottom of each leg to give them a more finished look.

11. Attach the legs to trim boards (from the inside as shown in the diagram at right) with construction adhesive and three 2-inch deck screws.

   For each leg, drive in one screw, then square the leg before driving in the others. The screws holding the legs to the longest side will need to be driven in on a slight upward angle because of the tight corners, or you can secure them through the front trim board.

12. To prevent water damage, finish the stand with a coat of deck stain or exterior paint.

   Now all you need is potting soil that drains well and a few of your favorite plants to fill those empty pots. Dig in!

Step 9: Fastening angled pieces can be tricky, but clamping them to a workbench or table will make it much easier.

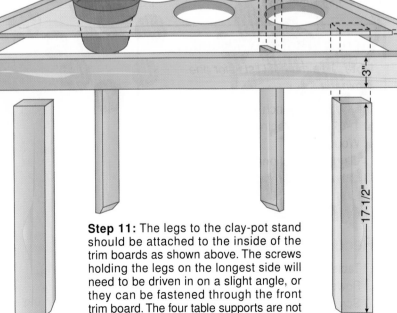

CLAMP

PLYWOOD TOP

TRIM BOARD

WORKBENCH TOP

3"

17-1/2"

Step 11: The legs to the clay-pot stand should be attached to the inside of the trim boards as shown above. The screws holding the legs on the longest side will need to be driven in on a slight angle, or they can be fastened through the front trim board. The four table supports are not pictured in this drawing.

BEST READER PROJECTS

2005

PULLING ITS LEG...and everything else. This reader needed a little help (above) to get his 7-foot bear replica (left) to its hilltop home.

A Bear of a Move

MY 84-YEAR-OLD father, Harry Hartvigsen, built a huge replica of a black bear to stand watch over his rural home in Mansfield Township, New Jersey.

He cut the bear's contours from plywood, covered that with mason wire and lath, and coated the frame with cement plaster. Then he applied black roof cement, combing it to make it look like fur, and added brown detailing on the nose and paws (see photo above).

But when he'd finished, Dad found the job was only half-completed. He wanted to place it in a natural setting—at the top of a hill. But the bear is 7 feet tall and weighs 800 pounds, so getting it up the 45-degree incline was an event in itself.

Dad and my husband, Kevin, created a complex setup that included a pole, guide wires, tracks and a winch. Dad built a wooden frame so the bear could ride along the tracks without getting scratched (above inset).

The neighbors on Dad's sleepy country lane gathered to watch this spectacle, breaking into applause when the two finally settled the bear into place.

The bear looks right at home on its lofty perch. In fact, several people have mistaken it for a real bear—including a police officer.

Knowing my dad, I'm sure the wheels are already turning on his next big project. Maybe a bear cub to keep this one company?
—*Karen Sferra, Field Editor*
Mansfield Township, New Jersey

Creative Downsizing Keeps Memories Alive

MY HUSBAND and I live on the farm where I grew up, so when we had to cut down a maple tree in the yard, I hated to see it go. My sister and I had climbed and swung from that tree as children, and I'd watched my own son play there.

Since only the top part of the tree need-ed to go, we decided to save a large section of the stump. A few days later, I heard my husband's chain saw. I looked out the window and saw he was turning the stump into a bird feeder. He cut out a section in the center where we now place seed. We also hang suet feeders from it as well.

I don't know how long the stump will last, but for now we can enjoy the birds it brings...and reminisce about the past. —*Georgia Stalnaker, Grantsville, West Virginia*

"Hatching" Outside and in

I MADE THIS simple birdhouse (left) about 7 years ago, but my friend Diane Berger gets the credit for making it so colorful and cozy.

The birdhouse roof is covered with screening and moss. Diane planted hens-and-chicks and oth-er succulents in the moss. Now the house is an eye-catcher.
—*Edward Wilson*
Sheridan, Oregon

Ladybug, Ladybug, Fly into These Homes

WE GROW 33 varieties of sunflowers in our yard to provide a buffet for birds in fall and winter. But we had one nagging problem. We used to lose many of our plants to the aphids that devoured the leaves.

So my husband, Tim, decided it was time to fight Mother Nature *with* Mother Nature. He started raising ladybugs, which can gobble up thousands of the tiny aphids.

These beautiful houses (with Tim above left) encourage ladybugs to stay near our sunflowers and feast on the aphids. With fewer aphids, our yield of sunflowers has increased, preserving them for the birds.

—*Carolyn Twombly*
Cape May, New Jersey

Fill It and Forget It

MY HUSBAND generally has a "relaxed" attitude (some might call it lazy) about completing projects around the house.

Despite this, he likes to make sure our backyard birds are well fed.

Recently, he came up with a solution that allows him to catch some extra shut-eye and still keep the birds happy. He designed a feeder that holds enough seed to last the birds an entire week—while he sleeps in.

The feeder is 10 feet long, 2-1/2 feet wide and 4 feet high (that's it, and my sleeping husband, above). Each of the two feed hoppers holds 35 pounds of black-oil sunflower seed or 50 pounds of shelled sunflower.

A roof protects it from the weather, and debris falls on the Teflon-lined tray below, so it can be easily swept or washed away…when he gets around to it.

—*Jeanne Simpson, Sanford, Connecticut*

Tree Lives on as Bird Haven

WHEN THE LARGE white pine next to our house died, I decided to turn it into a decorative tree for us and the birds to enjoy. I cut it back and left 2-foot sections of limbs on its trunk.

My husband and I make lots of birdhouses, so we hung several of those from the limbs, along with odds and ends I had around the house.

I collected dried vines from the woods to make a wreath for the top of the tree, and added a birdhouse that looks like a sunflower head. After we took this photo (right), I hung pinecones on the tree. In winter, I spread peanut butter on the cones and sprinkle them with birdseed as a special treat for the birds.

The birdhouses and feeders attract many kinds of birds to our yard all year long. This area is surrounded by iris, black-eyed Susans, touch-me-nots, daisies, daylilies, primrose and hosta, so it's especially pretty—and busy with plenty of winged activity—in spring and summer.

—*Lois Ann Shehan*
Gainesville, Georgia

Rain-or-Shine Sunflowers

WHEN I SAW these machine parts at an auction, I said to my husband, "sunflowers!" He just rolled his eyes and bid on them for me. The pieces are very heavy, so he carried them to the truck. From there, however, they were mine.

I hadn't welded before, so my husband gave me lessons. With his instruction, I created a sunny crop of sunflowers (above) that shines no matter what the weather's like. The best part is, they never stop blooming!

I love looking out the back window on a rainy day and seeing their bright faces smiling back.

—*Wendy Drotos, Mazomanie, Wisconsin*

Treating Birds to Real Bavarian Hospitality

WHEN Klaus Liebig from Encinitas, California sets out to make a bird feeder, he doesn't cut corners.

Klaus built this classic Bavarian-style bird feeder to look like his family's home in Germany. As a Master Woodworker, he built it to last a lifetime.

The feeder (left photos) took 3 months to complete. Klaus used all the tricks of the trade, including laser cutting and fine finishing techniques. No detail was left out. The windows are made with Plexiglas, while copper tubing forms rain gutters. Numerous other accents like window boxes and animals were painstakingly created.

The birds get to the seeds through open slots along the sides and in front of the main entrance. And the detachable roof allows for easy refilling.

"The birds love this feeder, which now sits in the garden of some family friends in Los Angeles," Klaus says. "When I see many birds using it, it reminds me of festive Bavarian parties in Germany."

Can you put a price tag on this bird feeder? Well, Klaus estimates there's about $250 of materials in it. As for a Master Woodworker's time…let's just say it's "priceless".

MINI MARVEL. Klaus Liebig built this bird feeder as a replica of his family's home in Germany. Birds eat seed from side slots, right next to animals and flowers just their size.

Critter Creations

DURING A VISIT to a museum one year, Richard Babbitt of Vineland, New Jersey spotted a display of tiny critters made from natural materials like pinecones and seedpods. He thought it was such a clever idea that he decided to try to duplicate the process at home.

For a retired glassblower and lifelong naturalist, creating miniature animals with items found in nature turned out to be a perfect fit.

Richard started by copying the critters he'd seen, but soon created his own designs.

"He uses seeds, pods, grasses, cobs, cones—whatever he can find," writes Theodore Craig of Livonia, Michigan, a fan of Richard's designs who took this picture (at right).

Richard keeps some of his whimsical menagerie in his yard, he gives most of his creations to family and friends. His latest efforts are more like sculptures, complete with natural settings for his critters.

"His clever designs and genius are endless," Theodore says.

Lincoln Logs a Perfect Fit

I WANTED to build a wooden birdhouse, but I didn't know much about woodworking, so I made one out of Lincoln Logs.

I bought two large kits to supply plenty of pieces. My husband, Dan, altered some of the logs by cutting off one or both ends. That enabled me to build a tight-fitting rectangle, using the other logs to anchor the pieces together.

I used exterior wood glue to hold everything in place.

Dan added the platform and a hinged roof. Then I spray-painted the pieces we'd cut off and added them to the roof for decoration. The perch is made from one long log and two short ones, and the "windows" are Popsicle sticks.

I'm pleased with the result (above). Now all our house needs are occupants.

—Elaine Jastredowski, Mentor, Ohio

BUILD THIS BIRDHOUSE BENCH

It's the perfect porch decoration.

Y ou'd have a hard time finding a decorative bench that packs more old-time country charm than this one.

The birdhouse bench pictured above was inspired by a well-weathered bench spotted at a bed-and-breakfast in the heart of Amish Country—Holmes County, Ohio. The beautiful bench had so much homespun appeal we decided to make our version out of untreated lumber.

Give it a more nostalgic feel by making it with hand tools and using galvanized nails (where appropriate).

When you're finished, stain or paint the wood for a more formal look, or leave it as is and let nature and time "finish" it for you.

Before starting this project (directions begin on page 132), make sure your lumber is dry. If it feels heavy, wet and cold, give it extra time to dry out before building this treasure.

Here's What You'll Need...

- ❏ Two 8-foot 4 x 4's
- ❏ Three 8-foot 2 x 4's
- ❏ Five 8-foot 1-inch x 8-inch boards
- ❏ 3-1/2-inch and 2-1/2-inch galvanized nails or 3-1/2-inch, 2-1/2-inch and 1-1/4-inch galvanized deck screws
- ❏ 1-1/2-inch galvanized finishing nails
- ❏ 1-1/4-inch wire brads

Recommended Tools...

- ❏ Table saw
- ❏ Saber or coping saw
- ❏ Rafter square
- ❏ Combination square

Let's Start Building

1. Cut a 4 x 4 in half, giving you two 48-inch-long pieces for the back posts.

2. Use a combination square to mark two 45° angles on one end of each post to form the peaks of each decorative "birdhouse". Make the angle cuts with a miter saw or a hand saw.

   If you're using a hand saw, draw the 45° lines, then use the combination square to extend the lines straight along the adjacent sides of the post. This will provide a guideline to help you cut straight.

3. For the front posts, cut a 4 x 4 into two lengths of 27-3/4 inches and set them aside.

4. Build the seat and bottom frames from 2 x 4's. These frames will be the same size, so from three 8-foot 2 x 4's, cut four pieces 14 inches long and four pieces 38-1/2 inches long.

   On a flat surface, assemble the rectangular frames (as pictured in the plan on the next page) with 3-1/2 inch nails or 3-1/2-inch deck screws. Make sure to square each frame as you assemble it.

   If using nails, blunt them first by turning them upside down and hitting the tip lightly with a hammer. This will help keep the 2 x 4's from splitting. If the wood still splits, drill pilot holes.

5. Attach the bottom and seat frames to the 4 x 4 posts. Start with the bottom first, squaring the frame to

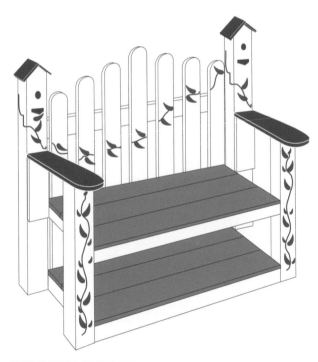

BENCH WITH CHARACTER. You can add your own one-of-a-kind touches to this birdhouse bench by painting it (as shown above) or staining it (as pictured on page 131). You can even use pointed "pickets" instead of rounded ones.

each post (clamp to hold in place). Predrill holes in the frame, then attach to the posts with two 3-1/2-inch deck screws.

   To help as you attach the seat frame, temporarily tack a small block of wood to the inside of each 4 x 4 post 14-1/4 inches from the bottom. Then set your seat frame on the blocks, square the posts and clamp in position. Drill pilot holes and fasten. Remove the blocks from the post when finished.

6. From 8-foot 1-inch x 8-inch boards, cut six bottom shelf and seat boards measuring 38-1/2 inches long.

7. Before nailing the boards in place, orient the growth rings so the curves resemble a rainbow (see the next page for an illustration of this). If the boards begin to cup, the water will run off.

   Fasten the boards to the bottom frame with 2-1/2-inch nails or 1-1/4-inch deck screws. Begin with the front board, positioning it flush with the front of the frame. Fasten the back board (flush with the back of the frame), then rip the third board to fit between the two.

   Nail the seat boards in place using the same method.

8. Make a seat support measuring 3 inches x 14 inches from a 1-inch x 8-inch board. Center the support below the seat boards and between the frame's front and back boards. Use 1-1/4-inch deck screws to fasten the support to all three seat boards.

9. Cut two rear arm supports measuring 3-1/2 inches x 13-1/2 inches from a 1-inch x 8-inch board. Fasten them to the faces of the back posts with 1-1/4-inch deck screws or 2-1/2-inch nails so the bottom of the supports are 14-1/4 inches from the bottom of the posts.

10. Make the pickets by ripping two 1-inch x 8-inch boards into 3-1/2-inch-wide boards. Cut the center picket 49 inches long. Then cut two measuring 46 inches long, two 43 inches long and two 40 inches long.

11. Create the rounded picket tops by tracing a pint paint can on one end of a single picket. Carefully cut along the curved line with a saber or coping saw and sand smooth. Then use that picket as a pattern for the others.

12. Before attaching the pickets, locate and mark the center of the bottom frame on its back board. Then center the longest picket on this mark 1 inch from the bottom and square it to the seat with a rafter square. Screw or nail the picket to the seat and bottom frames just enough to hold it in place. Then lightly tack the two shortest pickets close to the back posts. Evenly space, square and tack the four remaining pickets, placing each one 1 inch from the bottom.

   Step back to make sure they all look straight and

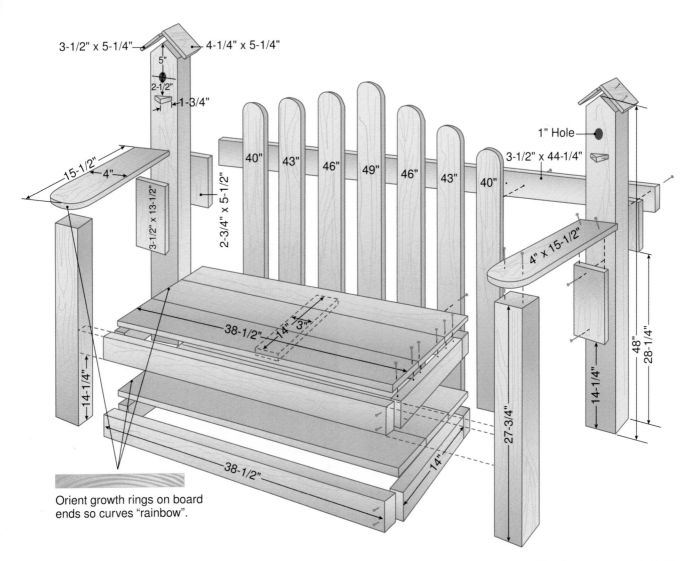

3-1/2" x 5-1/4"

4-1/4" x 5-1/4"

5"

2-1/2"

1-3/4"

15-1/2"

4"

3-1/2" x 13-1/2"

2-3/4" x 5-1/2"

40"

43"

46"

49"

46"

43"

40"

1" Hole

3-1/2" x 44-1/4"

4" x 15-1/2"

48"

28-1/4"

14-1/4"

14-1/4"

38-1/2"

14"

3"

27-3/4"

14"

38-1/2"

14"

Orient growth rings on board ends so curves "rainbow".

are properly spaced. Drive fasteners home.

13. From a 1-inch x 8-inch board, cut two spacers measuring 2-3/4 inches x 5-1/2 inches. Attach them to the back side of the rear posts so the bottom of the spacers sit 28-1/4 inches from the bottom of the posts. Drill pilot holes and attach them to the rear posts with 1-1/4-inch deck screws or 2-1/2-inch nails.

14. From a 1-inch x 8-inch board, make a horizontal picket support measuring 3-1/2 inches x 44-1/4 inches.

15. Center and attach the picket support to the spacers with 2-1/2-inch deck screws or nails. Screw the pickets to the horizontal support from the back with 1-1/4-inch deck screws or nails. If you use nails, fasten from the seat side.

16. Cut two armrests measuring 4 inches x 15-1/2 inches from a 1-inch x 8-inch board. You can either round the ends (we used a quart paint can as a template), leave them square or dog-ear the corners.

With 2-1/2-inch finishing nails, fasten the arm-

rests to the front post and back arm support. Drill pilot holes first and let the outermost edge of the armrest overhang the post by about 3/8 inch.

17. Make a decorative birdhouse entrance hole in the face of each back post. Measure 5 inches down from each peak and bore a 1-inch hole centered about 1 inch deep with a spade bit.

18. Cut triangular "perches" from the corner of a scrap board. Measure 1-3/4 inches in each direction from a corner of the board, then cut between the top points to make a triangle. Cut the pieces and attach the perches 2-1/2 inches below the center of the holes. Predrill holes through the perches to keep them from splitting. Nail them into place with 1-1/4-inch wire brads.

19. Cut the roof pieces from a 1-inch x 8-inch board. The two wide roof sections measure 4-1/4 inches x 5-1/4 inches, and the two narrow pieces measure 3-1/2 inches x 5-1/4 inches. The wide roof will overlap the narrow roof at the peak. Fasten with 1-1/2-inch finishing nails.

Now have a seat and admire your handiwork!

FEATHERING HER NEST

Artist transforms pieces of torn paper into exquisite bird portraits.

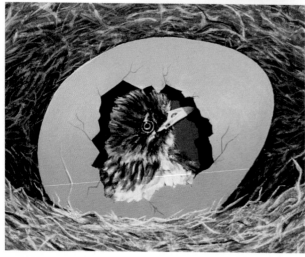
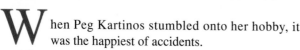

Whuen Peg Kartinos stumbled onto her hobby, it was the happiest of accidents.

After a career of teaching chemistry to nursing students, she was looking for a more creative pursuit. She started painting classes, something she'd always longed to do.

Then in the mid-1980s, while browsing through a shop in Chicago, she spotted a display of Oriental paper. Intrigued by its potential for art projects, Peg picked up a small book of sample papers to take home to Park Ridge, Illinois.

As she examined the samples in her studio, one of the papers got wet, so she pulled it out. To her surprise, the moisture weakened the paper's strong fibers so they separated,

creating a fringed edge that reminded her of bird feathers.

Excited by this discovery, Peg dampened more of the samples, tore them into pieces and used them to make a small collage. She was happy with the effect, but disappointed the papers weren't brighter.

"Then it occurred to me that I could paint them," she says. "Eureka! That's how it all started."

Realistic Results

For a lifelong bird lover, using torn paper to create three-dimensional bird portraits was the logical next step.

Peg painted the papers with thin feather veins and shad-

PORTRAITS SPRING TO LIFE. Artist and bird lover Peg Kartinos found a way to combine her two pastimes. She assembles bird portraits using paper feathers. First Peg (at far left) makes the feathers with torn paper and paints them. Then she places them on watercolor backgrounds to create the finished pieces. Clockwise from far left are: an American robin, great-horned owl, snowy egret, eastern bluebird and northern cardinal.

ing variations, then attached them to watercolor backgrounds. She used as many as eight layers of color to achieve the lifelike look.

The results were so realistic that when Peg started exhibiting her work at galleries, people often mistook her paper feathers for the real thing.

"One time I had my pictures in a gallery and somebody came in and complained to the owner, saying it was illegal to use bird feathers in art," she chuckles. "They had to put up a sign saying the feathers weren't real.

"Now I have little tags I put on things that say, 'These aren't real feathers—they're torn paper'."

Hands-on Art

For children, she added another sign: "Please touch."

"When I exhibited at art fairs, I'd put out a tray full of leftover paper feathers," she says. "Parents were always telling their children not to touch them."

Peg not only reassured them the feathers were safe, but

encouraged each child to take one home.

Although Peg has demonstrated her feather-painting technique at schools, workshops, art league meetings and senior centers, she has yet to convince anyone else to try it.

"I think people realize it takes a lot of time to do this," she says.

Peg has sold many of her portraits, and has done work on commission. But she says the occasional sale isn't what drives her to create.

"If I were trying to make money at this, I'd starve," she laughs. "I've always loved birds, and I do this because I thoroughly enjoy it. My reverence for nature dominates my life, and painting is a way of expressing that."

LET YOUR IMAGINATION SOAR

These fanciful feathered friends will bring cheerful notes to your garden.

WINGED WONDERS. R.L. Porter of Des Plaines, Illinois designed these easy-to-make garden decorations. Because they move with the breeze, they bring both color and action to your garden.

Want to add a little wooden wildlife to your gardens? Give this plan a try. These charming bird ornaments are a snap to create and add a welcome touch of whimsy to any garden or yard.

R.L. Porter of Des Plaines, Illinois came up with the whimsical design while recuperating from an accident. "I'd seen some decorative birds similar to these 3 or 4 years ago and thought making some might be good therapy," he recalls.

Since then, he's made several of these cheerful garden companions for neighbors and relatives.

For the most striking effect, R.L. suggests placing them among flowers, along borders or at the edge of a low shrub. "They also look good indoors, stuck in among large potted plants," he adds.

Once you make one, you won't be satisfied until you've made a whole flock of these birdie companions.

TIME FOR TAKEOFF!

1. Photocopy the pattern on the next page, or carefully trace it onto a sheet of paper (make two copies for the wings and one for the body). Trim each paper pattern with scissors, leaving 1/2 inch of white space outside the cutting lines.

2. Position the patterns on a 13-inch 1-inch x 6-inch board (see board layout above right). If you plan on painting them, we recommend using pine. The wood grain should run parallel with the longest dimension of each pattern. Glue each pattern in place with glue stick.

Here's What You'll Need...

- ❑ One 13-inch 1-inch x 6-inch rough-cut cedar or No. 2 pine board
- ❑ One 3/16-inch steel rod, about 3 feet long
- ❑ Glue stick
- ❑ Waterproof construction adhesive
- ❑ 1-1/4-inch finishing nails or brads
- ❑ Paint or outdoor stain (optional)

Recommended Tools...

- ❑ Saber, band saw or scroll saw
- ❑ Power drill

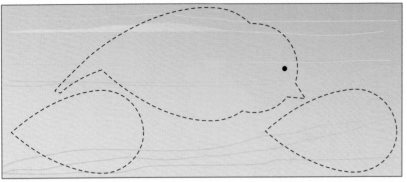

Step 2: The wood grain runs parallel with the longest dimension of each piece.

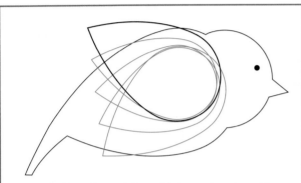

Step 5: The wings of these birds can be placed in a variety of positions to make each one unique.

3. Mark the eye of the bird with an awl, then drill a straight hole through the wood at this point with a 3/16-inch bit.

4. Cut out all the pieces with a saber, scroll or band saw, cutting through the paper pattern along the cutting lines. Drill a 3/16-inch hole in the bottom edge of the bird for the steel rod. The angle of the hole determines how the bird will perch.

5. Peel away the paper patterns and sand off any glue remaining on the wood. Attach the wings in the position you like best with waterproof construction adhesive. Tack each wing in place with 1-1/4-inch finishing nails or brads.

6. If using pine, paint the bird whatever color you like. Bright colors make it stand out in the garden.
   R.L. likes to use rough-cut cedar for his wooden birds. To give them an instant weathered look, he adds a little black acrylic paint to a bucket of water and dips the completed birds into the mixture. This darkens the wood slightly to give the just-cut edges an aged appearance.

7. Mount the bird on a 3/16-inch steel rod about 3 feet long. The rod will have an oily coating (it's there to inhibit rust). R.L. wipes this coating off with a cloth so the rods rust, giving them a more weathered look. Then simply push the rod into moist soil and the birds will take flight!

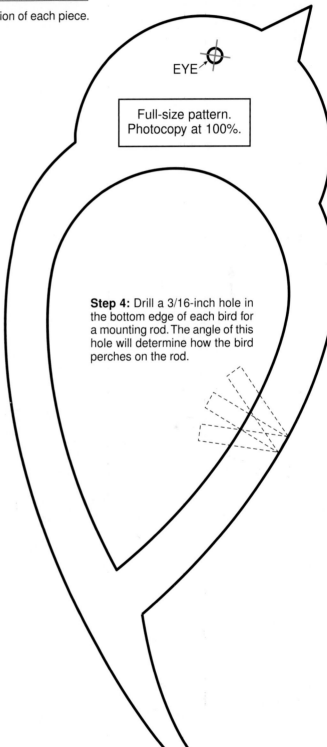

EYE

Full-size pattern.
Photocopy at 100%.

Step 4: Drill a 3/16-inch hole in the bottom edge of each bird for a mounting rod. The angle of this hole will determine how the bird perches on the rod.

Workshop Wisdom
Paper Pattern Pointer
CUT OUT paper patterns, leaving 1/2-inch white space beyond the guidelines. Glue to the wood, then cut on the guideline, sawing through the paper and board at the same time.

diluted liquid fertilizer to container plants throughout the season to ensure strong growth and prolific blooms. Be sure to water regularly, too.

Once young plants are vigorously growing, pinch the stems back to encourage fullness—and then pinch some more. This forces the plant to produce side branches, which you can also pinch back. Stop pinching 8 to 10 weeks before you want it to flower.

Efforts Pay Off

Yes, all this feeding, watering and pinching takes time, but it's definitely worth it. At bloom time, you'll have a full well-shaped plant that's as dazzling as anything you could buy in a nursery.

For continuous blooms, remove the faded flowers regularly. And don't panic if flowering stops during hot spells. It will resume as soon as the weather cools.

To produce extra plants, try taking tip cuttings. Snip off the last two or three joints at the tip of a growing branch, dip the cut end in rooting compound, then place it in a damp rooting medium. You can also grow fuchsia from seed,

which is usually available through specialty seed catalogs.

If you grow fuchsias as annuals, you can overwinter them in a cool dark basement. That way, you won't need to buy new ones next year. Prune lightly before storing and leave them in their containers, watering about once a month.

Then cut back to live wood when you return the plants outdoors in spring. Northern gardeners may want to jump-start the dormant plants inside. You can grow fuchsias as houseplants, too.

Join the Club

Fuchsias have an avid following throughout the world, so it's easy to find information and guidance from experienced growers. One of the oldest groups, the American Fuchsia Society (you'll find them at *www.americanfuchsiasociety.org*), maintains a registry of all the new hybrids developed each year.

My local society also has a Web site (*www.ccfuchsia.net*) that contains a lot of tips about growing fuchsias. Visit us anytime. We'll tell you everything you need to know so you can enjoy this wonderful plant, too!

PLANT PROFILE

Common Names: Fuchsia and lady's eardrops.

Botanical Name: *Fuchsia.*

Bloom Time: Summer to first frost.

Hardiness: Zones 8 to 10; grow as annual elsewhere.

Flower Colors: Pink, white, red, purple and orange.

Flower Shape: Tubular and pendulous single or double blossoms.

Height: Trailing varieties: 6 to 24 inches; shrubs: 8 inches to 10 feet.

Light Needs: Full sun to partial shade.

Soil Type: Rich, moist and well-draining.

Prize Picks: *Fuchsia magellanica* has abundant red and violet flowers on 3-foot stems and can be grown as a perennialas far north as Zone 6 in a sheltered location with mulch for winter protection. Thalia fuchsia is an upright form that works especially well in planting beds when paired with Dropmore Scarlet honeysuckle.

Attracts: Hummingbirds and butterflies.

RED, WHITE & BLOOM

Get in the spirit with these patriotic garden ideas.

STRIKE UP THE BAND! You can parade your patriotic colors in full bloom right in your own backyard.

Cheryl Richter of Lincoln, Nebraska came up with these red, white and blue flower combinations that would make Uncle Sam proud. Most are annuals, which means you can plant them this spring and summer and have a brilliant explosion of colors in time for Independence Day.

What better way to make America beautiful?

White *Zinnia linaris*, Red Spider *Zinnia tenufolia* and Blue Danube ageratum (photo at right)

Red and white pentas and Victoria Blue salvia

Petunias in Big Daddy Blue, Mini Flora red and white

Telstar Red dianthus, White Wave petunia and Blue Danube ageratum

Accent Series red and white impatiens and Crystal Blue and white lobelia

SWEET PEAS

Try these flowers for an old-fashioned treat.

By Carol Graham
Vancouver, British Columbia

I t doesn't take long to develop a taste for sweet peas. Not only do these annual climbers have a luscious scent, but they're also easy to grow and will provide a season's worth of cut flowers for beautiful bouquets.

Sweet peas originated in Sicily, but quickly caught on in England, where gardeners grew them for their delightful aroma as well as the diverse palette of flower colors—from pinks and purples to blue and white.

Although there are some perennial varieties, the most common is an annual climbing vine. This flower's fragrance is so distinctive that even its botanical name, *Lathyrus odoratus*, refers to its aromatic quality.

Sweet peas also have a unique flower shape. Each bloom has one large upright petal, two narrow side petals and two lower petals, creating a distinctive ruffle-like effect.

Try These Tips

Sweet peas are easy-care flowers that can thrive without special attention, but I've learned a few green-thumb tricks over the years. These tips will help you grow the best sweet

144

peas in the neighborhood—in no time!

● Choose a spot that's sunny all day, or perhaps gets a little afternoon shade. Then mix plenty of organic matter into the planting hole. I use well-decomposed manure, but other organic materials like peat moss or compost will work, too. Because sweet peas grow long roots, this well-prepared soil keeps the plants happily producing healthy flowering stems.

● Most gardeners grow sweet peas from seed. There's a wide variety available at most garden centers, so finding ones with the colors or characteristics you desire is easy. Since I like the fragrant ones, I usually look for "old-fashioned" varieties because some of the newer cultivars have less scent.

● One gardening legend holds that if you sow your sweet peas before sunrise on St. Patrick's Day, the blossoms will be larger and more fragrant.

Superstition aside, however, when to plant sweet peas largely depends on your region's climate.

These charming climbers thrive in cool weather, and the seeds germinate in cool soil. It's part of the reason the

---

"Sweet peas perform best if you regularly pick the flowers…"

---

flowers are so popular in England, where the temperate climate is ideal.

● For spring blooms, get planting as soon as the soil is manageable. You can sow them directly in the garden, soaking the hard seeds in water for at least a day before planting.

In warmer regions, plant sweet peas in late fall for flowers in winter and early spring.

In British Columbia, spring doesn't arrive until April, so I start my sweet peas indoors in February so they're ready to transplant as milder weather arrives. By mid-April, they're already vigorously sprouting, and I pinch off the tips to encourage them to branch out.

Nowhere To Go But Up

Sweet peas' twining vines will grow on a trellis, a teepee of bamboo poles, or in rows along wire, string or strong netting. The plants can reach 6 feet, so make sure your support is tall and sturdy enough for the full height of the plants.

To avoid damaging the roots, I've found it's best to put the trellis up before planting the seedlings. Efficient gardeners secure the trellis in place while they're digging organic matter into the flower bed.

Plant the seedlings 6 to 8 inches apart. With seeds, you can plant them as close as 1 inch, then thin the small plants to 6 inches. This allows each plant to have better access to soil nutrients, and, in my experience, seems to result in

healthier plants and top-quality blossoms.

Keep them well-watered, thoroughly soaking the plants without getting the leaves too wet, and fertilize as needed.

About a month later, the flowers bloom and I gather handful after handful of sweet-smelling bouquets and enjoy them throughout my home. The more I pick, the better they bloom.

In fact, sweet peas perform best if you regularly collect the flowers. This prevents them from going to seed, which hampers their growth. You can use the flowers in bouquets as I do, or simply prune off the spent flower heads.

The sweet-scented show lasts until hot weather arrives. Like garden peas, sweet peas prefer the cooler weather of spring and early summer, gradually declining under hot August skies.

It's a short, but very sweet, season.

PLANT PROFILE

Common Name: Sweet pea.
Botanical Name: *Lathyrus odoratus.*
Bloom Time: Typically spring, but varies by region.
Hardiness: Annual.
Flower Colors: Wide variety of colors including pink, purple, salmon, blue, red and white. Yellow is the one hue not available.
Flower Shape: Unique ruffle-like bloom.
Height: 4 to 6 feet.
Light Needs: Full sun or partial shade.
Soil Type: Moist and well draining.
Propagating: Plant presoaked seeds 1 inch deep and 6 inches apart in garden, or start seeds indoors and transplant outside after about 6 weeks.
Prize Picks: Fragrant varieties include Noel Sutton (blue), Pink Cupid (pink with white wings) and the bicolor Quito. Royal Mix and Mammoth Mix have large blossoms and are heat tolerant.
Warning: Sweet pea seeds are toxic and may cause nausea.

ANGELS' TRUMPETS

Create a heavenly paradise.

I t's a jungle out there—especially when your garden boasts a showy display of angels' trumpets.

These tropical plants unfurl captivating bell-shaped blooms that are 6 to 12 inches long, and flower prolifically from spring to autumn. But the sheer number of blooms surprised Maxine Blackburn of Blanco, Texas.

"By mid-September, I'd counted 1,000 blossoms, and the plant continued to grow and bloom daily," Maxine writes. "What prompted this amazing performance? I think it was the compost…and 37 inches of rainfall!"

Flower colors range from white to red to yellow, and many—like the one in Gretchen Changelon's yard in Austin, Texas—are most fragrant at night.

Gretchen Changelon

"It releases a heavy sweet fragrance when the temperature cools in the evening," she says. "The scent not only fills my patio, but my entire backyard."

Angels' trumpets can reach heights of 12 feet and grow 8 feet wide, with some topping out at 30 feet tall and 12 feet wide. Their size makes them especially attractive at the back of a border garden, but they'll provide a striking accent anywhere in the landscape.

The Name Game

Although gardeners who grow these plants easily agree about their beauty, their name can cause a bit of a debate.

Until recently, angels' trumpets were divided into two botanical groups, *Brugmansia* and *Datu-*

Mark Turner

146

ra. Now, however, the American Horticultural Society has combined the two under the *Brugmansia* name, even though some nurseries—and gardeners—continue to use both.

Adding to the confusion are the different common names for these plants, a problem that's multiplied by their varying appearance. Some are tall trees with drooping flowers (photos at left and right), and others are shorter shrubs with upright-facing blooms (photos below). The shrublike variety is often called moonflower (not to be mistaken for moonflower vine, which is a relative of the morning glory).

Luckily, you don't have to keep the names straight to enjoy these tropical plants. Gretchen has several types in her yard and is happy with them all.

"One produces a multitude of pendulous yellow blooms starting in May," she writes. "It's over 10 feet tall with seven trunks—and still growing!

"Another plant is much shorter and has double purple blooms that don't have any scent, but are quite beautiful and unusual.

"A third plant that I purchased when it was small has grown to about 11 feet tall and 10 feet wide," she continues. "The blooms are brilliant white and stand straight up when they open and then lean over and close as they fade. It produces hundreds of blooms in May and June."

Warm Reception

To grow angels' trumpets in your yard, take a cue from their native habitat of Central and South America. They thrive amid scrub growth and along streams—locations that offer shelter from the wind, yet plenty of sunshine.

Richard Shiell

Given their tropical origins, angels' trumpets can't handle temperatures below 45°. So they're best grown in containers that you can bring indoors during cold weather.

If moving heavy containers isn't for you, there's another way to enjoy angels' trumpets—treat them like annuals. They grow quickly from seed, just plant new ones each spring, starting them indoors for an earlier bloom outside.

One word of caution, however. Angels' trumpet belongs to the nightshade family and is highly toxic. You should keep the plant away from children and pets, and gardeners should wear gloves to prevent contact with the plant's sap.

With these simple precautions, you can turn your landscape into a tropical paradise, just as Gretchen has.

"These plants need a lot of room and a certain amount of nurturing, but I think they're well worth it," she says. "I just love them—and my neighbors do, too." ✒

PLANT PROFILE

Lou and Kay Drouant

Common Names: Angels' trumpets, moonflower, datura.
Botanical Name: *Brugmansia*.
Bloom Time: Late spring to autumn, varies by species.
Hardiness: Annual in most areas.
Flower Colors: White, yellow, apricot, pink and red.
Flower Shape: Trumpet.
Height: Typically 3 to 12 feet.
Spread: Typically 3 to 8 feet.
Light Needs: Full sun.
Soil Type: Rich well-draining soil or a soil-based potting medium used in a container.
Propagating: Sow seed in spring, or root cuttings in summer.
Prize Picks: *Brugmansia arborea* provides a long blooming season, producing 6-inch white fragrant flowers from spring to autumn.
Warning: All plant parts are poisonous. Keep away from children and pets, and wear gloves when handling.

their extended bloom time, provide a whimsical note when planted along a garden path or driveway.

A member of the daisy family, it attracts a variety of birds and butterflies, including monarchs and painted ladies, but people will appreciate the blooms, too, when used as a cut flower.

Colorful Choices

Compact and tidy or loose and wild, cosmos' appearance depends on the species and cultivar.

Named after its sulfur-yellow flowers, *Cosmos sulphureus* delivers an impressive blast of color. Yielding showy single and double blossoms in

---

"It attracts a variety of birds and butterflies..."

---

shades of yellow, orange and red, it can grow up to 6 feet tall.

Certain varieties, including Diablo, Crest Red, Ladybird Dwarf Gold and Dwarf Klondike are ideal choices for smaller spaces, since they only reach 1-1/2 to 3 feet tall.

Cosmos bipinnatus has feathery leaves and produces 2- to 3-inch single flowers in shades of pink, white and red. Straight species can grow 8 feet tall, but improved varieties, including Purity, Dazzler and Gloria, grow 3 to 6 feet tall. For even smaller plants, choose the popular Sonata Series, which grows 12 to 18 inches tall.

A third and lesser-known variety is *Cosmos atrosanguineus*. Affectionately called "chocolate cosmos", this tuberous-rooted perennial produces silvery foliage and 2-inch brownish-red flowers that have a chocolate or vanilla aroma in late summer and fall.

Start from Seed

To grow these beautiful blooms, sow seeds indoors 4 weeks before the last spring frost or plant directly in the garden in late spring.

When seedlings emerge, generally in 5 to 10 days, thin to 12 inches apart. In 8 to 10 weeks, you should have a plethora of candy-colored cosmos.

Cosmos grows best in full sun and well-draining soil. It is drought tolerant, and generally needs additional water only during long dry spells.

You can apply starter fertilizer when setting out transplants in the garden or 4 to 6 weeks after sowing seeds, but

Mark Turner

UNIVERSAL FAVORITE. The many varieties of cosmos provide a colorful palette of hues, from pinks and white (above and far lower right) to fiery orange (far right inset, with a clouded sulphur butterfly). In the garden (above right), its feathery foliage provides an airy appearance.

keep in mind that cosmos won't live up to its potential in soil that's too rich.

Though usually self-supporting, taller cosmos need reinforcement to stand up against heavy rain and wind, so plant them near a fence or choose sturdy stakes that are as tall as the eventual height of the plant.

To encourage reseeding, leave some flowers on their stems at season's end, and don't disturb the soil over winter and early spring. When the soil warms, your cosmos will once again leap from the earth in a dazzling array of colors.

Don't be surprised if the seedlings of hybrid cosmos don't look the same as the original plants. That's perfectly normal for hybrids that revert to

Ann Trulove/Unicorn Stock Photos

> ### READER TIP
>
> To support tall cosmos varieties, plant them near a fence or provide sturdy stakes that are as tall as the eventual height of the plants.

traits of their parent plants. They may even grow to a different size.

Many gardeners bring the beauty of cosmos indoors by including it in floral arrangements. For the best-looking blooms, cut the flowers just after they open and immediately place them in a container filled with cool water.

With its bright flowers and easy-going nature, it's no wonder this Mexican wildflower has captured the hearts and minds of gardeners for centuries.

PLANT PROFILE

Common Name: Cosmos.
Botanical Name: *Cosmos.*
Bloom Time: Summer to late fall.
Hardiness: Annual.
Flower Colors: Pink, white, red, purple, yellow, orange and orange-red.
Flower Shape: Single or double daisy-shaped blossoms.
Height: 1 to 6 feet.
Spread: 1 to 2 feet.
Light Needs: Full sun.
Soil Type: Well-draining.

Richard Day/Daybreak Imagery

Prize Picks: The semi-double orange blossoms of Diablo and the yellow, orange and red blooms of Bright Lights are two good selections of *Cosmos sulphureus*. For *Cosmos bipinnatus*, try Sea Shells for fluted white, pink and crimson flowers or the compact Sonata Series.
Attracts: Birds and butterflies.

Donna and Tom Krischan

CHRISTMAS CACTUS

Spread the holiday cheer.

Mark Turner

Looking for an alternative to the traditional poinsettia to brighten your home over the holidays? Consider a Christmas cactus. This inexpensive houseplant can deck your halls with hundreds of blossoms during the festive season—and beyond.

When it's mature, this vigorous plant spreads up to 3 feet wide, and with proper care it can last for generations. Some *Birds & Blooms* readers have heirloom plants that have been in their families for over a century!

Patricia Engelhardt of Hockessin, Delaware is the caretaker of a healthy Christmas cactus that her great-aunt purchased in 1888! (That's it above right.)

"One year, it produced more than 500 blossoms," Patricia says. "I've sent cuttings to relatives around the country so they can enjoy this plant in their homes, too."

Christmas cactus, known botanically as *Schlumbergera*, makes an ideal holiday gift—and an economical one. Just take a stem cutting, pop it into a container with well-draining potting mix, and it will keep on giving for decades.

Family Heirloom

Julie Zeid of Palmdale, California received a start from her mother-in-law's 49-cent plant more than 20 years ago, and both plants are still going strong today. Julie's pro-

The fleshy, truncated stems may be scalloped or deeply notched, and they arch and droop as the plant grows. A hanging basket displays the plant nicely and allows room for it to spread.

Three-inch trumpet-shaped blossoms appear at the tips of the leaf segments from late fall through late winter, depending on the species. As Julie discovered, some cultivars even bloom several times a year. The flowers may be red, pink, orange or white.

duces up to 300 blossoms at a time and flowers year-round.

Although Christmas cactus has a reputation for being somewhat temperamental, Julie and Patricia say their plants aren't particularly fussy and require minimal care.

"Christmas cactus will grow almost on its own, without a lot of extra help," Julie confirms.

Ruth Waterman of Newport Beach, California, agrees.

"They thrive on neglect," she notes. "I just keep mine where they're cool during the day and receive some sun."

Brighten Your Indoors

In their native environment of southeastern Brazil, these "air plants", known as epiphytes, grow much the way orchids do, on trees or amid clusters of rocks. Since they can't tolerate temperatures below 50°, they're used primarily as houseplants in North America.

Virtually any home will provide the ideal indoor environment for a Christmas cactus. All it needs is bright but indirect light, with moderate humidity. In summer, the plant is perfectly happy being moved outside, as long as it's in partial shade. Be sure to bring it back indoors well before the first frost, however, or your cactus is history.

Unlike many cacti, the Christmas cactus has no spines.

Prepare a Holiday Display

Most plants will bloom around Christmas without special effort on your part. To increase the odds, just cut back on watering in fall. Keep the cactus in a cool spot, and water only after the potting soil dries out.

Overwatering is the most common mistake when caring for a Christmas cactus. As a general rule, water regularly when the plant is blooming or actively growing, usually in spring. Otherwise, water only after the potting mix has dried out. For a nutritional boost, apply a high-potash liquid fertilizer just after flowering, or when the plant is producing new growth.

These tropical plants prefer porous soil. The best medium is an epiphytic cactus potting mix (available at garden centers), but any well-draining potting mix will do.

If you follow these simple guidelines, you'll find Christmas cactus is an easy-care selection that requires little special attention. Even diseases and pests aren't a real issue with these productive and colorful plants.

So why not spread some cheer with a Christmas cactus this season? It just may become an heirloom to pass on to the next generation of green thumbs.

PLANT PROFILE

Mark Turner

Common Names: Christmas cactus, Thanksgiving cactus, crab cactus, holiday cactus and Easter cactus.

Botanical Name: *Schlumbergera.*

Bloom Time: Most bloom from late fall to late winter, but some flower in spring and late summer.

Flower Colors: Red, white, orange and deep or pale pink.

Flower Shape: Trumpet-shaped.

Height: 2 feet.

Spread: 3 feet.

Light Needs: Bright to indirect light indoors. Partial shade if placed outdoors in summer.

Soil Type: Epiphytic cactus potting mix or any well-draining potting soil.

Propagating: Place stem cuttings in potting soil.

Prize Picks: *Schlumbergera orssichiana* produces white blossoms with a purplish-pink tinge at the tips. This small species has a particularly long blooming period, from late summer to winter.

SETTING THE TABLE

Try these ideas for a flurry of winter bird activity.

Her Cookies Are for the Birds

ONE COLD WINTER DAY, when the animals had a hard time finding the birdseed at the feeders, my Aunt Bev and I spent the day cooking for the critters. We invented what we call "wildlife cakes" (right)—a mix of apples, birdseed, dried bread, bagels and raisins. We even added some old cat, hamster and dog food to the mixture and decorated them with grapes.

My aunt found suet and bacon drippings for fat and we added eggs and flour to the mix.

After greasing cookie sheets, we shaped the "dough" into squares, decorated with grapes and baked them at about 350° until cooked through.

After they cooled, I put the cakes outside on old plates and watched the animals enjoy our special treat.
—*India Fowler*
Port Dalhousie, Ontario

Bev McCullen

the paper just before hanging outside. I've been doing this for 20 years, and they've always been my most successful feeders. —*Gloria Lariviere*
Edgemoor, South Carolina

A Real Treat

LAST WINTER, I was trying to come up with a use for the gingerbread house my grandchildren made for Christmas. I broke up a few small pieces and put them on my deck railing to see if the birds would be interested. They gobbled up every crumb!

Within a few days, the birds devoured the entire gingerbread house. Now I buy gingersnaps at the store for a special bird treat.

Tufted titmice are our most frequent visitors, but the gingersnaps also attract blue jays, dark-eyed juncos, nuthatches, red-headed woodpeckers and chickadees.

The birds look forward to this daily treat. On mornings when it's too rainy to put the cookies out, they sit on the railing and wait for us. Talk about being spoiled!
—*Pat Hughes, Manchester, Pennsylvania*

READER TIP

I always save the cotton packing from medicine bottles and toss them near my birdhouses when the weather turns cold. I've seen sparrows use it in the entrance of a birdhouse at night to block out the chilling wind. Pretty smart! —*Norman Vierk*
West Lafayette, Indiana

Simple Suet Cups

BACON AND BIRDSEED are all you need for easy-to-make suet cups. Just drop a length of heavy string into a 5-ounce paper cup, making sure to curl one end around the bottom and letting the other end hang over the top.

Pour in bacon grease (it must be warm enough to be a liquid) until the cup is half filled, then add birdseed and stir carefully. Place cups in the freezer until needed—then rip off

Snow Show

AFTER a late season snowstorm, my wife and I were shut in. For entertainment, we pulled up a chair and gazed out the windows at our active feathered friends.

The cedar waxwings (at right) were the most interesting. They came by the hundreds to feast on

our pyracantha and holly berries. Mockingbirds did their best to scare the waxwings away, but there's strength in numbers, and the waxwings eventually won. The plants were completely stripped by the time the waxwings finished.

I'm sure glad Mother Nature gave us the day off. Otherwise, we would have missed this amazing show.

—*Paul Brinson, Irving, Texas*

These Snowmen Feed Birds

HERE'S A WINTER project that's lots of fun for kids and adults—make a snowman that stands in as a bird feeder. There are unlimited possibilities, but to get you on track, we thought we'd share a couple of clever ideas sent by readers:

Jessica Iskierka of Andover, Minnesota (pictured below), sculpted this snowman that serves up treats to the backyard birds while wearing a charcoal smile.

"I asked Jessica to make me a bird-feeder snowman, and she created this frosty gentleman," says her mother, Pam. "The snowman holds a pie pan where we place the birdseed. It didn't take long for the backyard birds to warm up to him."

In London, Kentucky, Meghan Stallcup built her grandmother Agnes a snowman feeder, but was disappointed when the birds didn't arrive to eat any of the seed she set out.

"I suggested she put birdseed on the rim of his hat," (left) Agnes says. "That's all it took for the snowman to become a big hit with the birds in our yard. We enjoyed watching the winged action for several days."

Set a Place at the Table

WE MAKE SURE we take care of "ground eaters" as much as the birds that use our regular feeders. In winter this is important, especially after a snowfall.

We came up with this method after waking one morning to 8 inches of fresh snow. I dug a path to the patio and cleared off the picnic table near our "feeder tree". Then I spread seed for the ground birds on the tabletop and benches.

It's easier to clear heavy snow from a table, and we're rewarded with an excellent view of the birds as they eat.

—*Sharon Leaidicker, Coatesville, Pennsylvania*

Clean Feeder Idea

LOOKING FOR an inexpensive homemade feeder? Try recycling an empty laundry detergent bottle into a simple bird feeder like this one (below, with a chickadee).

After a thorough cleaning, cut out the middle of the bottle as pictured. This creates a covered "porch" when you mount it upside down, protecting the birds and your seed or suet mix from the weather. Don't forget to drill a few drainage holes in the bottom of the feeder to help keep the seed dry.

—*Al Hanson, Eau Claire, Wisconsin*

Frost-Free Water

HERE IN MINNESOTA, winter birdbaths must be heated to keep them from becoming miniature ice rinks. A variety of birdbath heaters are available, but I couldn't find one suitable for the fountain I already had.

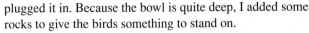

Then, while shopping for birdseed one day, I found an unlikely alternative to the standard birdbath heater—a heated pet bowl, complete with thermostat and insulation. I had to give it a try.

I simply placed the dish inside my existing birdbath and plugged it in. Because the bowl is quite deep, I added some rocks to give the birds something to stand on.

So far, so good. In temperatures down to -10°, my new winter birdbath has kept the water from freezing.

—*Roland Jordahl, Pelican Rapids, Minnesota*

A Protected Perch

IN WINTER, we attach branches trimmed from our cedar trees to our feeders. The simple addition provides birds with protective cover and seems to draw more activity to them. —*Sue Bogart, Topeka, Kansas*

Peanut Butter Spread

IF YOUR HOME is made of brick, spread a mix of peanut butter, cornmeal and birdseed into the mortar joints. Woodpeckers love it, especially in winter. It's also a good mixture to spread onto the bark of trees.

And, contrary to popular belief, peanut butter is perfectly safe for birds. They won't choke on it. —*Lisa Scott*
Bloomington, Indiana

A NEARLY NATURAL WONDER

Utah gardeners use wildflowers and a splash of water to give Mother Nature a helping hand.

By Becky Yeager, Field Editor, Nibley, Utah

When Pam and Kevin Fife moved into a quaint rural neighborhood in Logan, Utah in 1995, they found their new house a delight. It was the 3-acre lot that made them a little uneasy.

The long-neglected yard was filled with weeds and rocks. Poor soil conditions, coupled with dry summers and harsh winters, only made the situation worse.

With the serene Blacksmith Fork River bordering one side of the property and mountains looming on the horizon,

the Fifes knew their backyard had potential to be a real beauty. They also knew the remedy to their dilemma—hard work and a passion for gardening.

Over the next few years, Pam and Kevin transformed their landscape into a lush sanctuary filled with extensive flower gardens, a pond and productive vegetable plot. The grounds are tidy and well maintained, yet look as natural as if Mother Nature planned it herself.

The Fifes started by installing a fence for their dogs,

Photos: Linda Sargent

which helped define the yard, and then began the slow process of removing the "field of weeds".

"We used a garden hose to outline where I wanted the flower beds," Pam recalls. "We had a bunch of topsoil brought in to get everything leveled out and added lots of compost. Then I planted trees in the beds."

Planning a Path

Before the main flower bed even had anything growing in it, Pam was already thinking ahead. She created a wide pathway through the bed to make maintenance easier when the plants matured. Then she scattered handfuls of wildflower seeds to create an almost instant mass of color.

The following year, the Fifes began landscaping in earnest, laying sod and adding shrubs and perennials. They installed a sprinkler system to ensure their plantings got enough moisture. Pam says that made all the difference.

"I really wanted my garden to start growing, especially the trees," Pam says. "After we installed the sprinklers, everything just took off."

The Fifes dug a pond in the middle of the main flower bed

and enhanced it with water-loving plants. They created a fenced-in vegetable garden (see photos on page 178) near the back of the yard, and built a coop for chickens and ducks.

Nature Lends a Hand

By the third year, nature was beginning to take its course. The wildflowers reseeded, filling in the remaining bare areas of the flower beds.

In the main garden, visible from the road, asters and other flowers reach out from between the fence rails. The same garden can be seen from a secluded patio, where the Fifes like to relax and watch the animals, including a dazzling array of birds that flit in and out of the vegetation—and the birdhouses that tower above it.

Pam's only problem now is keeping her native plants in check.

"The wildflowers were a great idea, but they're still coming up, and sometimes they take over," she chuckles. "I planted purple coneflower because the birds like the seeds, and now I've got it everywhere!

"Now I'm concentrating on thinning out flowers that are interfering with other plants or coming up where I don't want them, like on the pathway. I'm gradually digging those up and giving them away to the neighbors."

Using Their Resources

The only task left to complete was moving the river rocks that covered most of their property.

"Since we live on a riverbed, everything was covered with small to good-sized rocks," Pam says. "We've been removing them gradually over the years."

While the rocks have been a bit troublesome, the Fifes have found ways to put them to use.

"I outlined the path through the garden with rocks, we put some rocks around the garden itself, and we used some for a waterfall," Pam says. "They've come in handy."

With most of the landscaping complete, the Fifes now devote their time to building a business.

Set against the beautiful backdrop of mountains and gardens, the barn they added to the landscape is now the home

> ### READER TIP
>
> Use a garden hose to outline the space for a new flower bed. It's easy to adjust the shape and size until you find a layout you like.

HILLY HAVEN. The Fifes' backyard is a respite for birds, including domestic fowl like the well-hidden chicken above, as well as wild birds that flock to their birdhouses (top). It's also the perfect place to raise llamas and alpacas (like the one with Pam, above left).

ALL DECKED OUT. Margaret Buch is always looking for more room for her flowers, so she packs them into every possible space. This blooming deck (above) is her pride and joy. Her deck railings hold planters overflowing with pink and white geraniums and purple lobelia, and even more containers of annuals adorn the deck itself.

but try telling that to the folks who receive jars of Margaret's superb grape jelly for Christmas each year.

Her secret is winter protection. She packs leaves around non-hardy plants and covers them with plastic containers as extra insulation.

Margaret also looks for plants that provide interest for more than one season, like the Virginia creeper that cascades over her fence.

"It's nice and green in summer, and turns a beautiful red and orange in fall," she says.

Her shade garden features a large assortment of hostas. Margaret controls the ever-present slug population by picking them off by hand at dusk and dropping them into a coffee can that contains a little bleach.

Look on the Bright Side

There have been a few setbacks over the years, but Margaret turns each one into a green-thumb opportunity.

"The most devastating loss was our weeping birch, which

> ### READER TIP
>
> Coax some non-hardy plants through winter using this method: Pack leaves around the tender plants and cover them with plastic containers for extra insulation. —*Margaret Buch Regina, Saskatchewan*

was absolutely beautiful," she recalls. "It was only 3 feet tall when we planted it, and it grew to cover a large area of our backyard. But when birch borers got to it, we had to cut it down.

"I couldn't bear to part with it, so we saved the stump. Now I use it as a stand for a container of cascading petunias every summer."

When they had to remove a low-growing mugo pine, she turned the space into an additional flower bed.

"I grow roses, hardy lilies, calla lilies, clematis, fern peonies and Lenten roses there," she says.

For Margaret, gardening is a tonic for both body and soul.

"It's great therapy, and keeps me in good shape," she says. "I'm alone now, and a senior, but I'm still able to shovel soil, dig the garden and drag large bags of peat moss into the yard.

"When I ask my sons to do chores for me in the house, they ask how I can work in the yard but not do things indoors. I always tell them the yard isn't 'work'. It's an act of love—for the flowers and the beauty I've created." ◢

DETERMINATION OVER DROUGHT

Colorado transplants learn how to embrace the wild weather of the West.

By Gary L. Shaufler
Field Editor,
Pueblo, Colorado

When Andre and Anita Fredette (at left) bought their home in Pueblo, Colorado 8 years ago, they inherited a weary yard that had seen better days. Neglected for 20 years, the back lawn was a neighborhood eyesore and in desperate need of a green thumb.

Hailing from Vancouver, British Columbia, Andrea and Anita were accustomed to the lush surroundings of the temperate Northwest. Adapting to the arid conditions of southern Colorado, however, was a challenge they were both willing to take head on.

In addition to the harsh growing conditions and an unkempt yard, the couple soon found themselves facing an even more daunting backyard threat—one of the worst summer droughts the area had seen in decades.

Real Work Begins

Determined to turn their slice of desert into a gardener's dream, the couple set out on a landscaping adventure. They gathered design ideas from home shows and magazines, and researched plants and flowers that were known to thrive in the area.

The two began their outdoor renovation by adding on to an existing concrete patio. When the work was complete, a two-tiered patio with brick retaining walls and sprawling curvaceous flower beds (top) made for an impressive backyard centerpiece. Always keeping in mind the dry conditions, the patio was constructed with a slight slope to encourage rainwater to run off into the plantings.

Next, they removed dead shrubs and pruned back overgrown evergreens to encourage new growth. They selected

annual and perennial plants to give the drab landscape much-needed color—tea roses, golden-tipped junipers, begonias, marigolds, African daisies, snow in summer and phlox. Between the cascade of colorful blooms, they mixed in strawberry and tomato plants as well.

By summer's end, however, Andre and Anita found themselves facing another challenge—government-ordered watering restrictions. Andre reluctantly stopped watering the lawn, but was elated when the drought-resistant Bermuda grass he'd selected held its lush green color into the fall.

Waste Not, Want Not

To further minimize water consumption, Andre and Anita came up with several other solutions, including restricting water pressure to the sprinkler heads to minimize over spray and planning a drip system, which will use about one-third less water than regular sprinklers.

Their good thinking has paid off, as Anita now has more perennials than she can handle. Every year, she divides the overgrown plants and repots them, selling them at her annual garage sale. Not only does this allow her to share the beauty she nurtured with her community, but the extra pocket money gives her the freedom to buy more perennials for her ever-growing garden.

Andre and Anita's yard is a true beauty, and neighbors still drop by with praise for a job well done. Together, the two have educated themselves by doing research, and learned even more by trial and error. One look at their bright desert oasis, and there's no doubt their efforts were worthwhile. ◄

WATER-WISE GARDENING

Get more color with less water.

By Damian Fagan, Moab, Utah

Water! That's my first thought when I see areas around my town landscaped with Kentucky bluegrass and landscape plants that demand well-moistened roots.

That's fine in areas with sufficient rainfall (or incredibly cheap water rates). But here in the arid Southwest, water is a precious commodity.

To help educate people in this area about "water-wise gardening"—also called "xeriscaping" (*xeri* is Greek for dry)—the Moab Information Center in Utah offers visitors a showcase of plants that can create a colorful garden without extensive watering.

The center's educational garden, which features drought-tolerant plants arranged in a pleasing and colorful way, was created by Janis Adkins of High Desert Gardens, a local nursery.

Many of the plants she selected share the same characteristics—broad root systems, small leaf sizes, waxy coatings on the leaf surfaces, spring growth, seed longevity and other unique traits that help them survive in sandy, rocky soil.

More Than Cactus

There are over 100 plants in the gardens. Surprisingly, most of them *don't* belong to the cactus family!

The display gardens cover 14,000 square feet and include many varieties of perennials, succulents and drought-resistant trees and shrubs. It's clear gardeners have many choices.

Janis' plan has been so effective, the gardens are watered only once or twice a month—even in summer.

The lawns at the center also fit the plan. Buffalo grass and blue grama grass are used extensively because they require 60% less water than bluegrass. They're extremely drought-resistant because they're native to the prairies of the Great Plains.

Once established, these grasses need minimal watering and can be mowed or left to grow wild.

A Few Pointers

Whether you live in a desert climate or just want to reduce your own water bill, Janis offers these tips for water-wise gardening:

- Plan before you plant. Group plants with similar water, sun and soil needs. Direct water runoff into planting beds.
- Choose plants that are drought-tolerant. Many are readily available at nurseries. (See box below.)
- Limit lawn areas and select native grasses.
- Mulch and improve soil with compost and other organic matter. This helps hold moisture.
- Use drip irrigation or soaker hoses to water deeply. Don't overwater.
- Maintain landscape by mowing, pruning and controlling pests and weeds.

A Few Water-Wise Plants for Your Garden

Annuals	Perennials	Shrubs	Trees
Amaranth	Bearded iris	Butterfly bush	Goldenrain tree
California poppy	Daylily	Cotoneaster	Hackberry
Coreopsis	Evening primrose	Firethorn	Locust
Cosmos	Gaillardia/blanketflower	Juniper	Oak
Marigold	Liatris/gayfeather	Smoketree	Sweet bay
Nasturtium	Mexican hat (at left)	Western redbud	

GET UP & GROW

Three readers overcome garden obstacles.

Stuck on Cactus

"CACTUS" is a nickname I acquired at a young age.

My mother had a beautiful flowering cactus that simply fascinated me. Every day I tried to grab it, and every night my father had to tweeze the prickers out of my hands.

Although my parents eventually got rid of that cactus, the nickname stuck.

My love for cactus plants—or, more accurately, my obsession with them—has only grown over the years. I have cacti in my house, on my patio and in my 40- by 60-foot backyard garden (see the photo above).

I've received many cacti as gifts, and have rescued many others friends didn't want. It's hard to choose a favorite, but the longer the thorns, the more appealing they are.

I guess you could say I'm really stuck on cactus, and cactus certainly is stuck on me...ouch!

—Jennifer Gregory
Acampo, California

Plant-Packed Corner

HAVING MINIMAL gardening space shouldn't keep you from enjoying plants and flowers. It sure hasn't stopped me!

My apartment has a small shaded balcony, but I packed it with plants (above). I have 20 pots of hostas, ferns, coleus, ivy and impatiens in a space that measures only 5 by 7 feet. I cover all the pots with chicken wire to keep the squirrels at bay.

The space may be small, but it's my little slice of heaven. *—Robin Brown, Chatham, Ontario*

Staked Her Claim to Year-Round Gardening

HERE'S A CLEVER idea from Patricia Fears from Yelm, Washington, who found a way to spend more time in her garden all year long. To protect herself from the elements, Patricia cut the bottom out of this old tent (left), which shelters her when the weather just doesn't cooperate with her garden plans.

"With the tent in place, I can garden no matter what the weather," Patricia says.

To keep clean, Patricia kneels on an old piece of carpet. "Then all I need to do is grab my tools, and a-weedin' I go—wind, rain or snow."

FIT FOR FLOWERS. Anything can become a planter in Carolyn's yard. Flower-filled teapots provide a colorful welcome out front (above). Recycled items and souvenirs come together in an eclectic collection (left). She has even used items like a butter kettle, wooden toolbox and a tire-testing tank as flower containers.

and rock formations. The Dreamcatcher Garden includes a "peace pole"—an upended hog trough painted with messages of peace in various languages —plus a bent-willow arbor and Native American sculptures.

"When people walk through the garden, they love the whimsy," Carolyn says. "Around every little bend, they see something new—wind chimes, stained-glass butterflies, a calf tank turned into a water garden. You're just in a state of wonderment, never knowing what you're going to meet."

Alive with Wildlife

For birds, bees, butterflies and other wildlife, this organic landscape (Carolyn doesn't use any chemicals) is an urban oasis. With 36 birdhouses, four butterfly boxes, seven small water gardens, butterfly "puddling" areas, plentiful

ground cover and dozens of tree and shrub species.

It has been certified as a Backyard Wildlife Habitat by the National Wildlife Federation since 1984 and recognized by The Wild Ones, an organization that encourages natural landscaping. It was honored by the Willowbrook Wildlife Foundation's 2003 Blazing Star Award for urban wildlife-friendly landscapes. The Finzer yard has also been on the Illinois Audubon Society's butterfly garden tour and The Garden Conservancy's Open Days Tour.

"It's a sensory place," she says. "You go out and close your eyes and you can hear the birds chirping, the chipmunks running, the leaves rustling. When you lie in the hammock and look up into the tulip tree, with the green leaves silhouetted against the blue sky, it's just like being on a retreat.

"Some people go to a spa. I go to my yard." ✦

MAKING THE GRADE

Turning an eroding yard into a terraced treasure.

By Kelly Walsh, Shelton, Connecticut

There's some good in poison ivy, stinging nettles and wild grapevines, after all. They're the only things that were keeping my steep lawn from sliding into the Housatonic River!

I bought my home from an elderly woman who owned it for decades. The yard leading to the river was eroding badly, so I knew I had to do something before it was history.

The growth was so thick it blanketed long-forgotten discarded items—fence posts, a cable wheel, a 55-gallon metal drum, even the missing 25-foot section of rain gutter from the house. It was an overgrown neglected mess...and I loved the challenge.

Buying the house left me with nothing to spend but imagination and sweat. So I went for broke.

Rock-Solid Plan

At the time I decided to take on the project, a road crew was widening the highway I took to work each day. So I routinely filled up my trunk with rocks blasted from the roadside cliff. My husband, Richard (we were engaged when I

started the project), soon caught rock fever, too. It wasn't long before the side yard became a mountain of hand-picked boulders to make stone walls.

Once the slope was cleared, I started terracing it so I could have some garden space. I dug a trench for the retaining wall foundation. I placed the largest rocks I could handle in the trench, then staggered the next layers. To fill in the back of the wall, I poured in buckets of small stones, then packed in sandy soil. One wall after another, the once useless bank began to take shape.

At a flower show, I ran into a Ferry-Morse Seed Co. representative and told him about our project. He was impressed with our enthusiasm and generously gave us a shoebox full of flower and vegetable seeds for $20.

We started the seeds indoors in anything that would hold soil—mushroom containers, Styrofoam cups and cans. Although we carefully labeled everything, eventually we lost track of the plants as we repotted them. I ended up with a garden of hollyhocks in front of lobelia, nicotiana dwarfing strawflowers, marigolds buried under tomatoes. It was beautiful anyway!

It Pays to Have Friends

Plant donations from friends and neighbors also flooded in once they heard about our project. Someone sent bishop's weed and hostas. Another gave us moonbeam coreopsis and red-hot pokers. A third came with lilac shoots.

My best friend, Sharon, dug up some of her rose of Sharon and a hydrangea bush. My brother encouraged me to take whatever plants I wanted from his place. I was in heaven, planting peonies, iris and ornamental grasses until midnight that day.

To control the weeds, we used mulch made of newspaper, leaves and household vegetable scraps. Then we covered it with a thick layer of hay.

To keep costs down, we collected lots of leftover "freebies"—with permission, of course. Bricks came from a demolition site, cobblestone from a nearby street project and slate from a church where the roof was being rebuilt.

With a little help and luck, we transformed this overgrown, eroding slope into a beautiful backyard for less than $80—and that included the $15 co-pay for a visit to the doctor to treat my poison ivy!

STEEP AND CHEAP. Kelly Walsh tamed the incline in her backyard for pocket change by using donated plants and materials.

A CUT ABOVE THE REST

Clients at this home hair salon are treated to a beautiful backyard view.

By Joanne D. Wells, Savannah, Georgia

One of my neighbors here in Savannah, Georgia found a charming way to combine business with pleasure. Ginny Dubose's home hair salon overlooks her backyard garden (above), giving her customers front-row seats to an ongoing parade of blossoms, birds, butterflies and wildlife.

Customers of Ginny's Hair Design sit in front of a huge picture window, enjoying the changing panorama of several distinctive "garden rooms".

"The garden took on my personality," Ginny explains. "It's a way of

194

TAKE A SEAT. Chairs (like the ones at right) are a frequent theme in Ginny Dubose's backyard, which she planned as a series of garden "rooms". Her latest project is a water garden (top left) that features towering umbrella grass in the water and variegated privet onshore.

expressing my inner self. I've always liked being outdoors and getting involved with nature. Having a business with a garden view lets me share that beauty with my clients."

For years, Ginny's shop was at another location, and working away from home left her little time for gardening. When she decided to build a shop on the back of her house, her first goal was to provide an attractive entrance.

She lined the walkway that leads to the salon with thick borders of lush holly ferns and planted seasonal flowers in the window boxes. In early spring, pink blooms hang from a magnolia, providing a beautiful contrast to the tree's silver-gray branches.

Sprucing up the entry area inspired Ginny to give the entire backyard a makeover, and she slowly restyled it over a period of 5 years.

Putting It All Together

Ginny planned her gardens carefully, considering bloom time, drainage, light needs and whether plants would attract butterflies. She also looked for plants that would help her create different themed "rooms".

"I'm not a one-track person," she says. "I like expressing myself in a variety of ways, and gardening by rooms gives me that option. I established the rooms around things I liked and nostalgic items, such as the weathered wooden chair in the garden room."

The chair, now a planter for annual vinca, came from a South Carolina schoolhouse where her mother-in-law once worked. A log-cabin birdhouse and a cushioned swing surrounded with jasmine tie the elements together for an old-fashioned country look.

The garden rooms aren't defined with walls or hedges. Instead, they're casually arranged throughout the yard. One is devoted to tropical plants, and another uses hydrangeas

to create a romantic Victorian atmosphere.

Every arbor in the garden features two climbers with different bloom cycles for ongoing color. In the Victorian room, Ginny chose the combination of spring-blooming gloriosa lilies and sweet autumn clematis.

Ginny's latest project is a small water garden. Her grandchildren Julia and Christian supplied the goldfish to swim among the umbrella grass and waterlilies.

All these delightful areas are visible from Ginny's shop. Some clients arrive early to stroll in the garden first. Inside, talk at the salon is as much about gardening as it is about hairstyles. They share ideas and promise to swap seeds and plants.

As Ginny works, red-bellied woodpeckers, tufted titmice, chickadees and hummingbirds flock to the feeders just outside the window. Clients often ask her to turn their chairs for a better glimpse of these familiar visitors.

Just beyond the feeders, monarchs, sulfurs and swallowtails flit through the butterfly garden. Ginny made the most of this small space by adding parsley and fennel plants, which many butterflies seek out for laying eggs.

Never Enough Time

Ginny still doesn't have as much time to devote to garden maintenance as she'd like, so she has learned to set priorities. She tries to focus on existing plants, making sure they're well established before she moves on to another project.

"This is still a work in progress, but there's a feeling of accomplishment in bringing this together," Ginny says. "It's peaceful and soothing.

"Gardens are made for sharing with friends and family. I want my clients to be relaxed, and my family to have a feeling of well-being. My garden does all of that for me." ◄

> ## READER TIP
>
> Because time is limited, I try to focus on existing plants, making sure they're well established before moving on to another project.
> —*Ginny Dubose*
> *Savannah, Georgia*

BACKYARD
SHOWPIECE

Darryl R. Beers

LIVE OAK

Towering trees grace our eastern coastal regions with Southern charm.

Perhaps no other tree is more cherished in the American South than the graceful and majestic live oak. These sprawling trees with gigantic moss-covered canopies and huge gnarled limbs belong to an earlier era and conjure up visions of Southern plantations and scenes from *Gone with the Wind*.

Live oaks are a true all-American with Southern charm. While other species of oak are found throughout the world's temperate northern regions, live oaks are only native from Virginia south to Florida and west to Texas. Georgians proudly honored the live oak, naming it their state tree.

They appear in their greatest numbers on coastal islands throughout the South, thriving in the heat and humidity typical of this area.

American Legends

Live oaks survive for hundreds of years and some have become local landmarks, noted as the sites of treaty signings and other historic events.

The famed Treaty Oak in Austin, Texas is about 500 years old. While there's no real proof, it's believed the state's founder, Stephen Austin, signed the first Native American boundary treaty under this tree's spreading branches in 1824.

Then there are the famous twins at The Live Oak Inn, a bed-and-breakfast in Georgetown, South Carolina. A pair of 500-year-old live oaks flank the historic inn.

But those trees are mere youngsters compared to the legendary Angel Oak (pictured at left) near Charleston, South Carolina. Scientists believe the Angel Oak is more than 1,400 years old. (Its exact age can't be determined because heart rot, a disease live oaks are susceptible to, makes tissue sampling useless.)

The Angel Oak's trunk has a circumference of more

Derek Fell

Photos: Derek Fell

than 25 feet, and its massive canopy covers 17,000 square feet. And most striking of all, the lower limbs of the Angel Oak actually rest on the ground. The largest single limb on this tree is 89 feet long with a circumference of more than 11 feet!

Distinctive Looks

Live oaks are evergreen and grow in Plant Hardiness Zones 8 to 10. They have smooth-edged leathery leaves 2 to 5 inches long. The shiny leaves are dark green on top, with fuzzy white undersides.

The old leaves drop in spring, when new ones begin to emerge. However, some live oaks can be deciduous at the northern edges of their habitat.

> **READER TIP**
>
> When adding a live oak to the backyard, give it plenty of room. As it grows, the tree's width often doubles the size of its height!

Its branches are often draped with Spanish moss (above), giving the trees a captivating appearance. And its bark is reddish brown, with grooves.

Live oaks can be planted in the landscape by seed using its acorns (above right)—which the trees bear in great numbers—or by purchasing container-grown trees from a garden center.

When adding one to a backyard, give live oaks plenty of room—its spread is usually double the tree's height!

Planted in groups or rows, live oaks eventually form an interlocking canopy for a captivating "cathedral effect". While young live oaks have an upright appearance, with full rounded crowns, they appear to become more stout, with thick twisted limbs that slowly lower as if overpowered by the tree's weight.

Live oaks tolerate occasional dry weather, but do best with regular watering. An irrigation system that ensures deep watering as needed is ideal for helping these true Southern belles shine for generations to come. 🦅

David Liebman

PLANT PROFILE

Common Names: Live oak, Southern live oak.

Botanical Name: *Quercus virginiana*.

Height: 40 to 80 feet.

Spread: 60 to 100 feet.

Flowers: Dangling catkins of male flowers.

Fruit: 3/4- to 1-inch acorns, grown singly or in clusters.

Hardiness: Zones 8 to 10.

Light Needs: Full sun.

Soil Type: Either acidic or neutral and well-draining.

Planting: Plant acorns in fall and protect from rodents. Small container-grown trees transplant easily. If planting more than one tree, space 25 to 30 feet apart so the branches interlock to create a canopy.

200

HOW TO PLANT THE BIG STUFF

By Melinda Myers, Contributing Editor

Picking the perfect tree for your yard is only half the job. Proper planting once you bring your selection home is essential. But with a little know-how, it's easy to get your tree off to a good start so you can enjoy its beauty for years to come.

Trees and shrubs are available as bare-root, container, potted or balled-and-burlapped plants. They present a challenge because of their size, weight and handling issues.

Soil preparation for trees is different from flowers because of their larger root system. Their roots could eventually extend 2 to 5 times the height of the tree, so it's next to impossible to amend the entire root zone.

And you don't want to amend the soil in the planting hole. This creates more problems than it solves.

Adding lots of peat moss and compost creates a wonderful growing environment that the roots will never leave. When the roots hit the heavy clay or dry sand outside the planting hole, they turn and stay within the highly amended planting hole. This leads to girdling roots and early death.

Your primary focus for trees and shrubs is making sure the hole is the proper size. There's an old horticultural saying, "It's better to place a $50 tree in a $100 hole than a $100 tree in a $10 hole." Take time to dig a proper hole for your investment. Trust me—I've seen many gardeners waste time and money replacing failed plants just because they skimped on the planting hole. The illustration (at left) shows the proper way to plant a tree. Remove the burlap, if possible, and stake only if necessary.

Be sure to dig a hole at least 2 times wider than the diameter of the root ball on shrubs, and 2 to 4 times wider than the diameter of the root ball of trees.

But don't dig deeper than the height of the root system. Otherwise, your heavy plant will sink. Sunken planting holes collect water, and the plant's health could quickly decline.

Before placing your large plant, scratch the sides of the planting hole with your shovel to make it easier for roots to penetrate the surrounding soil.

Then place your plant centered in your hole and backfill with the existing soil.

Shrubs should be at the same depth they were growing in the container. On trees, look for the root flare—the area where the trunk widens into roots. (You may have to gently dig through the soil around the trunk to find it.) Keep the root flare at or slightly above the soil surface. Burying the flare leads to trunk decay, root rot, early decline or even death.

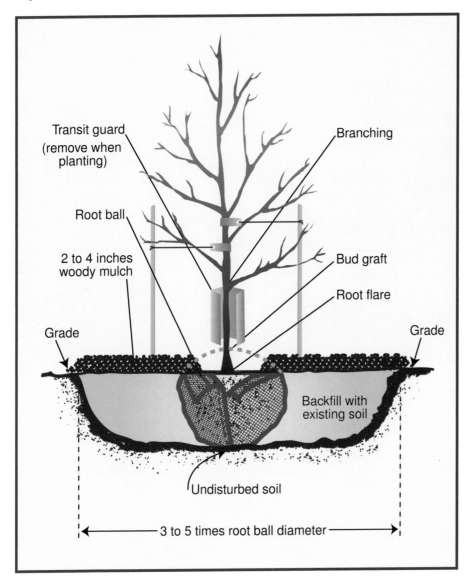

Transit guard (remove when planting)

Root ball

2 to 4 inches woody mulch

Grade

Branching

Bud graft

Root flare

Grade

Backfill with existing soil

Undisturbed soil

3 to 5 times root ball diameter

SMOKETREES

It's tough to extinguish their dusky beauty.

By Deb Mulvey, Greendale, Wisconsin

Mark Turner

Have a burning desire for an easy-care plant that provides a lot of drama? A smoketree might be just the ticket.

These deciduous trees and shrubs guarantee a stunning display in summer, when clouds of downy plume-shaped panicles seem to envelop the foliage in a smoky haze. As the weather cools and the panicles disappear, the leaves become bold shades of orange, red or yellow. Best of all, this unusual show will unfold with virtually no effort on your part.

Smoketrees perform best when simply left alone. Giving them too much attention—overwatering, for instance, or pruning—can even damage their growth and appearance. They seem to thrive on neglect, as my family discovered.

The smoketree at my childhood home in southern Ohio sat right next to a busy rural highway. Lumbering farm equipment coated it with grain dust and debris. In winter, snowplows sprayed it with salt. And summer road crews spread bubbling hot tar on the pavement no more than a yard away.

Other landscape plants might have withered under these conditions. But our smoketree flourished in the same unlikely spot for more than 40 years, reliably producing clouds

of dusky pink panicles every summer (like those at left).

Tough growing conditions are no sweat for these plants, which hail from rocky regions in southern Europe to southern China. Botanically known as *Cotinus coggygria*, these types are generally called smokebush.

A species native to the southeastern U.S., American smoketree is botanically classified as *Cotinus obovatus*.

Alarmingly Simple

Both types are easy to transplant and will grow in almost any sunny spot, including less-than-perfect planting sites. They're susceptible to only a handful of pest and disease problems, none of them serious.

And, as my family's experience proves, temperature extremes and pollutants don't faze them.

The flowers are insignificant, but they're responsible for the plant's distinctive look. The tiny yellow-green blooms appear in June or July, then fade, leaving long fuzzy stalks that form showy panicles.

Over summer, the panicles cycle through a series of color changes. They emerge as delicate green, then turn soft fawny brown and become smoky pink as they mature. Depending on the variety, the panicles may be tinged with brown, beige or purple and generally remain on the tree through September.

As the panicles wither in fall, the leaves put on a show of their own, changing to yellow, orange and shades of scarlet from their summer hues of green, red or reddish purple.

One purple-leafed variety (similar to the one at right), Royal Purple smokebush, has leaves that emerge as a rich maroon and then darken, sometimes turning almost black. In autumn, the leaves become a rich red-purple.

Hands-Off Approach

Smoketrees generally have a loose, open growth habit and may be wider than they are tall. They're naturally shapely, so minimal pruning is needed.

Most varieties top out at 15 feet, making smoketrees a good choice for small spaces.

The largest species, the American smoketree, soars to 30 feet with a 25-foot spread. It produces 6- to 10-inch panicles that stay on the tree well into autumn.

Hardy in Zones 4 through 8, these plants aren't fussy about soil, and actually seem to perform best when somewhat stressed. They'll flourish in dry or rocky locations, especially if the soil is moderately fertile and drains well.

With their unusual summer display, these plants are equally effective in borders or as the center of attention. When used in groups, the feathery panicles guarantee a striking summer show wherever they're planted.

After admiring this tree while growing up, I'd say it's almost impossible to extinguish their beauty. ✦

PLANT PROFILE

Photos this page: David Liebman

Common Names: Smoketree, smokebush, Venetian sumac and chittamwood.
Botanical Names: *Cotinus coggygria* and *Cotinus obovatus*.
Height: Most are 15 to 20 feet tall.
Spread: 10 to 15 feet for most varieties.
Leaves: Oval green or purple leaves that become yellow, orange, scarlet or purplish red in fall.
Bloom Time: Insignificant flowers appear in June and July, followed by showy panicles through September.
Hardiness: Zones 5 to 8.
Light Needs: Full sun to partial shade. Purple-leafed varieties produce the best color in full sun.
Soil Type: Moderately fertile and well draining.
Planting: Plant container-grown trees anytime during the growing season.
Prize Pick: One of the showiest varieties is Daydream smokebush, which produces heavy drifts of fluffy brownish-pink panicles and has a dense growth habit.

ORNAMENTAL GRASSES

They'll make waves in your yard.

By Heather Lamb, Editor

Mention ornamental grasses and many people envision amber waves on an endless prairie. It's not an image that fits most backyards.

But in reality, these diverse plants—some native and some not—provide a way to make the grass on your side of the fence greener…or golden or blue or burgundy.

There has been a surge of interest in these versatile plants in recent years, in part because of the wide range of choices available and their ability to handle extreme conditions.

"They're virtually maintenance- and pest-free and can grow without much water," says Robert Bowden, director of the Harry P. Leu Gardens in Orlando, Florida, which has an extensive collection of grasses. "Not only that, but you can use them in a variety of ways—as ground covers, borders or accents—and they're great companion plants, too."

Hard to Resist

With hundreds of types to choose from and a range of sizes, colors and flower characteristics, it's no wonder ornamental grasses are riding a wave of popularity.

But there's more to it than practicality. Ornamental grasses have an eye-catching allure that makes them uniquely attractive to gardeners.

"Grasses have a restful and natural quality I think is appealing to people," says Mary Meyer, a University of Min-

> ### *"Grasses have a restful and natural quality…"*

nesota associate professor of horticulture who has been studying ornamental grasses for 30 years. "It's an informal look that changes with the seasons."

The first rule of thumb when considering ornamental grasses: Relax! Mary says gardeners should treat grasses like any other backyard plant.

"People tend to worry too much about the placement of grasses because they're not thinking of them as just another perennial," Mary says.

You don't have to dedicate an area of your yard to grass-

AT HOME OFF THE PRAIRIE. A collection of ornamental grasses (far left) provides autumn interest, while blue fescue (above) and fountain grass (below) add natural appeal to flower beds.

READER TIP

Grasses tend to look best among other perennials. Many people think grasses will take over the garden, but the majority aren't invasive.
—*Mary Meyer*
University of Minnesota
Associate professor of horticulture

BREEZY BEAUTIES. When it comes to ornamental grasses, the possibilities are endless. At top, Pumila pampas grass waves in the wind, while Karl Foerster feather reed grass (above) creates a striking profile and muhly grass (below) is hard to overlook.

206

es. This isn't even the best course of action, especially when you're just starting to plant them.

"Grasses look best among other perennials," Mary says. "Many people think grasses will take over the garden, but the majority aren't invasive."

So, where to start? Mary suggests a trip to your local garden center. You'll discover what's available in your area, and if there's a display garden, it will give you ideas of how to use them.

Then think about the same types of factors you would when selecting other plants, such as form, sun exposure, soil conditions and climate.

Plant form—and how it will fit in your landscape—is one of your first considerations. Ornamental grasses vary from 6-inch-tall fescues to varieties that reach 20 feet. The foliage is just as diverse, with shades of green as well as blue, yellow, brown, red and variegated.

In addition, the foliage exhibits assorted silhouettes. Some have short spiky blades, while others grow in an upright column or produce mounds of curving leaves.

Focus on the Flowers

But on many ornamental grasses, the leaves are only part of the picture. The characteristics that really stand out are the flowers.

Yes, flowers. Only these aren't flowers like we might typically think of them. Ornamental grasses rely on the wind to carry their pollen, so they don't need brightly colored blooms to attract insects for pollination.

But these flowers, more commonly called inflorescence, are just as attractive. The clusters of tiny flowers offer a diverse range of choices for the backyard, from the fuzzy spikes of fountain grass to the airy plumes of Japanese silver grass. Some, like the purple clouds of muhly grass (below left), are so striking they meet what Robert calls his "jogger test".

"If I have a grass in the front yard that makes the joggers stop to take a look, then I know it's something special," he says.

And unlike many garden flowers, these clusters keep their appeal year-round. Many exhibit rich autumn color and then provide a wonderful accent in winter landscapes as well.

Climate is another important factor, both in terms of winter hardiness and heat tolerance. Many types aren't hardy in northern areas, while other varieties fall victim to disease in humid regions.

Consider, too, that some grasses are a little too carefree.

Most of the common types have so-called "clump forming" roots, which slowly expand in diameter. But "creeping" grasses spread through more aggressive rhizomous roots and can quickly get out of control. Ribbon grass, giant reed grass

WITH HUNDREDS of varieties to choose from, there really is an ornamental grass for almost any situation, whether it's sun or shade, wet or dry. Here are 13 selections for different regions and conditions. One—or two—will surely work in your yard.

● **Blue fescue** (*Festuca* species) has blue tufts 6 to 10 inches tall. This is a good choice for dry sunny sites, especially in northern gardens. Most are hardy in Zones 4 to 8.

● **Blue oat grass** (*Helictotrichon sempervirens*) is an alternative to blue fescue that's more tolerant of clay soil. It has 16- to 20-inch blue tufts with tall panicles of summer flowers (right) up to 4-1/2 feet tall. Zones 4 to 9.

● **Crown grass** (*Paspalum quadrifolium*) forms a mound of bluish foliage up to 3 feet tall and adapts to a variety of soils. It performs especially well in humid regions. It's hardy in Zones 8 to 10.

● **Feather reed grass** (*Calamagrostis* x *acutiflora*) is fast growing, but slow spreading and withstands partial shade. Karl Foerster is a popular cultivar with upright stems 2 to 6 feet tall and wheat-like seed heads. Hardy in Zones 4 to 9.

● **Fountain grass** (*Pennisetum setaceum*) is one of the most common ornamental grasses, with different varieties producing fuzzy flower spikes in a range of hues. It grows 2 to 5 feet tall and can handle partial shade. Zones 8 to 10; grow as an annual in North.

● **Japanese silver grass** (*Miscanthus* cultivars) is a large family of tall grasses, some of which can spread quickly. Select a specific cultivar like Morning Light or Zebrinus (zebra grass, right) for a less

aggressive plant that tolerates moist soils. It's hardy in Zones 4 to 9.

● **Little bluestem** (*Schizachyrium scoparium*) is a compact native, 1-1/2 to 3 feet tall, with silvery-white flower heads in fall that complement the foliage as it becomes reddish-orange. Works well in Zones 3 to 7.

● **Muhly grass** (*Muhlenbergia*) is a native grass that produces an eye-catching cloud of wispy purple to red flowers. It's a good choice for dry gardens and grows up to 3 feet tall. Most are hardy in Zones 7 to 9.

● **Pampas grass** (*Cortaderia selloana*) is a large plant with an eye-catching plume of flowers. For a more contained grass, select a dwarf variety like Pumila or Compacta, which produce 6-foot plants hardy in Zones 7 to 10.

● **Prairie dropseed** (*Sporobolus heterolepis*) is a mounding grass (right) about 2 feet tall with drooping flowers that are unique because they produce a fragrance, which has been compared to buttered popcorn. It tolerates a variety of regions from Zones 3 to 9.

● **Switchgrass** (*Panicum virgatum*) is a native grass that's a fitting selection for wet conditions or areas in partial shade. It is narrowly upright, reaching 3 feet tall with drooping spikes of flowers in early fall that stick around to provide winter interest. It adapts to a variety of climates, from Zones 4 to 9.

● **Spike grass** (*Spodiopogon sibiricus*) has a bamboo-like appearance and grows 4 to 5 feet tall. Its tall flowers emerge in summer high over the foliage. This variety prefers moist and cool areas, good for Zones 4 to 9.

● **Tiger grass** (*Thysanolaena maxima*) grows up to 8 feet tall in full sun or part shade and in a wide range of soils. This tropical grass flowers in summer. Zones 9 to 10.

and Japanese blood grass are a few examples of these.

Once you've selected a few grasses you'd like to grow, adding them to your yard is fairly simple.

"Just plant, water, fertilize and stand back," Robert says. "The best way to learn about them is to grow some."

They require little upkeep, just extra water during the first year until they're established. In spring, you can cut most types back to the ground to make room for new growth.

It's just what you'd expect from plants with such natural good looks.

JAPANESE MAPLE
Create an instant tranquil oasis.

By Melinda Myers, Contributing Editor

Close your eyes and picture a beautiful Japanese garden. A weeping willow gracefully cascades over the edge of a small pond. A wooden footbridge traverses the water, and in the foreground, a Japanese maple completes the serene scene.

Now imagine adding a piece of this tranquil oasis to your own backyard. It's as simple as planting a Japanese maple.

These graceful trees work in traditional landscapes as well theme gardens. Their unique form, delicate and often colorful leaves, and smooth gray bark give them year-round appeal.

Japanese maple, botanically *Acer palmatum*, is one of the most versatile members of the maple family. With over 300 cultivars, a low-growing habit and a range of sizes, these trees are perfect for many ornamental uses.

When shopping, look for a variety with a size, shape and color that suits your landscape design and tolerates the growing conditions.

Endless Possibilities

Osakazuki is an old favorite with bright-green leaves and outstanding crimson fall color. It has a rounded top and grows 15 to 20 feet tall.

If you're looking for season-long color, try Bloodgood. It maintains deep reddish-purple leaves throughout the growing season. Plus, it has colorful red fruit and an even brighter red fall foliage display. Although it grows slowly, this rounded tree eventually reaches heights of 15 to 20 feet.

The cutleaf forms, known to horticulturists as the dissectum group, have leaves with seven, nine or 11 narrow fin-

HARD TO MISS. With a range of sizes and outstanding fall colors, Japanese maples provide a unique accent in any backyard. They're a natural in Asian-themed gardens, like the bright-red specimen in the Japanese Garden in Portland, Oregon at far left, but they're equally attractive in home settings (left). Varied leaf forms, like the delicate cutleaf types (above) offer home owners lots of choices.

ger-like lobes, giving the plant a fine texture. This characteristic, along with its often smaller size, makes it a nice addition to perennial beds, small landscapes, Zen gardens or planted in containers.

Waterfall is considered the best of the green cutleaf forms and tolerates heat found in Plant Hardiness Zone 8. Its leaves turn gold with red tones in autumn. It has a nice form and grows 10 feet tall by 12 to 14 feet wide.

Red Dragon, a new introduction from New Zealand, holds its maroon color throughout summer, even in the South. This vigorous small tree has a nice cascading form.

Filigree is a variegated cutleaf variety. The green leaves have cream and gold flecks that turn golden in fall. This 6- to 9-foot tree does a fine job of brightening a shade garden.

Give It Some Shade

Selecting a planting site for Japanese maple is not just about designing a pretty garden. These delicate trees tend to be a bit picky about their growing location.

Dappled sunlight provides the best looking leaves from spring to fall. Full sun and high temperatures can fade purple-leafed varieties and even cause the leaf edges to become brown and crispy, called scorch.

Avoid further leaf damage by planting Japanese maples in a spot protected from late spring frosts and winds.

Those of us who garden in the extreme North or South

> ## READER TIP
>
> Dappled shade provides the best looking leaves from spring to fall. Full sun and high temperature can fade purple-leafed varieties and even cause the leaf edges to become brown and crispy.
> —*Melinda Myers*
> *Contributing Editor*

Derek Fell

may have to settle for tranquil pictures of Japanese maples in our heads. This tree struggles through the winter cold and late spring frosts in Zone 5, and won't tolerate the summer heat of Zones 9 and above.

Though tolerant of clay, Japanese maples prefer well-drained soils. In heavy or poorly drained soils, plant in raised beds or on slight slopes to improve drainage.

Also make sure the soil is moist, but not wet. Apply a mulch like wood chips or shredded bark to conserve moisture and protect the trunk from lawn mowers and weed trimmers.

In addition, eliminating grass around young trees will reduce competition for water and nutrients, getting your tree off to a faster start. This is especially important with a slow grower like the Japanese maple.

READER TIP

To get Japanese maples off to a faster start, eliminate any grass around the young trees. This reduces competition for water and nutrients.

Mini Marvel

Japanese maples also look good and perform well in large containers. Use them on a deck or patio or as an entryway accent.

Container plantings will need more attention than trees growing in the ground. Water the soil thoroughly whenever it dries. Those in colder regions will need to move planters into an unheated garage or enclosed porch for winter. Or surround the container with bales of hay to provide added insulation for the roots.

With so many options, it's difficult not to daydream about the possibilities of Japanese maples.

Go ahead—picture one of these serene beauties in your landscape.

Alan and Linda Detrick

PLANT PROFILE

Common Name: Japanese maple.

Botanical Name: *Acer palmatum*.

Height: 15 to 25 feet (can grow 40 to 50 feet in the wild).

Spread: 15 to 25 feet.

Leaves: Deeply lobed leaves with five to 11 "fingers". Summer colors range from green to reds and purples, with autumn hues of various reds and golds.

Flowers: Small red to purple clusters in May or June.

Hardiness: Zones 5 or 6 to 8, depending on cultivar.

Light Needs: Prefers dappled shade, but will tolerate full sun.

Soil Type: Moist and well-drained.

Planting: Plant balled-and-burlapped or container-grown trees in late winter or early spring. This gives the trees a chance to establish themselves before the stress of summer's heat or winter's cold.

PLANTING HISTORY

Some trees have historical roots.

By Jodi Webb, Pottsville, Pennsylvania

"WITNESSES TO HISTORY". Jeff Meyer, founder of the Historic Trees Project, has seen his dream fulfilled as thousands of trees started from the seeds of famous American trees have been planted. Volunteers collect the seeds from these trees (left).

Many years ago, nurseryman Jeff Meyer and his young son picked up an acorn beneath the Treaty Oak in their hometown of Jacksonville, Florida and planted it in their backyard. Jeff liked that they planted a piece of history right out the back door.

That gave him an idea. Why not propagate seedlings from some of the nation's most historic trees and make them available to the public? From that seed of an idea the Historic Trees Project took root. Since 1992, the project has sold about 500,000 seedlings from trees that have witnessed centuries of American history.

Volunteers and park rangers gather the seeds and cuttings from specimens on the National Registry of Historic Trees. The Historic Tree Nursery in Jacksonville tends the plants for 2 years and sells them when they reach 1 to 3 feet.

Famous Offspring

The project sells direct descendants of more than 200 historic trees, including seedlings to the honey locust that shaded Abraham Lincoln as he delivered the Gettysburg Address. More interested in a tulip poplar? Why not buy one grown from the seeds of the trees George Washington planted at Mount Vernon in 1785?

Gathering the seeds isn't always easy. The tulip poplars at Mount Vernon are so tall that bees can't fly high enough to pollinate them. Volunteers now do the honors as they reach the flowers in lift buckets and pollinate them with cotton swabs.

Trees with more recent roles in American history are included, too, such as sweet gum and pin oak from Elvis Presley's Graceland mansion to a sycamore whose seeds traveled to the moon on *Apollo XIV*.

Home owners are welcome to buy the seedlings. Many are also sold to communities interested in creating historic groves. In Sanford, Florida, retiree Howard Jeffries led an effort to replace a rundown, unused basketball court with a park filled with more than 100 historic trees.

Community Pride

An elementary school in Quarryville, Pennsylvania has been adding to its historic grove for several years. Landscape contractor Scott Peiffer helped his daughter's school start the grove by planting 11 trees in 1999. Three years later, they staged a "tree walk" to celebrate the plants' growth.

As historic trees begin to grow all across the country, Jeff Meyer has seen his dream come true. He travels around the U.S. telling people about historic trees and attends many plantings. He recently filmed *TreeStories*, a PBS series, and published *America's Famous and Historic Trees*.

"My goal is to make trees exciting," Jeff says. "Historic trees are every bit as important as historic buildings. They're the oldest living witnesses to history."

TREE PEONIES

No longer an ancient Chinese secret…
these shrubs brighten up spring.

From the mountains and palaces of China to your back-yard, tree peonies provide beauty in any landscape. Sure, they may be fussier than the popular "herbaceous peonies" found in Grandma's garden, but their eye appeal makes them worth the extra effort.

The Chinese have grown tree peonies for over 1,500 years. They were initially grown for medicinal purposes, but soon their beauty moved them into the garden setting.

Today's tree peonies are the result of 900 years of breeding several different types of woody peonies native to the mountains of central and western China. Hybridizers have improved their flower size, color and fragrance.

In 1994, the tree peony was adopted as China's official flower, and its popularity spread throughout the world.

To be more accurate, tree peonies are more shrub-like. Their woody base provides the framework for its broad leaves

Dick Keen/Unicorn Stock Photos

Karen Bussolini

and fragrant flowers. Though not as big as a tree, these plants do need room to grow. They can reach 6 feet tall and wide.

An individual tree peony certainly provides a focal point in any spring garden. And its attractive size and foliage make it a nice backdrop for summer- and fall-blooming plants. This season-long appeal makes tree peonies the perfect choice for just about any landscape style.

Tough Beauties

Because they're native to the mountains, tree peonies are tough plants that are used to the cold and snow. They're well suited for areas with tough winters. Many tree peonies can tolerate temperatures as low as 20° below zero!

The plants also need at least 500 to 1,000 hours of 32° to 40° temperatures to set flowers. Southern gardeners should pay attention to selecting cultivars suited to areas with mild winters.

If planted properly, tree peonies will last a lifetime. All you have to do is look to China for proof—some plants there are 700 years old and produce 200 flowers each year.

Increase your growing success and bloom time by planting tree peonies in fertile well-draining soils. If you have heavy clay soil, add organic matter to improve drainage.

Avoid placing tree peonies in windy locations. This will stress the plants and damage their large flowers as they sway in the breeze. And you'll want them to be in the shade in the afternoon to keep the blossoms fresh and long lasting.

Tree peonies are typically grafted onto the hardy roots of herbaceous peonies. It's important to protect this union, so be sure to plant the graft 5 to 6 inches below ground level.

Mulch newly planted tree peonies with organic matter. This will help keep the soil warm in winter, cooler in summer and moist, which encourages root growth. Northern gardeners will need to provide a bit more protection from the cold, but wait until the ground freezes.

For greater insulation, surround the plant with hardware cloth sunk several inches into the ground. This keeps the mulch in and most hungry critters out. Once the ground freezes, fill the cylinder, covering the plant with evergreen boughs or straw. Remove the mulch in spring once the temperatures start hovering around freezing.

Be Patient for Flowers

It's important to wait a year to fertilize new plantings to avoid root damage and excessive top growth at the expense of root development. Don't worry—your properly prepared soil will have enough nutrients to establish the plants.

Tree peonies require very little additional care during the growing season. Deadheading keeps the plants tidy and allows energy to go into the root growth.

It takes several years for tree peonies to start blooming. The first set of flowers may be slightly smaller and fewer in numbers, but once established, you'll have a lifetime's worth of large fragrant blossoms to enjoy.

PLANT PROFILE

Ray Packard

Common Name: Tree peony.
Botanical Name: *Paeonia suffruticosa*.
Height: 3 to 6 feet.
Width: 3 to 6 feet.
Flowers: Spring blooming round single and double flowers.
Hardiness: Zones 3 to 9, depending on variety.
Light Needs: Full sun to partial shade. Protect from hot afternoon sun, especially in South, to prolong bloom.
Soil Type: Moist organic soils with good drainage. Prefers neutral to slightly alkaline soil (pH of 6.5 to 7.5).
Planting: Transplant container stock from spring through fall. Northern gardeners may want to plant earlier in the season to establish plants before winter. Fall planting bare-root tree peonies, especially in the South, gives plants time to root and establish before the hot summer. Plant so the graft union is 5 to 6 inches below ground level.

CRABAPPLE

New varieties serve up stunning spring flowers and long-lasting fruit.

By Deb Mulvey, Greendale, Wisconsin

Last summer, I was offered a deal too good to pass up—10 free trees from the National Arbor Day Foundation. My yard wasn't big enough for all of them, so when a friend said she'd take a few off my hands, I gladly surrendered the extras. The flowering crabapples were the first to go.

Although I love seeing these trees bloom in our neighbors' yards every spring, I hate the mess that follows. My kids and I know the location of every flowering crab within a 2-mile radius of our house—and we have the spattered bikes and stained shoes to prove it.

I figured, crabapples—who needs 'em? Besides, these trees are notoriously susceptible to many diseases, right?

Not necessarily.

It's true that a lot of crabapples are vulnerable to a laundry list of ailments, from fireblight and leaf drop to powdery mildew or apple scab. And unfortunately, some of the most popular varieties are the most likely to succumb.

The Next Generation

But every season, growers introduce new crabapples they've bred for insect and disease resistance, plus fruit that stays put. With some 700 crabapple varieties to choose from, even persnickety gardeners like me can find one that's a good fit without the typical problems.

Known botanically as *Malus*, crabapples come in a wide range of shapes and sizes, from densely mounded shrubs to 25-foot-tall upright, weeping or spreading trees. Their spring display is second to none, with a heavy blanket of red, pink or white blossoms that dominate the landscape. In fall and

Darryl R. Beers; opposite page: Paul A. Hein/Unicorn Stock Photos

winter, the small apple-shaped fruits attract a variety of birds.

"We have three crabapples—a red, a pink and a white," says Mary Ellen Van Slembrouck of Sterling Heights, Michigan. "The white one is so dense with blossoms the neighbors often ask to take their children's First Communion pictures next to it. It's stunning and has a wonderful scent. And later the cedar waxwings come, 50 to 60 birds at a time, to feed from the trees."

These fruits, which can be red to orange and even yellow, provide an attractive buffet in fall and winter for American robins and bluebirds as well.

Technically speaking, these trees with fruit that is 2 inch-

es across or less are crabapples, while anything larger is considered an apple.

Picking the Right Tree

If you're in the market for a crabapple, ask your local garden center or nursery which varieties offer the characteristics you want along with disease-resistant qualities that fit your growing conditions. For instance, fireblight is more likely to be a problem in humid regions, while other gardeners may be more concerned about the leaf drop caused by apple scab.

And don't just consider the spring flowers when making your selection. The blossoms last for only a week or two, but the fruits will linger for months. When in doubt, the Asiatic crabapple varieties are dependable choices that are generally more resistant than their North American cousins.

One of the most popular Asiatic trees, the Japanese flowering crab (*Malus floribunda*), boasts a stunning display of deep-pink or red buds that fade to white, with yellow fruit that turns brownish-red in fall.

For maximum disease resistance, consider Adams, which features pink flowers and long-lasting red fruit; Beauty, with its white to pink flowers plus large dark-red fruit; or Baskatong with purplish-red flowers and fruit.

If you're worried about the mess from falling apples, these varieties hold on to their fruit, as does the white-bloomed Donald Wyman (that's a flowering branch of it below).

Another resistant variety, Callaway, is ideal for Southern landscapes, where disease can be more of a problem. This white-flowered beauty overcomes that factor and blooms beautifully.

For a big impact in small spaces, plant a shrub crabapple. The densely mounded, white-flowered Sargent crabapple (*Malus sargentii*) reaches a height of 10 feet and spreads to about 15 feet, with bright-red fruit.

Derek Fell

Easy Care

Crabapples prefer a sunny spot that drains well, but need little upkeep. They should be pruned in late winter, but only for shaping. Aggressive pruning will promote small vertical branches called water shoots, creating a messy tree.

As a reward for your efforts, you can coax the trimmings to bloom indoors. Just recut the stems, place them in warm water and you can enjoy an early breath of spring when the fragrant buds open.

With careful selection and proper care, it really is possible to enjoy the beauty of crabapples without all the headache.

Maybe I'll find room for one in my yard after all.

Richard Shiell

Richard Shiell

PLANT PROFILE

Common Names: Crabapple, flowering crabapple.
Botanical Name: *Malus.*
Height: 8 to 25 feet, depending on the variety.
Spread: Up to 25 feet, depending on the variety.
Flowers: Red, white or pink cup-shaped flowers.
Bloom Time: Spring.
Fruit: 1/4- to 2-inch red, yellow or orange apples.
Hardiness: Zones 2 to 8.
Light Needs: Full sun, but will tolerate light shade.
Soil Type: Moist, rich and well draining.
Planting: Transplant in spring, with root flare at or just above the soil line. Dig the planting hole to the same depth as the root system, and 3 to 5 times wider.
Backyard Benefits: Fruit attracts birds.

ENCHANTED FOREST IS A WORK OF ART

Reader's magical facelifts bring this orchard to life.

By Jennifer Goering, Platte City, Missouri

Children's storybooks are filled with tales of enchanted forests where trees magically spring to life. Here in Platte City, Missouri, those fairy tales came true.

Five mature trees at Alldredge Orchard have come alive, thanks to creative makeovers crafted by my talented neighbor Christa Turner. She created trees with facial expressions that are so real you expect them to talk!

Christa discovered the faces on trees concept on a trip to Toronto, Canada. Once she returned home, she knew it was something she had to try. She began looking for timber that could use a "facelift".

Bark Worse Than Their Bite

Because the trees in our subdivision were all too small, Christa set her sights elsewhere—and what better place to look than in an orchard?

Curt Alldredge, who owns the orchard, had plenty of mature trees on the property and was looking for a way to make it more fun for the many children who visit. So he listened intently to Christa's idea and gave her the go-ahead.

"When I started the first tree, Curt really wasn't sure how it was going to turn out," Christa chuckles. "But when it was finished, he loved it and wanted more trees done."

Christa has no artistic training, but that does not stand in her way. She relies on her creativity, patience and inspiration from her kids' favorite toys and television characters.

Before she begins, Christa carefully examines a tree from every angle to determine exactly where its natural "face" is. Then she sketches an appropriate expression.

Once she finds the perfect look, the finished designs are transferred to foam board, cut out and tacked to the trunk.

The Creative Process

Christa creates the lifelike effect by placing pieces of window screen over the facial features, giving them a 3-D appearance. She'll cover the screening with fiberglass and blend the features with custom-mixed exterior paints that match each tree's bark.

The faces withstand both weather and children's curious hands. And most importantly, the process is limited to one side of the tree, allowing it to continue to grow.

PUT ON A HAPPY FACE. Christa Turner (above left) brought trees to life at Alldredge Orchard in Platte City, Missouri. She uses fiberglass to create the facial expressions, and blends them into the trunk with custom paints.

As the faces begin to age a bit, many people have told Christa they look even more real.

"When school tours come to the orchard, they're told it's enchanted and are encouraged to keep their eyes out for the 'magic trees'," she says. "Many of the kids say if you listen hard enough, you can actually hear them talk. What wonderful imaginations."

KLAMATH BASIN

Eagles soar over these expansive refuges.

By Donna Ikenberry, South Fork, Colorado

Every year starting in November, they arrive, like clockwork, to dine and relax in the Klamath Basin.

Soaring on wings as broad as a man is tall, bald eagles from throughout the Northwest drift into this area along the California/Oregon border. As cold weather approaches, their numbers swell to between 500 and 1,000, creating the largest winter population of bald eagles in the contiguous United States.

Joining these colossal birds are up to a million ducks and geese. Some spend winter in the basin, while others continue on to warmer climates.

Such get-togethers prompt area residents and visitors to raise their eyes to the sky. I myself have watched endless congregations of geese and ducks stream by, and at

Photo: Jeffrey Rich Nature Photography

night I've heard them honking on their southward journey.

There are six national wildlife refuges in the Klamath Basin, covering over 168,000 acres in northern California and southern Oregon. The Klamath Marsh, Upper Klamath and Bear Valley refuges are in Oregon, and Lower Klamath, Tule Lake and Clear Lake are located in California.

Frequent Fliers

All the refuges are on the Pacific Flyway, one of four major migration routes in North America. Millions of birds use these flyways during spring and fall migrations.

To date, more than 350 bird species and 470 total wildlife species have been observed at the refuges. Many stick around to raise young there in summer.

The Tule Lake and Lower Klamath refuges are famous for massive concentrations of waterfowl. You'll see the largest number of birds in early November and again in March. Eagles are typically in the basin from mid-November through March.

There are vehicle routes through these two refuges that allow visitors to observe wildlife from various points.

The Upper Klamath and Klamath Marsh refuges are wetland habitats that are traversable mostly by canoe. Bear Valley and Clear Lake are set aside for wildlife habitat and aren't open to the public.

Donna Ikenberry; all other photos: Jeffrey Rich Nature Photography

Wings Fill the Air

Klamath Basin is a place where I could sit in the same spot all day long and never tire of the winged spectacle.

Flocks of snow geese move over the land in masses so large they sometimes block out the sun. When the geese settle in an area field, their countless bodies create the illusion of a moving snowfield.

Swans descend onto a lake already filled with thousands of bobbing migratory ducks. There are hundreds of northern shovelers, their scoop-like bills making them easy to identify.

I've seen coyotes trotting across the landscape, a lone porcupine sitting in a bare tree near the shoreline and a great horned owl peering at me with its wide staring eyes.

Standing there amid such diverse wildlife, I feel I'm a part of the massive gathering. And like the birds, I'll be back next year.

Oregon

Klamath Basin

California

Want to Visit? The Klamath Basin National Wildlife Refuges are near the California/Oregon border and are accessible via U.S. Hwy. 97, Oregon State Hwy. 39 or California State Hwy. 139. The Refuge Headquarters and Visitor Center, located at 4009 Hill Road in Tulelake, California, can provide maps and guidance for your visit.

The refuges are open year-round, from 8 a.m. to 4:30 p.m. Monday through Friday and 10 a.m. to 4 p.m. on weekends. Admission for the vehicle tours is $3.

For more information, call 1-530/667-2231 or write to Klamath Basin National Wildlife Refuges, 4009 Hill Road, Tulelake CA 96134. You also can visit the Web sites at *http://klamathbasinrefuges.fws.gov* or *www.klamath birdingtrails.com.*

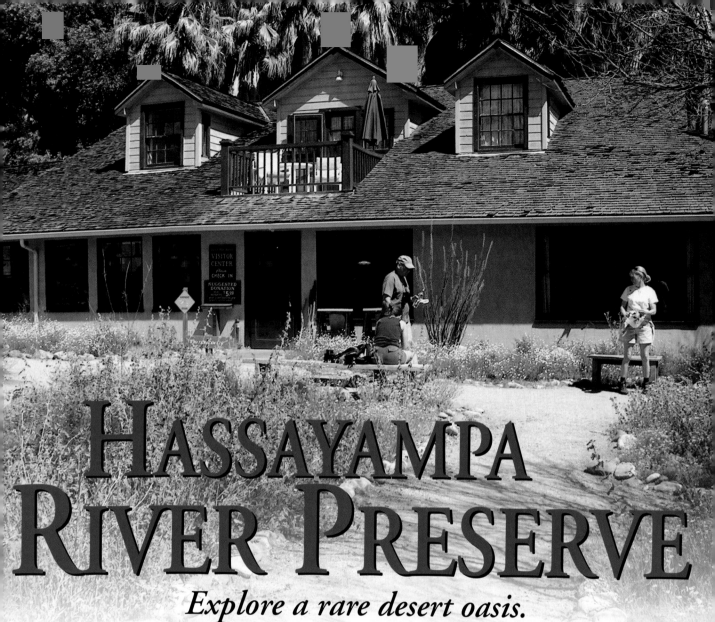

HASSAYAMPA RIVER PRESERVE

Explore a rare desert oasis.

By Pamela Conley, Cazadero, California

Photo: Michael Rigney, TNC Arizona

Driving home over an unfamiliar road near Wickenburg, Arizona, my husband and I realized we were alongside a ribbon of lush green habitat. We followed it for miles, looking for a way to enter this desert oasis.

Suddenly my husband slammed on the brakes, threw the truck into reverse and grinned. He'd spotted a sign.

We followed a single-lane dirt road lined with a split-rail fence to the entrance of the Hassayampa River Preserve, one of the last remaining "riparian forests" in the state.

These rich habitats, which are located on the banks of natural waterways, were once a dominant feature along Arizona's major desert rivers. Today, only 5% to 10% of this habitat remains, yet 80% of the state's wildlife depends on it for survival.

Among riparian forests, the cottonwood-willow type is the rarest kind in North America, and Hassayampa is one of the best. Managed by The Nature Conservancy, this preserve is a bird-watcher's paradise, home to 230 avian species.

We followed the entrance road to the visitors' center, a wonderful four-room abode surrounded with wildflowers. Rancher Frederick Brill built this historic home in the 1860s, and also used it as a stagecoach stop. Inside, we found a rustic sitting area with a fireplace made of river rock, and a friendly guide who explained what we were about to see.

The guide told us the Hassayampa River travels underground for most of its 100 miles, surfacing at a thrust of bedrock near Wickenburg, where it runs crystal-clear through the preserve year-round.

The lush habitat surrounding the river is home to some spectacular wildlife, including one endangered species. Visitors can follow trails on their own, or take a guided tour to explore the preserve's nearly 4 miles of trails through river bottom, floodplain and forests.

Step Into Paradise

When we stepped outside with our trail map, giant trees shaded us from the beating sun, and the thickets throbbed with life. We were startled as bullfrogs and native lowland

David Liebman

DESERT RETREAT. A lush green stretch of habitat along the Hassayampa River helps support more than 80% of Arizona's wildlife. Visitors can explore the unique preserve, which is home to a variety of wildlife, including the javelina (left), mountain lion (above) and Harris's hawk (below).

Maslowski Photo

leopard frogs splashed into the water and lizards scampered underfoot.

We paused for a moment, taking it all in. Birdsongs filled the air, interrupted occasionally by the tropical whistles and cackles of yellow-breasted chats. Brilliant orioles flew to tall palm trees.

We decided to follow the Palm Lake Trail, which circles a spring-fed, 4-acre pond. Palm Lake attracts a large array of water birds and supports five species of rare native desert fish.

Bird Life Abounds

My heart pounded with excitement as we explored this busy environment. A male cinnamon teal duck came out of the shadows into the sun, his head a deep amber red. Bullfrogs croaked throatily, cactus wrens chortled from the mesquite trees and huge blue-backed carpenter bees buzzed around flower blossoms. A summer tanager flashed red as he flew to the top of a giant cottonwood tree.

Mississippi kites and yellow-billed cuckoos live here, as do great blue and green herons and pied-billed grebes. And the surrounding willows create nesting habitat for the endangered southwestern willow flycatcher.

Perched atop dead snags are some of Arizona's rarest raptors, like zone-tailed, common black-hawk and Harris's hawks as well as the only known nesting pair of red-shouldered hawks in the state.

Hassayampa supports many species beyond its avian population. Lizards and salamanders thrive here, including the evasive Gilbert's skink. Sometimes you can find tracks of mule deer, javelinas, raccoons, bobcats, ring-tailed cats and even mountain lions at the river's edge.

As we left the protection of the shade and walked back into the sun, we vowed to return. Next time, though, we'll make the Hassayampa River Preserve a destination rather than a stopping point on the way home.

Glenn Hayes/KAC Productions

Want to Visit? The Hassayampa River Preserve is open from 8 a.m. to 5 p.m. Wednesday through Sunday from Sept. 15 through May 14, and Friday through Sunday from May 15 to Sept. 14; closed on major holidays. Guided 1-hour nature walks are offered at 8:30 a.m. the last Saturday of each month, except during summer.

Admission is free for Nature Conservancy members; a $5 donation is requested from other visitors.

The preserve is located at 49614 U.S. Highway 60 (at mile marker 114) in central Arizona, 3 miles southeast of Wickenburg and about 50 miles northwest of Phoenix.

For information, call 1-928/684-2772 or visit *www.nature.org/arizona.*

Arizona

Hassayampa
● River
Preserve

LOCAL LOOKOUTS

These birding destinations are reader favorites.

Count on It

IN ARIZONA'S beautiful Verde Valley, birds sometimes outnumber people—and we have the statistics to prove it!

One year, the Audubon Society's annual bird count documented 14,090 birds from 97 species in Jerome. The town's human population is about 400.

Volunteers spotted bald eagles, cactus wrens (below, our state bird), merlins, cedar waxwings, American robins, dark-eyed juncos, white-crowned sparrows, a red-naped sapsucker, a green-tailed towhee, Brewer's blackbirds and many more.

The abundant bird life is only one of the benefits of living in north-central Arizona. Our area is filled with parks, waterways, canyons and other beautiful habitats, which provide a wonderful bird-watching backdrop.

—*Mary Ann Gove, Cottonwood, Arizona*

On Eagles' Wings

EVERY WINTER, our family packs up for some eagle-watching along the Mississippi River. Up to 2,500 bald eagles gather at the locks and dams between Minneapolis and St. Louis, hunting for fish in the open water.

The views are spectacular. We've seen 30 to 40 eagles at a time resting in trees, soaring over the river or diving into the icy water.

Our favorite spot is Concord Street in Davenport, Iowa, where the eagles in the trees are so close you don't even need binoculars. (Stay in your car so you don't disturb them.)

Adults are easy to recognize. They have white heads and tails and 6- to 7-foot wingspans. Young eagles are mottled brown or white and can be harder to spot. The white heads and tails don't appear until they're 4 to 5 years old.

Lock and Dam 13 in Fulton, Illinois is another excellent viewing spot. It has a raised platform that overlooks the locks.

Other good stops are Lock and Dam 12 in Bellevue, Iowa and Lock and Dam 11 in Dubuque, Iowa.

Often, we just "wing it", following the Great River Road from dam to dam. Information centers along the route will direct you to good viewing spots.
—*Bonnie Otto, Mukwonago, Wisconsin*

Martins Reign

TAKE A DRIVE through Griggsville, Illinois and there's no mistaking the town's claim to fame. A 40-foot-tall structure of purple martin apartments, fittingly dubbed "the Empire State Building of the bird world", can accommodate 1,200 martins and their young (see photo at right).

More houses for martins sit on almost every street corner, and still more are in residents' yards.

All this started in 1962, when loss of nesting sites was putting purple martins in danger of extinction. Local industrialist J.L. Wade suggested building martin houses to solve the town's insect problem—and help the embattled birds at the same time.

His company started building martin houses that year, and continues to be a leader in the field today, manufacturing dwellings for martins under the brand name Nature House.

It should be no wonder the town water tower proudly announces Griggsville as "the purple martin capital of the nation"!

—*Linda Cookson
Emporia, Kansas*

MORE TO EXPLORE. The Flower Fields grows a variety of perennials and annuals, which are showcased in the Theme Garden (left). But the ranch still is best known for the vibrant colors of the unique ranunculus flowers (above).

50 rose varieties. The Flower Fields is one of 130 accredited rose-testing gardens in the U.S.

More roses are on display in the Walk of Fame Garden, an unusual array of the 170-plus AARS winners that have been chosen since 1940. The fragrant Miniature Rose Garden, which opened in 2003, contains smaller specimens that have won American Rose Society awards.

The Color Project features gardens created by artists who use flowers as their medium. One has a reflection pool and aviary. Another offers a changing display of blooms in a maze-like circle with a footpath (that's it on page 226).

Events for Spring

The ranch's "public season" is short, but it's packed with activities. Kid's Days offers a variety of hands-on events to help children learn about growing plants and the nature around them.

The Strawberry Festival and Arts and Crafts Fair follows with a tempting array of strawberry treats and a variety of creations from skilled artisans. Numerous special events are held each year, so check with The Flower Fields for details.

For many area residents, a visit to The Flower Fields at Carlsbad Ranch has become a rite of spring—and a welcome way to escape the stress of urban life, if only for a single afternoon.

"With acres of beautiful ranunculus, themed gardens and landscapes featuring reflection pools, it's a great place to leave the buzz of the city behind," Jeanette says. "It's a place to feel tranquil and rejuvenated."

Want to Visit? The Flower Fields is open to the public each spring, typically between mid-March and early May. Admission is $8 for adults, $7 for seniors and $5 for children ages 3-10. Wagon rides are an additional small charge.

Guided tours are available, and the grounds are wheelchair accessible. Parking is free.

The Flower Fields is located at 5704 Paseo Del Norte in Carlsbad, California, directly east of Interstate 5 and about 35 miles north of San Diego. For more information, as well as a complete listing of the events scheduled at the ranch, log on to *www.theflowerfields.com* or call 1-760/431-0352.

California

The Flower Fields

VENICE ROOKERY

Photos by Gary Burdette

Discover a surprise nesting haven.

By Gary Burdette, Sarasota, Florida

W e rounded the last curve in the road, and suddenly the Venice Rookery appeared before us.

"Look at them!" exclaimed my wife, Naomi. "They're
everywhere!"

I was so unprepared for the sight that I couldn't even
speak. All I could do was nod. The birds *were* everywhere—
in nests, in the trees, on the ground, in the water and in the
air.

Even more amazing, we were in the middle of Venice,
Florida, just blocks from a busy highway. A trip of just 200
yards down a winding access road had deposited us in the

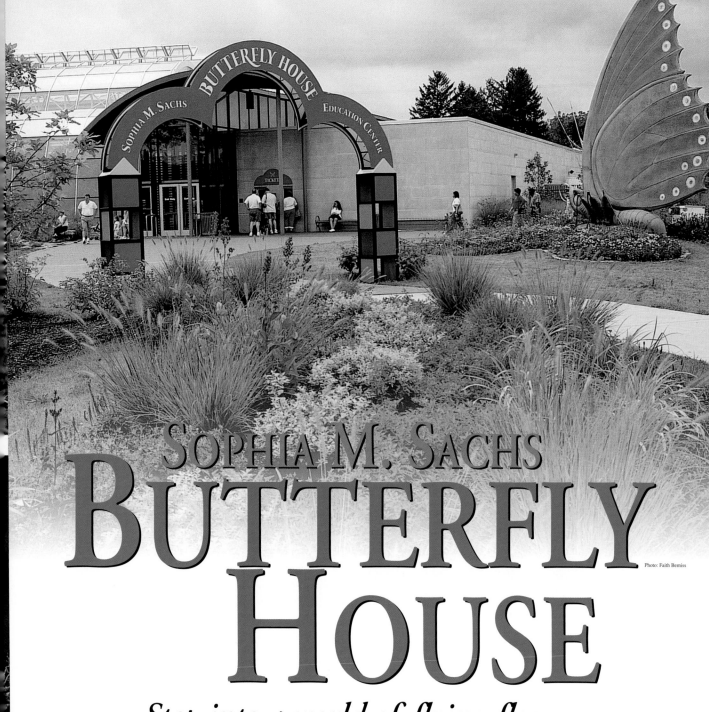

Photo: Faith Bemiss

SOPHIA M. SACHS
BUTTERFLY
HOUSE

Step into a world of flying flowers.

By Faith Bemiss, Sedalia, Missouri

Watching a butterfly emerge from its chrysalis is a wonder most people haven't had a chance to see. But a visit to a butterfly conservatory in Chesterfield, Missouri can change that.

The conservatory is part of the Sophia M. Sachs Butterfly House and Education Center, a non-profit facility operated by the Missouri Botanical Garden since 1998. With more than 1,000 tropical butterflies, representing as many as 60 species, flying freely year-round, there are up to 100 chrysalides waiting to open on any given day.

The conservatory's 150 tropical plant species provide hosts for the eggs and caterpillars, and nectar sources for adult butterflies. As a result, visitors see butterflies in every stage of development, from larvae to adults.

Step Into Another World

Butterfly curator Mark Deering says there are about 100 butterfly conservatories nationwide. What sets this facility apart is quality.

"It's the number of butterfly species and the ambiance

inside the Butterfly House, with all the insects and the great plantings," Mark says.

Guests enter the conservatory through a series of doors that keep the butterflies from escaping. Inside, the 8,000-square-foot garden resembles a fairy-tale scene, with iridescent butterflies fluttering amid lush vegetation.

Brochures with color photos help guests identify residents like the Grecian shoemaker, a delicate black and orange butterfly that's native to Central and South America.

Other striking specimens include the black and white paper kite from Southeast Asia, and the shimmering blue morpho from Central America.

Outside, carefully chosen plantings provide food and habitat for native butterflies. In the seasonal gardens around the Entry Plaza, which is paved with butterfly-shaped stones, "flying flowers" flit among black-eyed Susans, marigolds and Joe Pye weed, while children clamber over a 30-foot caterpillar sculpture and marvel at a replica of a monarch butterfly that's 28 feet tall (at left)!

Providing a delightful experience for butterfly enthusiasts is only part of the center's goal, however.

"We have a very strong educational and conservation message," Mark says. "We bring in close to 50,000 schoolkids a year."

A Leader in Education

Last year, the center became the first butterfly house in the U.S. to be accredited by the American Zoo and Aquarium Association, a designation reserved for leaders in butterfly conservation, education and research.

The Butterfly House is located in Faust Park, a 200-acre county facility bordering the Missouri River. Originally a farm owned by the state's second governor, Frederick Bates, the park includes a restored prairie and a 2-mile hiking trail through a wooded bluff that's dotted with wildflowers. Visitors can expect to see native butterflies in these areas, too.

With its peaceful storybook setting, exotic residents and tropical plants, the Butterfly House is an enchanting destination for nature lovers of all ages.

"If you're interested in butterflies, nature, conservation and plants, you should come visit us," Mark says. "It's a lot of fun."

Mark Deering/www.papiliophoto.com; all other photos: Faith Bemiss

TROPICAL ESCAPE. This butterfly house offers a lush indoor setting for tropical butterflies (like the kallima above) while the gardens surrounding it (photos above left) welcome native species. The dome houses 1,000 or so butterflies that visitors can view year-round (at top).

Want to Visit? The Sophia M. Sachs Butterfly House and Education Center is open Tuesday through Sunday. Hours are 9 a.m. to 5 p.m. from Memorial Day through Labor Day, 9 a.m. to 4 p.m. the rest of the year; closed on Thanksgiving, Christmas and New Year's Day.

Admission is $6 for adults, $4.50 for seniors, $4 for children ages 4 to 12, and free for children 3 and younger.

The Butterfly House and Education Center is located at 15193 Olive Blvd. (State Hwy. 340) in Chesterfield, Missouri, just west of I-270 and 21 miles west of St. Louis. For more information, log on to *www.butterfly house.org* or call 1-636/530-0076.

Butterfly House •
Missouri

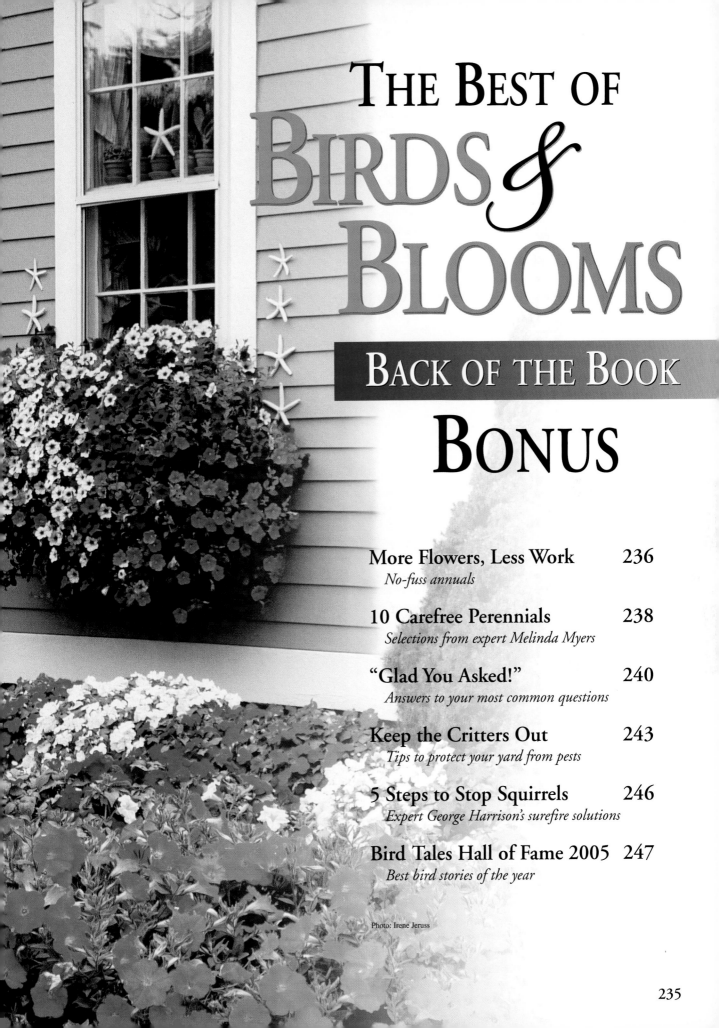

THE BEST OF BIRDS & BLOOMS

BACK OF THE BOOK

BONUS

Photo: Irene Jeruss

More Flowers, Less Work

These annuals are no-fuss beauties.

By Cheryl Richter, Lincoln, Nebraska

Annuals are an instant hit with busy gardeners. That's because a few flats of colorful annuals can make any yard look like a million bucks in no time at all.

Like other garden plants, however, some annuals require more care than time-challenged green thumbs can afford to give. On top of basic watering, fertilizing and weeding chores, geraniums, petunias and salvia, for example, need deadheading (removing flowers as they begin to fade) to keep them blooming prolifically all summer rather than going to seed.

For the gardener who wants less work and more enjoyment, there's still hope. You can have an easy-to-maintain kaleidoscope of color with these six annuals that keep giving, yet ask for little to nothing in return.

Wax Begonia

Wax begonia, also commonly called fibrous and everblooming begonia, is at the top of my no-fuss list—the only thing I need to give them is water. Even then, I can let the soil dry between waterings in shade.

They grow well in partial to full shade and flourish in borders, mixed plantings and containers.

Botanical name: *Begonia semperflorens*.
Size: 6 to 12 inches tall and wide.
Flowers: White, red, pink and salmon.
Bloom period: Summer to first frost.
Light: Partial to full shade.
Soil: Moist and well-draining.
Additional benefits: Attracts hummingbirds.

Flowering Tobacco

Many varieties of flowering tobacco produce fragrant blooms all season long on tall stems that sway in the breeze. Flowering tobacco is an excellent plant to attract hummingbirds and butterflies, livening up your no-fuss garden.

Botanical name: *Nicotiana alata*.
Size: 10 inches to 5 feet tall; 6 to 24 inches wide.
Flowers: White, red, pink, lavender, green and yellow.
Bloom period: Summer to first frost.
Light: Partial shade to full sun.
Soil: Rich, moist and well-draining.
Additional benefits: Attracts butterflies, hummingbirds.

Impatiens

If you have a shady area that needs color, impatiens are a no-brainer. They've made me look like a Master Gardener without me even trying, and can do the same for you.

Botanical name: *Impatiens walleriana.*
Size: 6 to 18 inches tall; 12 to 24 inches wide.
Flowers: A broad variety of colors, including white, orange, red, pink, lavender, coral and yellow.
Bloom period: Summer to first frost.
Light: Partial to full shade.
Soil: Moist and well-draining.
Additional benefits: Attracts butterflies, hummingbirds.

Sweet Alyssum

I love this annual because it blooms for months in full sun to partial shade. It does best in cool weather. After the heat of summer, cut it back to encourage new growth and blooms. It also works nicely in rock gardens and containers.

Botanical name: *Lobularia maritima.*
Size: 4 to 8 inches tall; 10 to 15 inches wide.
Flowers: White, pink, lavender and apricot.
Bloom period: Spring through frost.
Light: Full sun to partial shade.
Soil: Well-draining.
Additional benefits: Attracts butterflies.

Ball Horticultural Company; all other photos: Cheryl Richter

Wave Petunia

While most petunias need extensive deadheading to continue flowering, Wave petunias and many other newer introductions seem to defy the laws of nature. They produce continuous blooms all summer, even when you don't remove the spent flowers.

Botanical name: *Petunia* x *hybrida* 'Wave'.
Size: 4 to 6 inches tall; spreads 3 to 4 feet wide.
Flowers: Purple, blue, lavender, lilac, pink and rose.
Bloom period: Spring through frost.
Light: Full sun.
Soil: Well-draining.
Additional benefits: Fills in large areas.

Annual Vinca

If you experience lots of heat in summer, annual vinca, also known as Madagascar periwinkle, is the perfect plant. It flourishes in full sun and doesn't need excessive watering or deadheading.

An upright plant that spreads with age, it's perfect in the garden or as a container planting. Its heat tolerance and appearance make annual vinca a perfect substitute for impatiens in hot dry locations.

Botanical name: *Catharanthus roseus.*
Size: 6 to 24 inches tall and wide.
Flowers: White, pink, rose-pink, red, lilac and some with a contrasting eye.
Bloom period: Early summer.
Light: Full sun.
Soil: Well-draining.
Additional benefits: Drought tolerant.

10 CAREFREE PERENNIALS

Easy-care plants from expert Melinda Myers.

Perennials are a great way to grow an easy-care garden. They usually bloom with little effort, plus the plants return—and expand—year after year. But with so many flowers to choose from, where do you start?

For help, we turned to *Birds & Blooms* Contributing Editor Melinda Myers. She sorted through the thicket of possibilities and came up with these 10 fantastic flowers. Some are newer varieties that offer a different look to old favorites, while other plants are solid performers that just get better with age.

Alan and Linda Detrick

Russian Sage: Little Spire

Little Spire (at left) provides the eye-catching beauty of Russian sage in a smaller package. A profusion of tiny lavender-blue flowers covers its stems from mid- to late summer.

Its upright growth habit makes it a good fit as a focal point in a sunny perennial border.

Botanical name: *Perovskia atriplicifolia* 'Little Spire'.
Size: 24 to 30 inches tall and 18 to 24 inches wide.
Light needs: Full sun. **Hardiness:** Zones 4 to 8.

Tall Garden Phlox: Flame Series

These flowers provide the beauty of phlox without the disease problems that sometimes plague this variety. With a smaller stature, the Flame Series is perfect for perennial borders and cottage gardens. It blooms in mid- to late summer, with sweetly scented lilac, purple or pink flowers that attract hummingbirds.

Botanical name: *Phlox paniculata* 'Lilac Flame', 'Purple Flame' or 'Pink Flame'.
Size: 12 to 18 inches tall and 10 to 12 inches wide.
Light needs: Full sun. **Hardiness:** Zones 4 to 8.

Daylily: Strawberry Candy

One of the thousands of daylily varieties, Strawberry Candy (right) stands out with its pink flowers with red eyes and yellow-green throats.

It unfurls new ruffled flowers each day from late spring to midsummer. The flowers rise above its tall grassy foliage. Works well in a variety of garden locations.

Alan and Linda Detrick

Botanical name: *Hemerocallis* 'Strawberry Candy'.
Size: 26 inches tall and 12 to 24 inches wide.
Light needs: Full sun.
Hardiness: Zones 3 to 10.

Showy Upright Sedum: Purple Emperor

This variety's purple-red leaves form a striking contrast with its dusty-red flower heads when they bloom in late summer. The upright plant is perfect for sunny borders, cottage gardens and rock gardens.

Botanical name: *Sedum* x 'Purple Emperor'.
Size: 15 inches tall and 18 to 24 inches wide.
Light needs: Full sun. **Hardiness:** Zones 4 to 9.

Variegated Japanese Sedge: Ice Dance

This ornamental grass has fine-textured dark-green leaves with strong cream-colored edges.

It's an attractive addition to brighten shady areas and contrasts nicely with other low-light plants. It even thrives in wet locations along streams and ponds.

Botanical name: *Carex morrowii* 'Ice Dance'.
Size: 12 inches tall and 12 to 18 inches wide.
Light needs: Partial sun to partial shade.
Hardiness: Zones 5 to 9.

Dick Garbe/Shady Acres Perennial Nursery

Coral Bells: Plum Pudding

A favorite for shade gardens, this variety (above) has both attractive foliage and outstanding flowers. Silvery plum-purple leaves provide the backdrop for sprays of tiny pink bell shaped flowers in early summer.

The attractive foliage and low growth habit make it ideal for the front of a perennial garden, as well as in rock gardens, along pathways or in woodland settings.

Botanical name: *Heuchera* x 'Plum Pudding'.
Size: 8 inches tall and 12 inches wide.
Light needs: Partial sun to partial shade.
Hardiness: Zones 4 to 8.

Fringed Bleeding Heart: King of Hearts

King of Hearts provides season-long interest as well as the distinctive heart-shaped blooms of common bleeding hearts.

It has a compact habit that remains tidy all season and unfurls flowers all summer. This variety forms a dainty mound that fits well into a shady border garden, along pathways or in a container. Also, its leaves are a unique bluish-green hue.

Botanical name: *Dicentra* x 'King of Hearts'.
Size: 8 to 12 inches tall and 12 to 18 inches wide.
Light needs: Partial to full shade.
Hardiness: Zones 3 to 9.

Hosta: Inniswood

This hosta variety has gained popularity for its resistance to slugs. Its large, heart-shaped and puckered leaves

are yellowish-green with dark-green edges—very attractive in the shade garden or planted in masses under trees. Pale lavender flowers emerge in late spring.

Botanical name: *Hosta* 'Inniswood'.
Size: 20 inches tall and 40 inches wide,
Light needs: Partial to full shade.
Hardiness: Zones 3 to 8.

RDA Inc./GID

Bigroot Geranium: Ingwersen's Variety

This perennial geranium has something to offer throughout the growing season. Dainty pink flowers bloom from summer to frost, then its glossy-green leaves become bronze and scarlet in fall.

It works well in a variety of light conditions and is perfect for rock gardens or border plantings.

Botanical name: *Geranium macrorrhizum* 'Ingwersen's Variety'.
Size: 12 to 15 inches tall and 20 inches wide.
Light needs: Full sun to partial shade.
Hardiness: Zones 4 to 8.

Threadleaf Coreopsis: Zagreb

For a profusion of sunny flowers with a compact size and little upkeep, try threadleaf coreopsis. It has fine foliage and small yellow daisylike flowers from early summer to fall.

RDA Inc./GID

It also tolerates dry soil and is hardier than its cousin, the larger *Coreopsis verticillata* 'Moonbeam'.

Botanical name: *Coreopsis verticillata* 'Zagreb'.
Size: 12 to 18 inches tall and 18 inches wide.
Light needs: Full sun.
Hardiness: Zones 4 to 9.

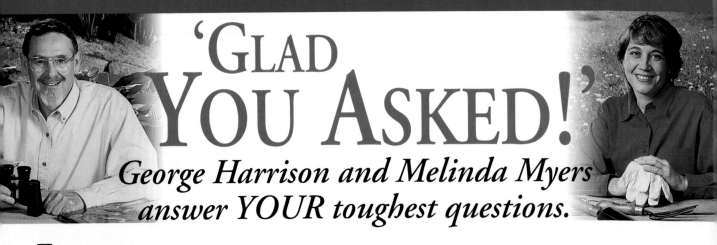

'GLAD YOU ASKED!'

George Harrison and Melinda Myers answer YOUR toughest questions.

In their popular "Glad You Asked!" column, contributing editors George Harrison and Melinda Myers provide expert answers to readers' birding and gardening dilemmas.

Some questions come up again and again. That's why we've provided these three pages of their answers to common problems, so others can benefit from their expertise.

So Long, Sparrows
Is there a birdseed that house sparrows won't eat? I use mixed birdseed, and the sparrows eat it all and scare away the other birds.

George: House sparrows love most of the ingredients in wild birdseed mixes. The solution is to offer seeds the sparrows don't like, such as nyjer (thistle), safflower and sunflower in the shell (though some house sparrows are able to crack sunflower shells).

Also, sparrows usually can't feed from tube feeders without perches. Unfortunately, the same is true for cardinals.

Out, Out Black Spot
How can I get rid of the black spot on my roses?

Melinda: Black spot is a fungal disease common to roses.

One solution is to replace your roses with one of the many newer varieties that resist black spot. Just check with your local garden center.

Or, minimize its impact by applying a fungicide weekly at the first sign of the disease. Select a product labeled for use on roses to control black spot.

In fall, rake and destroy the fallen rosebush leaves. Reduce the source of the disease for the next season by picking off infected leaves before applying winter protection.

Peanut Butter Dilemma
Is it safe to feed peanut butter to birds?

George: Yes, peanut butter is safe for birds. It's a misconception that birds will choke on it.

In fact, peanut butter is a nourishing food, and many species of backyard birds flock to this snack. However, many people are still concerned, even after I assure them peanut butter is safe. So I recommend mixing peanut butter with cornmeal for a high-energy treat.

How to Plant Under Trees
I want to plant flowers under my tree, but the roots make it difficult to plant. How much topsoil should I add to grow flowers?

Melinda: None. Adding as little as 1 inch of soil around them can kill some trees, although the damage doesn't show up for 5 to 10 years. You'll know a tree is declining if its leaves turn color early in autumn and fall prematurely.

Try growing perennials and ground covers around trees and shrubs. The digging will be difficult, but you only have to do it once.

You can also brighten up the area with pots filled with annuals, or set pots amid ground covers for a different look.

Unique Visitor
We spotted this strange red and white bird (at left) in our yard. What is it?

Virginia Vojtas

George: The bird is a northern cardinal with partial albinism. The lack of pigment in some of its feathers is a permanent condition, and it will look that way throughout its life.

Partial albinism is fairly common among backyard birds. A true albino bird, which is all white with pink eyes, bill and legs, is much more rare.

Ready to Get Growing
We live in a new house on a virtually empty lot. What are some fast-growing plants that will attract birds and other wildlife?

Melinda: A mix of annuals, perennials, trees and shrubs will provide the food and shelter that wildlife need.

Annuals offer immediate results. Here are some that do well in most soil conditions: sunflower, dahlia, marigold, zinnia, verbena, nasturtium, petunia and spider cleome.

For perennials, choose yarrow, hollyhock, pearly everlasting, rock cress, butterfly weed, coneflower, black-eyed Susan, daylily, phlox, lupine, bee balm or sedum. They'll start filling in and blooming the second year.

Then add evergreens and deciduous trees and shrubs like dogwood, viburnum, shrub rose, ash, crabapple, hawthorn and maple.

Wrens Wanted

How can I attract house wrens (like the one at left) to the birdhouses we put up for them?

George: You should be able to attract house wrens to nest in your backyard if you offer them several houses with entrance holes 1 to 1-1/8 inches wide. Attach or hang the houses from small trees, like fruit trees, about 6 to 8 feet above the ground.

Charles Housel

Male house wrens like to claim all available nesting sites in an area by filling every house with sticks. Then the female selects one for building her nest.

How to Build Raised Beds

I'd like to build several raised beds, but I'm not sure where to begin. Any suggestions?

Melinda: First select a location that will meet the light needs of the plants you want to grow. Then outline the shape of the flower bed and select a material for its border. Stone, plastic lumber and landscape timbers are a few commonly used materials that are long-lasting and environmentally friendly.

Cut the existing grass short and cover the area with several layers of newspaper. This will kill the grass and weeds.

Spread at least 12 inches of blended topsoil over the area. The soil will settle, so make sure to add a couple extra inches. Then lightly water the flower bed or wait 2 weeks for the soil to settle completely.

Now you're ready to plant!

Searching for Binoculars

Can you recommend good binoculars for bird-watching?

George: There are a few simple tips that will help you select perfect binoculars. The magnification and sharpness of the images are the most important considerations. Binocu-

lars have two numbers that describe these capabilities.

The first number is the power of magnification. For example, a bird viewed through 7 x 35 binoculars is magnified seven times.

The second number is the diameter, in millimeters, of the object lens (the front lens). Larger lenses gather more light, making the image you see clearer and brighter.

Bigger binoculars aren't necessarily better, however. Greater magnification and clarity require more glass, which makes binoculars heavier. And higher magnification can make it difficult to quickly spot a bird because the image is so close.

Therefore, 7 x 35 or 8 x 40 binoculars are the best choices for most birders.

Help Stop Slugs

Slugs are devouring my zinnias! How can I keep them away from my flower beds?

Melinda: Traps are the most effective way to combat slugs. You can make them yourself by filling shallow containers with beer and placing them throughout your flower beds. The slugs are attracted to the fermenting yeast, crawl inside and drown.

Here's another method that works particularly well: Place half-empty beer bottles on their sides in garden areas that show slug damage. This trap has a convenient "roof" to keep rain from diluting the bait. In either case, tuck the containers below plants to keep your garden looking tidy.

You also could try some of the new iron phosphate poisons, such as Sluggo and Escargo. These products eliminate slugs without harming pets, birds or wildlife.

Birdseed Is All Wet

No matter what kind of feeder I use, I can't seem to find one that keeps the birdseed dry in our wet climate. Any ideas how I can prevent the seed from getting damp?

George: Wet seed is a hassle for anyone who maintains bird feeders, and it has to be an even greater dilemma for people who live in wet environments.

One way to protect seed from rain is to provide roofs over your feeders. For tube feeders, simply hang a squirrel baffle above them. For tray or hopper feeders, make sure the roof extends over the entire platform.

Roofs will help, but the only foolproof way to keep the birdseed dry is to change it often.

Phoebe Beiler

Water Lilies in Winter

I live in Zone 5 and am wondering how to keep water lilies (like the one at left) over the winter.

Melinda: Unless you live in Zone 10 or 11, tropical water lilies must be wintered indoors. Place the lilies in a pool or tank and suspend a daylight-type fluorescent light fixture 12 to 15 inches above it. Leave the light on for 16 hours each day.

Hardy water lilies, however, can stay outdoors as long as their roots don't freeze. Ponds that are at least 2 to 5 feet deep, or equipped with a pump to keep the water from freezing over, make a nice winter home. If your water garden is shallow and freezes solid, however, you'll need to bring hardy lilies indoors for the winter.

Flight Safety
For the last several years, a male cardinal has been repeatedly flying into my friend's bedroom windowpane from dawn until about noon. What can she do to stop this bird?

George: Male and female cardinals often fight their own reflections in windows because they're trying to chase the "other bird" from their nesting territory. American robins, mockingbirds and many others will do the same thing.

To alleviate this problem, eliminate the reflection by rubbing soap on the window or hang streamers of some kind outside it.

Decna Haner

Leave the Leaves?
When is it okay to remove the leaves from spring-blooming bulbs (like the daffodils at left)? I know I should wait until the foliage dies, but sometimes that doesn't happen until late summer—leaving little time to plant annuals!

Melinda: Have the best of both worlds by using your annuals to cover the declining bulb foliage. Some gardeners bend over and tie or braid the foliage to help disguise it in the garden. Of course, the plants will do better if the leaves are left completely intact until they turn yellow. I like to mix my bulbs with perennials so I don't need to disturb either planting.

Protection from Cats
The neighborhood cats often lurk near my bird feeders. How can I protect my feathered friends from these felines?

George: Free-roaming house cats cause enormous problems for backyard birds. The quickest solution is to convince your neighbors to keep their cats at home, preferably inside. This is no easy task, because cat owners often don't believe their pets are endangering avian wildlife.

You also can try planting thorny shrubs, such as barberry or roses, beneath pole-mounted feeders to keeps cats from lurking at the bases.

Wisteria Won't Bloom
We never get any blooms on our wisteria tree, which we've had in our yard for 4 years. Any suggestions?

Melinda: If you started your wisteria from seed, the first thing you need is patience. That's because seed-grown wisteria takes 7 to 10 years to bloom. If your plant was started from a cutting, then fertilizer containing too much nitrogen may be the problem. High-nitrogen fertilizers usually cause plants to produce lots of leaves but no flowers.

A soil test will tell you exactly what type and how much fertilizer you should use. If soil tests aren't available, try applying a moderate amount of 5-10-5 fertilizer in early spring. (These numbers appear on the fertilizer bag and correspond to the percentage of nitrogen, phosphorus and potassium, respectively, in the fertilizer.)

A Home for Butterflies
Do butterflies actually use butterfly houses (like the one at right), or do they just make nice garden decorations?

RP Photo

George: Butterfly houses are primarily for decoration because the kinds of butterflies that frequent gardens won't use houses for shelter or roosting.

However, there are woodland species of butterflies that might use the houses, such as mourning cloaks and common wood nymphs, which overwinter in the protective cover of wood piles and tree cavities.

Issue with Algae
How can I eliminate the algae in my water garden without hurting the plants and fish?

Melinda: Make sure your pond includes plenty of oxygenating and floating plants such as starwort, fanwort, water violet and water milifoil to compete with the algae for food and light.

These plants will keep the problem under control while creating a better environment for the fish.

Also, be sure to keep leaves, plant debris and lawn fertilizer out of the pond. These all add nutrients that feed algae and help it grow.

KEEP THE CRITTERS OUT!

Varmint victims from across the country share plant protection tips.

Anita Wilson

We gardeners have been at war with animals ever since people first dropped seeds in the ground. And although we lose battle after battle, we never stop dreaming up ways to drive off the invaders.

Here's a collection of winning strategies passed on to us by readers, friends and neighbors. Just keep in mind that animals are unpredictable. The methods that have worked for others may or may not work for you.

When simple tricks fail, the only certain solution is to shield your plants with barriers like fences or cages. We'll describe some of those "sure cures" along with other more creative tactics.

First, Understand the Enemy

Your odds of victory depend on how hungry the critters are. In an area with plenty of easy meals, simple tactics can send the freeloaders elsewhere. But if animals are really hungry—due to overpopulation or drought, for example—only drastic measures will stop them.

Bear in mind that urban and suburban pests are tougher than their country cousins. They're less bothered by the sight, scent and sounds of people, so they're harder to scare off.

Animals grow accustomed to just about anything. Simple strategies like an old-fashioned scarecrow or noisy pie tins clanging in the wind might work for a while. But most animals will eventually learn that these things are harmless. Occasionally switching strategies will keep these garden attackers off balance.

Animals develop habits. Counterattack early, before your yard becomes part of their daily dining routine. The longer you wait, the more likely they are to bring along friends and family, and the harder it will be to stop them.

Oh, Deer Me!

Deer often do their dirty work under cover of darkness, so it can be hard to tell whether they're truly to blame for yard damage. Your first clue is the height of the damage—deer can reach up 6 to 8 feet. Most other garden grazers can't reach past 2 feet.

Secondly, deer teeth grab, pull and rip. Most other suspects have sharp teeth that leave clean cuts. If branches and

Jerry Howard/Positive Images

HOW MUCH CAN A WOODCHUCK EAT? Lots! They quickly devour almost any plant. Some spray-on deer repellents may keep these toothy visitors at bay.

stems look more torn than sliced, deer are probably guilty.

Some gardeners use motion-detector lights to frighten deer. Joe Mahoney of La Grange, Georgia took that trick one step further. He connected a radio to his motion detector. The light and radio turn off after just 4 seconds, but Joe figures the frightened deer are "probably in the next county by then."

We've heard several good reports about the Scarecrow sprinkler. It's basically a lawn sprinkler controlled by a motion detector (the same kind of detector that switches lights on). When it senses motion in the area, the sprinkler blasts out a cold 3-second shower.

It's not cheap (around $80), but gardeners tell us it works on deer and other invaders. To find a dealer in your area, contact *www.scatmat.com* or call 1-800/767-8658. Or you can buy one on-line at *www.deerbusters.com*.

Jim Novak of Sioux Falls, South Dakota solved his deer problem by chaining up his big mutt, "Pes", next to the garden on summer nights. Pes' presence not only kept the deer away, but he seemed to prefer camping out under the stars.

In hard times, deer will eat just about anything, even the

Christmas wreath on your front door. But they do have favorite foods. Next time you're plant shopping, ask about "deer-resistant" varieties. Many garden centers have lists of deer-discouraging plants that will grow well locally.

Sure Cure: Fences are the only certain solution for deer. Just how much fence you need depends on the hunger factor. Determined deer can jump an 8-foot tall fence without breaking a sweat.

But around smaller garden areas, a 4- to 6-foot-tall fence will send deer to easier feeding grounds. Some home owners have succeeded by fencing off only the one or two sides of their property where deer enter.

Rabbits, Gophers, Woodchucks

We've lumped all these critters together because they share likes and dislikes. Any weapon used against one of these garden raiders is worth trying on another.

Chipmunks and rabbits feasted on Fran Byron's flowers in Ellicott City, Maryland. "I tried mothballs and hot red pepper, but no luck," Fran reports. Sprinkling blood meal on the soil turned out to be the answer. To gardeners, it's just fertilizer. But the smell makes prey animals think of big hungry predators.

These animals can't resist seeking buried treasure in freshly churned soil. To protect just-planted bulbs, Janelle Zander of Harwood, North Dakota lays chicken wire over the planted area and weighs it down with a few rocks. "It's fun to watch confused squirrels try to dig through the wire," Janelle chuckles. Leave the wire in place and the protected bulbs will sprout right through it.

Joan Ungerer of Whiting, New Jersey makes bulbs less appealing before planting them. Here's Joan's bulb bath: Add 1/2 cup of Lysol to 2 quarts of water and soak the bulbs for about 10 to 15 minutes before planting.

For 40 years, Jan Lindhorst of Burt, Iowa has been surrounding her garden with Mason jars placed 3 feet apart. "Never had a rabbit problem…and we have rabbits everywhere else on our farm," says Jan. This might sound loony, but many other gardeners swear by Jan's jar trick.

Marie Marecki does battle with critters of all sizes on her 10 acres in Houghton Lake, Michigan. One of her successful strategies is a hair fence around her garden. Marie makes a ring of pet hair or clippings from a beauty shop and adds a covering of wood chips to keep the hair from blowing away. To garden raiders, hair carries the scent of danger.

Sure Cure: A short fence 4 feet tall will keep gophers, rabbits and most rodents out of your garden. These critters don't climb very well, but they dig like a backhoe.

So the key is to start with a trench that lets you extend your fence 6 to 18 inches underground. Pressure-treated

2x4s set at least 12 inches deep make sturdy posts.

Since rodents will chew right through wood or plastic, metal mesh is the best fence material. Hardware cloth with 1/2-inch openings will keep out everything but tiny mice.

Stop the Squirrels

To keep squirrels from feasting on fruit trees, all you need is a small roll of 14-inch-wide flashing (thin metal used by roofers). Loosely wrap flashing around the tree trunk 3 to 4 feet from the ground. Squirrels can't climb past it because they can't get a grip on that smooth metal. Remove the flashing after the harvest to prevent damage to the tree.

This won't work if squirrels can find a low-hanging branch or leap from nearby trees. For a less noticeable squirrel stopper, buy flashing that's painted brown.

"Squirrels don't like to travel far on the ground, especially if there are dogs or cats in the neighborhood," says Frank LaHaise of Winnipeg, Manitoba. Instead, they'll take the high road, jumping from tree to tree or scurrying along fence tops.

When Frank noticed that squirrels were using his fence as a safe route to the garden, he simply laid a 4-foot section of rain gutter upside down on top of the fence.

Sure Cure: Since squirrels can climb effortlessly, the mesh fence used for rabbits won't even slow squirrels down. But you can use the same hardware cloth to make protective cages for small or medium-sized plants.

Just bring both ends of a section together and join them with wire ties. Then set the round cage a few inches into the soil and cut a section of hardware cloth to make a removable lid.

Those Rascally Raccoons

Raccoons are tough customers. They climb anything and are nimble enough to unlatch gates. They can be dangerous, too. Big dogs have been sent away whimpering by small raccoons. They can also carry rabies.

Several gardeners claim that twinkling Christmas lights strung across cornstalks stop raccoon raids in the sweet corn patch. Lillian Marcotte of Hartland, Vermont says this works on deer, too, but only until morning. Unlike raccoons, deer don't stop their foraging after daybreak.

Michelle Petersen of Omaha, Nebraska takes her beagle out to the edge of her garden to do his business. The scent apparently keeps raccoons at a distance.

Experts say one way to keep raccoons out of your garden is to place garbage cans and pet food bowls in the garage rather than leaving them outside. Remove the main course, and raccoons won't stop off at your garden for dessert.

Ruth Schmerse of Janesville, Wisconsin puts a radio in her garden at night, keeping it dry with a plastic bag. "It's the only way we can get any sweet corn for ourselves," Ruth says.

Jerry Johnson of Bozeman, Montana set up his electric bug zapper in the garden to make raccoons buzz off. With its

Kathy Adams Clark/KAC Productions

RACCOONS ARE NIMBLE and can climb just about anywhere when they're looking for a meal.

noise and sparks, "It scares raccoons better than it stops mosquito bites," says Jerry.

Sure Cure: Truth is, we don't know of a surefire fix for raccoons. If you do, please let us know!

Bothered by Birds?

In most cases, birds are at their worst for short periods of time. They might attack as berries ripen, for example, and then lose interest until next year. That's why it's best to hold your fire. If you deploy your scare tactics too early, the birds will get used to them. That will leave you without a defense when you really need it.

It seems everyone has a wind-driven trick to scare off hungry birds: hanging pie tins, tinsel, balloons, gift-wrapping ribbon. But when the wind dies down, so does the scary movement.

Some readers suggest putting toy rubber snakes in the garden. Rita Christianson of Gleburn, North Dakota does not bother with a trip to the toy store. She just uses a 3-foot section of old garden hose. To make it more realistic, she adds stripes of colorful tape and makes sure to move the scary serpent daily.

Stuffed animals from the local thrift store keep birds away from Emmylu Lawrence's garden in Beaverton, Oregon. Now she enjoys watching the birds swoop in for a snack and then quickly turn tail when they see the stuffed defenders.

Sure Cure: Fruit and berry farmers drape huge nets—usually made from synthetics like polyester—over their crops to foil feathered freeloaders.

Squirrels and other critters sometimes chew holes in bird netting, but Martha Martin of Harriston, Ontario has found a cheap substitute. She finds sheer curtains at thrift shops and throws them over her cherry trees.

5 STEPS TO STOP SQUIRRELS

By George Harrison, Contributing Editor

Evelyn Ferguson

Squirrels! They're everywhere—eating from bird feeders, perched on utility wires and scampering through the yard.

Most are gray squirrels, but depending where you live, some may be red squirrels or fox squirrels. All can be pests.

While some people find squirrels fascinating to watch, others dream up countless ways to try to outsmart these intelligent and persistent creatures.

Over the years, I've perfected a number of methods that keep squirrels away from my feeders, but still allow them to be part of my backyard wildlife scene.

1. Rule of 5-7-9. Even squirrels have limits. I've found they cannot leap from the ground to a feeder that's higher than 5 feet; they cannot jump more than 7 feet from a tree or building to the side of a feeder; and they're reluctant to drop more than 9 feet onto a feeder.

Therefore, place your feeder 5 feet off the ground, leave 7 feet on each side from a launching place, and 9 feet below the closest overhang. Then protect it with squirrel baffles.

Do this, and 90 percent of squirrels should be unable to jump onto your feeder. Add another 6 inches to those dimensions, and you've locked out 100 percent of the squirrels.

2. Soda Bottle Roller. Squirrels are as famous for walking on high wires like circus performers. Bird feeders hanging from wires are easy pickings for any squirrel. But, if you string plastic liter-size soda bottles onto the wire on both sides of the feeders, the squirrels will be rolled off the bottles as they approach the feeders.

Follow the Rule of 5-7-9 when using this method, so squirrels can't leap directly onto the feeder.

3. Slinky on a Post. A "Slinky," the children's toy, makes a great post baffle. Thread the post through the Slinky and attach one end under the feeder to allow it to drape down the post. Shorten it if the Slinky touches the ground.

A squirrel that tries to climb the post will get a ride on the Slinky back to the ground every time. Again, first be sure to position the feeder following the 5-7-9 rule.

4. Birds in a Cage. Keep squirrels on the outside looking in by enclosing bird feeders in wire mesh that's large enough to allow birds to enter the cage, but small enough to exclude squirrels.

5. Don't Tempt Their Taste Buds. Believe it or not, squirrels don't like some kinds of birdseed. Safflower seeds, loved by northern cardinals, chickadees, nuthatches, finches and doves, are of no interest to squirrels. Nyjer (thistle) also seems to be disliked by squirrels.

BIRD TALES

We've gathered the most amazing bird encounters from the past year.

Hitching a Ride

DURING A CAR TRIP to Maryland, my radio went out as I drove through a tunnel on the Pennsylvania Turnpike. In the now quiet car, I detected another noise—bird chirping. Once through the tunnel, I pulled over to hunt for it, even peering under the hood. No bird.

Just then a Turnpike Commission employee, seeing the hood up, came by and asked if I needed help. When I explained, he helped me search, but the bird wasn't chirping anymore, so he couldn't find it either. (And I can just imagine what he told his coworkers about me when he got back to the office!)

For the next 2-1/2 hours, I kept the radio off, and the bird chirped the whole way. I found myself talking to it, urging my unseen passenger to "hold on" until we got to Maryland.

At my destination, I opened the passenger-side door to unload the car and discovered where my traveling companion had been hiding. That bird had ridden 250 miles sitting on the door hinge! It must have flown in when I was packing the car, but I still don't know how I avoided injuring it when I closed the door.
—*Mary Jo Kress*
Cranberry Township, Pennsylvania

Whirly Bird

WE WERE watching the birds at the feeders on our balcony when an evening grosbeak landed. It took a few seeds, then flew to our large and decorative multicolored pinwheel.

Just as it landed on one of the pinwheel's fins, a breeze started to turn it. To keep its balance, the bird did the cutest treadmill routine you could imagine. Its little feet and wings were going a mile a minute trying to keep up with the spinning pinwheel.

Finally, the grosbeak lost its footing and relied on wing power to get out of the jam.
—*Frances Kimball*
Dexter, Oregon

Purr-fect Playmate

WHEN MY HUSBAND put a bird feeder outside our dining room window, I knew our two cats would be delighted by the free entertainment. I never dreamed one cat would get a playmate in the bargain.

The cats watch the birds from a desk that faces the window.

The birds seem oblivious to the onlookers, except for one playful wren.

This bird flies back and forth in front of the window while our cat "Bramble" paces across the desk. When the wren perches in front of the window, Bramble watches for a while, then stands and puts her front paws on the glass. The wren flies to the feeder, waits for Bramble to sit, then returns to repeat the game.

They even appear to play peek-a-boo, taking turns hiding from each other. Usually the bird tires of this game first. When it flies away, Bramble gets so annoyed that she sometimes cries out in frustration.

The wren shows up even when the feeder's empty, so I'm convinced it doesn't stop by just to eat. It comes to play with my cat! —*Veronica Free, Asheboro, North Carolina*

April Fool!

I MAKE wooden birds from simple patterns. My son Dana especially liked my reproduction of a pileated woodpecker, so I made another one for him.

He mounted it on a tree at the edge of his property in the Ozarks, where he could enjoy seeing it from the house or the backyard.

One spring morning, he looked out the window and saw this scene (right) at the tree. The real male pileated woodpecker on the left returned daily for a week, pecking at the bark until it was almost bare.

He must've been puzzled about where his rival had come from—and why it never moved.
—*James Hoisington*
Warrensburg, Missouri

Easy Pickin's

ONE SUMMER, my neighbor planted a red currant bush in

her yard. When the fruit ripened, a mother American robin that was nesting nearby took notice of the bright berries and led her family to the bush. It was time to eat!

The little ones dutifully followed in a line behind her, then proceeded to devour every single berry within their reach.

When those branches were bare, the mother grabbed the higher ones with her bill and pulled them down so the little ones could pick off the fruit.

My neighbor and I quietly watched the scene. We didn't have a camera, but we'll always have a mental picture of this mother making sure her brood had enough to eat.

—*H. Newcomb, Limon, Colorado*

Peanut Butter Buddy

THIS CHICKADEE and I (above) met when it landed on my knife as I added peanut butter to a log bird feeder in my garden. After that, the bird flew to me whenever it heard the back door open. Of course, I always had some peanut butter handy.

If I stayed in the house too long, the black-capped chickadee would hop onto the kitchen windowsill and impatiently pace back and forth, looking inside until I finally emerged. When I was busy gardening, it would land on my head to get my attention.

I called the bird "Boldie", and enjoyed its company for about 3 months. Then my little friend vanished just as quickly as it'd appeared. Thanks for the memories!

—*Ursula Ratzkowski, Oakville, Ontario*

Two-on-One

I HAVE a platform feeder in the backyard that has a roof and a front rail. Two dark-eyed juncos were feeding there when a starling chased them out. Every time the juncos tried to eat, the starling pecked at them.

Finally, one junco perched on the roof while the other stood on the rail. Whenever the starling stuck its head out to chase the junco off the rail, the one of the roof pecked the larger bird on the head.

The starling finally tired of this treatment and flew off, leaving the juncos to feed in peace. Now that's teamwork!

—*Larry Gilletly, Tipp City, Ohio*

On Demand

WHEN I MOVED into a new house, I was excited to see two squirrels scurrying about my neighborhood. I decided to throw out peanuts in hopes of luring the pair to my yard. This seemed to be going well, as the peanuts I put out kept disappearing.

But as I watched from the front porch one day, I saw it was actually three blue jays that were enjoying my handouts.

The jays seemed quite happy…that is, until I ran out of peanuts! To let me know of their discontent, they sat outside my bedroom window and screeched until I was left with no option but to buy more peanuts.

Now if I forget to put out peanuts, those nutty birds will throw a fit until I go down to the porch and give them their treats.

—*Sheila Bird, Victor, Iowa*

Weigh to Go

MY BIRD FEEDER has a perch that shuts the feeder gate when heavier birds, squirrels and other seed thieves land on it. Sometimes it will even close if too many birds try to eat at once.

One morning, I noticed a group of sparrows had figured out a way around this mechanism.

Whenever more than three sparrows landed on the perch, the gate closed. After a few minutes, one sparrow jumped up about 2 inches in the air and the gate rose again. The bird landed gingerly, the gate stayed up and the birds resumed their feast.

I thought I'd imagined this behavior, until I poured a second cup of coffee and watched a while longer. The birds repeated what they'd learned every time their weight shut down the breakfast buffet.

—*Darla Sparks
Yukon, Oklahoma*

Special Delivery

WHEN THE HINGES on our brick mailbox rusted, my husband urged me to call a repairman and get them fixed. Apparently I waited too long.

After a few weeks, I saw a pair of bluebirds going in and out of the open mailbox. They were building a nest there. The photo shows the mother sitting on her eggs.

The mailman was very good-natured about holding my mail at the post office. When I'd stop to pick it up, most of the carriers would call me the "bird lady". —*Corky Willens
Tyler, Texas*

Earned Its Wings

IT'S HILARIOUS to watch other birds try to get a piece of the action at our busy, but small, hummingbird feeder. Have you ever seen a blue jay or grosbeak try to hover? It's quite a sight, believe me.

Several years ago, a yellow-bellied sapsucker rose to the challenge. Attracted by ants on the feeder, it perched nearby and observed the hummers for a while.

When the feeder was quiet, the sapsucker flew over. After some wild swinging, it managed to perch on the slippery surface to eat the ants. It wasn't long before "Woody" discovered the sweet nectar as well.

At first, it waited for the hummers to leave before approaching the feeder, but soon it became bolder, squawking at them from a distance or just flying in and forcing them to scatter. Whenever Woody overstayed its welcome, the hummers would band together and buzz the larger bird until it left.

Woody returned for several seasons, and the birds, big and small, shared the feeder as amicably as they could. I guess in the end, Woody became an honorary hummer.

—*Robin Leonard, Lyme Center, New Hampshire*

Watch the Birdie

THIS black-capped chickadee (left) found the ornamental camera hanging from our yard swing a picture-perfect spot to raise a family. We enjoyed watching her throughout the spring as she prepared the nest, laid her eggs, and flew back and forth to feed her brood.

The mother never seemed to mind when we sat on the swing to watch her take care of housekeeping duties.

Considering the spot she chose, I guess it's no surprise my daughter, Crystal, was able to get so many great photos of the nesting activities! —*Doris Sartini Lincoln, Rhode Island*

Frosty Pheasant

Years ago, I served on the State Patrol in Wisconsin. As I was out driving one cold and rainy day, I spotted something in the middle of the road. When I pulled over to see what it was, I was surprised to find a male ring-necked pheasant covered in ice.

Not sure if it was alive or not, I headed for the closest bird sanctuary. About halfway there, I noticed movement in the backseat. Apparently, the heat of the car had thawed the bird and it began flying around in the back of the squad car, upset it had been taking into custody.

I finally got him to the sanctuary, where he was placed

in a pen with some other pheasants. For months after that, I found feathers in every nook and cranny of my car, reminders of my out of the ordinary passenger. —*William Fredrick Pensacola, Florida*

Close Encounters

WHILE GARDENING one day last summer, I spotted a lone American goldfinch at the feeder. I started walking toward it, extending my hand and talking softly. I fully expected the finch to startle and fly away. To my surprise, it stayed where it was...and then climbed onto my outstretched hand!

I called for my husband, who took this picture (above). The finch then flew up to the roof and back, and I took pictures of it sitting on my husband's hand. We were so excited by the experience.

Maybe this well-fed little creature was showing its appreciation for all the seed we provide. —*Barbara Willis Kewaunee, Wisconsin*

Knock, Knock

YEARS AGO, the father of one of my friends was sitting in his backyard, watching a female flicker feed her young. She'd fly up with food in her bill and knock on the tree trunk, informing the babies that it was safe to poke their heads out to eat. When the mom flew away, the babies ducked inside.

After watching this for a while, my friend's father dug up some worms. When the mother was out of sight, he knocked on the side of the tree. The babies poked their heads out and he fed them.

In a flash, Mom was back at the tree. When the babies poked their heads out, she gave them a serious scolding. After she flew away, my friend's dad went back to the tree, knocked and not one nestling emerged.

We don't know what the mother said to her babies, but the little ones clearly understood they weren't to answer to door to strangers. —*Bonnie Hand, Sarasota, Florida*

Perfect Harmony

A FRIEND and I were at my house, practicing for a concert that featured a piano and flute duet of *Summer*, from composer Antonio Vivaldi's *The Four Seasons*. To keep my dog from interrupting us (she likes to "sing" along), I cracked open the sliding door to the backyard so she could come and go as she pleased.

As Carol and I practiced, the birds in the backyard seemed to get louder and louder. The song has several sections where flute notes are answered by silence, but instead we heard answering calls of "tweet, tweet". At one point, the calls were so loud we thought a bird was trapped in a house vent.

We decided to run through the song one more time. Bird calls answered the flute every time, right through to the final notes.

When we finished, there was a moment of silence, and then we heard the flutter of wings. Carol and I turned just in time to see a large male cardinal fly off the bookshelf and out the sliding door.

—*Sheila Guevin*
Montgomery, Alabama

Plea for Help

ONE SPRING, a pair of killdeer nested in the cemetery where my husband, Bob, is a groundskeeper.

Although he was careful to avoid the nest with the mower, whenever the machine came near the female always pretended to be injured. She'd run in front of it, flopping and dragging herself with one wing, until Bob moved away. Then she'd run back to the nest.

When the eggs hatched, Bob was pleased to see four little puffballs on toothpick legs running behind their mother.

One day, the mother ran in front of the mower and would not move. Bob had to stop to avoid running her over.

As soon as he stepped down, the killdeer ran to a headstone, looked down at the ground, then looked up at Bob. He followed, and found one of her chicks in an urn filled with cold water.

Bob gently lifted the chick to safety and laid it on a sun-warmed headstone. Before he could take his hand away, the anxious mother covered the chick with her own body to warm it.

That afternoon, Bob was delighted to see the killdeer family—with all four chicks—pecking for bugs in the grass.

—*Mary Lou Patrick, East Wenatchee, Washington*

Fur Thief

I WAS COMBING my cats on the patio last spring and left the comb in the same spot until the next day. When I returned, I noticed something was missing—matted fur that was stuck between the teeth.

I was puzzled, because I'd planned to remove the hair and wrap it in yarn for the birds.

I started combing my cats again, but this time I was interrupted by a phone call. As I talked, I looked out the window and saw a black-capped chickadee land on the comb and start pulling at the cat hair. That's when I grabbed my camera and snapped this photo (below left).

The cats unhappily sat through three or four more combings until the chickadee had enough to line the nest.

—*Linda Walter, Glenwood, Minnesot*

Who Was that Maskless Bird?

I WAS SO happy to see the "maskless" cardinal (below left) at our feeders this winter. He was very timid his first winter, and was easily scared off by the other male cardinals (like the one below right).

But this past year the unmasked bird has become a little more brave, frequenting the feeding tray on our deck more

often. He'd sit in our large Norway spruce for quite a while, waiting for the crowd of cardinals to vacate the feeder.

Cardinals are very territorial, but a little more tolerant during winter when they form loose flocks.

On cold snowy days, it's not unusual to have a couple dozen cardinals in our backyard, blazing like bright ornaments in the spruce tree. But it's the maskless one that outshines the others with its unique beauty.
—*Kathy Krattli*
O'Fallon, Missouri

Catch of the Day

WHILE FLY-FISHING one morning on the Eagle River in Colorado, I felt a tug on my line before I'd finished casting. The line hit the water with a splash. To my horror, I quickly realized I'd caught a small bird.

I immediately reeled the line out of the cold water. Luckily, the poor little fellow was only wrapped up in the line and not snagged on the hook. Was it actually going after the fly?

I held it carefully in one hand while I unwound the line with the other. The bird was beautiful, with green and purple feathers. It was very calm, although it was probably in a bit of shock. It didn't seem hurt, but it certainly wasn't ready to fly, either.

I gently placed the bird on an aspen branch so it could recover in the warm sun. About half an hour later, I picked up the bird and lifted it to the sky. It immediately flew off to join others soaring high over the water, catching insects.

When I got home I checked my field guide, I learned

this little beauty was a violet-green swallow. Ever since that day, I've been hooked on bird-watching.

—*Mark Pscheid, Nederland, Colorado*

Bird Buffet

I'D JUST STARTED mowing our 1-acre yard, when I noticed a bird swooping close to my head. What could it want with a noisy old lawn tractor?

After another pass, I realized the bird was following me, darting and gliding in the mower's wake. At first I couldn't figure out what this daredevil barn swallow was up to. Then it dawned on me—breakfast!

As the tractor moved through the tall grass, it kicked up hundreds of tiny insects. The swallow must have thought it had bellied up to the all-you-can-eat bird buffet.

Before long, I had at least six swallows dining around me, flying so close I could see the sunlight glinting off their deep-blue backs. Mowing isn't my favorite chore, but that day, the swallows transformed a mundane task into an unexpected joy.

—*Jill Richardson, Warrenville, Illinois*

No Place for Nap

JUST AFTER New Year's, this eastern screech-owl (see photo below) roosted in the Christmas wreath on our front

door. You can imagine my surprise when I opened it to get the newspaper and found myself face to face with the owl!

It stayed there all day, even when the UPS deliveryman came to the door.

At dusk, the owl flew off to go hunting and did not return. Maybe it needs a little quieter surroundings for its daytime roost.

—*Jack Odell*
Savannah, Georgia

Chip Shot

I WAS SITTING in my pickup in a parking lot, waiting for my wife to finish shopping. As I sat there, I spotted a blackbird that landed in a handicapped parking space, nibbling on a discarded potato chip.

When two drivers approached, looking for parking spaces, the bird picked up the chip, walked to a 3-foot-wide yellow striped area between two handicap spaces, dropped it smack in the middle and continued eating without worry.

I wondered—could the bird know the striped area indicated a safe zone?

My suspicion was confirmed when he accidentally knocked the chip to the far edge of the safety zone. To my amazement, the bird walked over, positioned his bill to the side of the chip, swung his head and, like a golfer taking a swing, deftly knocked his lunch back to the middle of the safety zone. —*David Camp, Wichita, Kansas*

Suet Standoff

FOR TWO SUMMERS, a pair of ornery gray catbirds monopolized our suet feeder, intimidating the smaller birds with their incessant mewing and swooping.

One July afternoon, a juvenile downy woodpecker perched on the feeder, unaware the catbirds considered it

their personal domain. As soon as it began eating, one of the catbirds landed on the suet holder, giving it a mighty swing.

To my surprise, the little woodpecker managed to hang on. The screeching catbird kept the feeder swaying and spinning, but the woodpecker didn't let go or even make a sound. Instead, it stared at the catbird and spread its wings (see photo above).

After a few minutes, the catbird realized it had met its match. It snatched a piece of suet and flew away. The catbirds' reign was over. —*Joyce Fleming, Reston, Virginia*

Fuel Efficient

SEVERAL YEARS ago, I took my first trip to the East Coast and toured Arlington National Cemetery in Washington, D.C. on a national holiday. All the while we were there, we kept hearing a weed trimmer going full speed.

We looked around several times for the unfortunate employee who was stuck working the holiday.

Imagine my surprise when we finally spotted the sounds coming from a northern mockingbird. What an imposter!

We got a good laugh out of it—that clever bird had us completely fooled.

—*Donna Peters*
Colorado Springs, Colorado

Piggyback Pair

I OFTEN SEE some unusual antics as I watch the birds at my feeder that's outside the dining room window.

On one such occasion, I looked up in time to spot a mourning dove land on top of the feeder. While I admired this beautiful creature, a charming little sparrow landed right on top of the dove! The two birds seemed in shock over the run-in, as the pair remained virtually motionless for some time.

The sparrow eventually flew away, but the dove remained perched with such a funny expression. One could only guess what might be going through its bird brain. —*Maxine Osburn*
Auburn, New York

INDEX

Index

255